CELTIC MUSIC

EDITED BY KENNY MATHIESON

CELTIC MUSIC
Edited by Kenny Mathieson

A BACKBEAT BOOK
First British edition 2001

Published by Backbeat Books
600 Harrison Street,
San Francisco, CA 94107
www.backbeatbooks.com

An imprint of The Music Player Network
United Entertainment Media, Inc

Produced for Backbeat Books by Outline Press Ltd,
115J Cleveland Street, London W1T 6PU, England.
www.balafon.dircon.co.uk

ISBN 0-87930-623-8

Art Director: Nigel Osborne
Design: Sally Stockwell
Commissioning Editor: Kenny Mathieson
Editor: Tony Bacon

Origination by Global Colour (Malaysia)
Print by Colorprint Offset Ltd. (Hong Kong)

01 02 03 04 05 5 4 3 2 1

CONTENTS

INTRODUCTION

What is Celtic music? If anything, it is a marketing strategy – and a very successful one. A less cynical and more practical answer is that it is the music produced in the so-called Celtic countries, drawing on the traditional musical culture of those countries, namely: Ireland, Scotland, Wales, the Isle of Man, Cornwall, Brittany, and the Spanish and Portuguese regions which in this book we have decided to call Celtic Iberia, as well as the music in exile of all those places but especially Ireland and Scotland. Celtic music is compounded from many elements, but the base is the traditional musical heritage of the various territories which we choose to identify as "Celtic". The brew is then seasoned with more ingredients, notably contemporary musical flavourings, from rock and jazz to techno and trance.

Apart from its inherent musical qualities, Celtic music has also been influenced by wide-ranging non-musical factors, such as a fashion for a kind of pseudo-Celtic new age mysticism – which is not given much credence in this book – and, on a more profound level, a new sense of cultural identity and political self-determination within the "Celtic" nations.

This survey will use that broad-ranging concept as its guiding principle. A word of caution, however. While traditional music and folk music (not necessarily synonymous) will form the backbone of much of the music discussed here under the heading of Celtic music, this is not a book about traditional music, far less an organised history of that music, and even less a history of the Celts, who have long since vanished from the scene but have left myriad tantalising glimpses of their life and culture.

This book focuses largely on the music made during the remarkable revival of interest and subsequent expansion of musical boundaries in traditional, folk and Celtic music that took place from the 1960s onward. Many historical antecedents are sketched in during the course of the various chapters, and the bibliography at the back of the book includes some further sources of historical information that will doubtless be of assistance to readers who wish to learn more about those particular aspects of the subject.

The interest in the music is very real, underlined by increasing sales of CDs and the expansion of huge international festivals such as the Festival Interceltique in Lorient in Brittany, or Celtic Connections in Glasgow, or Celtic Colors in Nova Scotia. In general, the organisers of these events take an all-encompassing view of their Celtic remit – and indeed they have every right to do so, given the murky issue of what is and what is not Celtic music.

Kate Woollard (opposite) of Rag Foundation at Pontardawe Festival, 2000.

In North America, for example, dispersed Celts have contributed to just about every significant corner of mainstream American music. The waves of immigration from Scotland and Ireland in the 18th and 19th century carried the indigenous musics of those countries over the Atlantic and began what is now a large, complex and probably inextricable interlacing of influences. The Celtic connections are real enough, but every time we make one it seems to be in the habit of breeding yet another layer of complexity in our understanding of the development of the music.

We tend to think of Celtic music as being the traditional musics of the territories covered in this book, including outposts of development which have been influenced by the old world – although much of Central and Eastern Europe was also homeland to the Celts, and shared common ground both in the music and the instruments used in playing it, including the ubiquitous bagpipes.

These influences have sometimes left authentic chunks of the imported tradition which have been preserved with even greater purity than in their homelands (as some argue happened with Scottish music, and with dance in Cape Breton), and have sometimes interbred with all manner of other influences to

■ *Paddy Keenan, with Tommy O'Sullivan on guitar, at Celtic Connections festival, 1998.*

produce a bastard tradition of their own. Formally identifying what Celtic music is, however, remains a musicologist's nightmare. And arriving at wide-ranging technical definitions for a music which often developed in highly individual fashion in isolated communities is well nigh impossible.

There are common factors evident in tune structures and in rhythmic patterns, often derived from dance, and there is the use of modality and shared scales. But if it is hard enough trying to isolate and classify the broad defining characteristics of the various national traditions – even if it is possible for you to hear the differences quite clearly – what happens when styles differ from region to region, or even village to village?

And then there is the assimilation of the music's increasingly hybrid existence into the global culture of today. At one end of the spectrum we have the authentic traditionalists singing the old songs and playing the old tunes as they have been handed down. These often feature running alterations, because a tradition is an evolving beast, not a fossil. At the other end are hi-tech, state-of-the-art fusions generated as folk meets rock, jazz, ethnic or dance-floor grooves head on.

Celtic has been in vogue these past couple of decades. But devotees of what used to be called the folk scene will not require long memories to recall a time when things were very different, when fundamental aspects of what now looks like a thriving tradition were threatened with virtual disappearance. Instead, we have a seemingly irresistible resurgence and, with a new century underway, we are faced with what looks like an ever-expanding rainbow-hued canvas that we choose to call Celtic music.

The blanket "Celtic" terminology seems to strike a particularly strong chord in the United States, where the immediate local connections are inevitably more distant, and the diluting influences more marked, thus perhaps giving additional weight to a notion of a more generalised Celtic inheritance.

Ireland has led the way in establishing an international audience, and as a consequence has the longest chapter in this book. The Irish have laid down highly influential models for the rest to follow or adapt in their own fashion, and have done so with considerable success.

Long eclipsed by the rampant Irish, the Scottish folk scene seems buoyant, with home-grown outfits like Deaf Shepherd and Old Blind Dogs following in the footsteps of pioneering bands such as Battlefield Band and Silly Wizard, or the Celtic-rock variations of Capercaillie, Wolfstone and Runrig, while bands like Shooglenifty, The Peatbog Fairies and John Rae's Celtic Feet push the music into new combinations.

Carlos Núñez has won a new audience for Galician music, and so the work of musicians such as his fellow Galician Xosé Manuel Budiño, also a piper, or the Basque accordionist Kepa Junkera, is now being more widely heard.

The ground-breaking iconoclasts of Cape Breton and Quebec, led by fiddlers Natalie McMaster and Ashley MacIsaac, and the wonderful La Bottine Souriante, continue to astound audiences wherever they play in an increasingly global reach. While no Breton artist has matched the international profile enjoyed by harpist Alan Stivell in the 1970s, the music continues to thrive and develop on an ever-expanding base, both at home and on the international concert and festival circuit which sustains much of this expansive growth.

Given the music's current state of rude good health, it is easy to ignore any nagging unease over the finer points of definition. Stretch the precise definition of Celtic music too far and it becomes meaningless, but that does not mean that the concept will not work just fine as a marketing strategy – and we live in an age where marketing strategies are king, even in the homely world of folk music. Folkies accustomed to lurking in back rooms of pubs have had to learn to cope with the glare of media attention and the application of more stringent critical standards, and some hard-liners have lamented the sacrifice of the music's grass-roots appeal in achieving its new high profile.

At the same time, audiences – and it is plural – have consistently grown, and for the most part have not been unduly concerned with definitions. Instead, they have taken the view that they may not know precisely what Celtic music is, but they do know what they like, and the artists covered in this book have succeeded in serving up precisely that, and in some style.

The structure of the book is territorial, and then with sub-divisions into the broad categories of voice, pipes, fiddle, other instruments and bands. I have happily sanctioned variations of that structure where the contributors felt that such variations would be a more accurate reflection of their area – notably in the case of Celtic Iberia. But I have not attempted to standardise contributors' text beyond matters of format, preferring to leave the individual voice in the prose as well as in the music.

The final chapter in the book, which goes under the title New Directions, is somewhat different from the rest. It is a brief survey of the latest fusions being formed in the continuing development and the transformation of Celtic music. Despite my early warnings about the vagueness of the category, the contributors to this book have succeeded in closely defining many of the elements which go to make up this music, and describing the unique conditions under which it is produced in the different regions.

My thanks go to all of the contributors for their hard work and expertise. Certain artists are discussed in more than one chapter, and for the most part I have let those overlaps stand, partly because what the writers have to say about them is intrinsically worthwhile, and partly as a reminder that the web of this music is increasingly interlinked in all manner of intriguing ways. **KENNY MATHIESON**

Kathryn Tickell.

IRELAND

BY KENNY MATHIESON

Ireland has been and remains a vibrant music-making area, and naturally deserves this wide-ranging and extensive chapter. Here we will meet all the great singers and bands, as well as the fiddlers, the pipers and the whistle players, the harpists and flautists, and the guitar players, accordionists and percussionists who make everything from traditional Irish music to the lushest orchestral settings or the latest fusions of Celtic-rock and beyond.

IRELAND: VOICE

The voice is the oldest of human instruments, and every musical tradition in the world has made central use of its expressive qualities. In Irish music the most famous traditional style of singing is sean-nós, a phrase usually translated as "old style", and sometimes applied to dance as well as song. The style developed over the course of several centuries in the Gaelic-speaking communities of Ireland and of Scotland, and although English-language songs are sometimes heard sung in the style, it is nonetheless intimately linked with the cadences and rhythms of the Gaelic language.

The purest form of the sean-nós style requires an unaccompanied solo voice with very personal embellishments of the melody – some of which also show distinct regional variations – and a song with a very specific shared local resonance for the listeners. It is essentially part of an oral tradition, rooted in a small community, and the songs were traditionally performed in an intimate social gathering, such as a house dance or céilí, a wedding, or a funeral wake. However, the growth of more public forums has taken the style into both the fleadh, or festival, and the competition arena.

A good taster of traditional sean-nós singing is available on the field recordings included on *Amhráin Ar An Sean-nós, 1948-65*, or *Buaiteoirí Chorn Uí Riada, 1972-96*, both issued on disc by RTE, the main Irish broadcasting organisation. There are also many records featuring individual singers such as Seosamh Ó hÉanaí (Joe Heaney), Máire Áine Ní Dhonnchadha, Daeach Ó Catháin, Nóirín Ní Riain, and many others.

Iarla Ó Lionáird has pushed sean-nós into new areas, including ambient backing tracks employing sampling and looping techniques on *The Seven Steps To Mercy* (Real World, 1997) and his work with Afro Celt Sound System (see the *New Directions* chapter, starting on page 176). The style has also exerted a major influence on more contemporary forms of folk-based singing, and remains a fundamental building block in instrumental Irish music as well as vocal.

If sean-nós is the pre-eminent traditional form in Irish music, it co-exists with a folk-song tradition of more recent origin, taking in ballads, macaronic songs (a mixture of Irish and English words in a single song), Irish rebel songs (Dominic Behan was a well-known exponent, as are The Wolfe Tones), sectarian songs, protest songs, the non-verbal vocalisation known as "lilting", and a range of songs brought in from Scotland, England and often much further afield – not to mention the seditious influences of rock, pop and jazz. The sharing of songs and "bothy ballads" between Scottish and Irish farmworkers was a long-established traffic, and each added distinctive flavourings to the cultural mix.

Joe Holmes was a singer and fiddle-player from County Antrim whose style and storehouse of songs has been influential on many modern singers. Holmes died in 1978, but not before he had recorded much of his repertoire with fellow Antrim-born singer **Len Graham**. Graham's work with his wife Pádraigín Ní Uallacháin, a noted sean-nós singer, and with Holmes in the group Skylark remain important as well as enjoyable resources, as do the field recordings Graham has collected in his *Harvest Home* series.

The Chieftains (opposite), pictured in concert during the late 1970s.

The folk-song revival of the 1960s brought ballad groups to the fore, with The Clancy Brothers and The Dubliners as the most popular exponents, although Limerick-born singer, banjo player and scholar **Mick Moloney** was also a major stimulus to the movement in Dublin in the 1960s, notably as part of The Johnstons. He later became an influential force on the Irish music scene in the US, where he worked with fiddler Eugene O'Donnell and multi-instrumentalist Séamus Egan, among others.

The blossoming of a wider interest in Irish traditional music from the 1960s onward allowed a new generation of singers to take the stage, and it is they who have become the most visible representatives of Irish song. At their head stands **Christy Moore**, a County Kildare native who formed a duo with Donal Lunny in his teens, an association that would be carried forward into two of the most important bands of the era: Planxty, and Moving Hearts. Indeed, the foundations of Planxty were laid in Moore's second album, *Prosperous* (Tara, 1972), which featured Lunny and fellow Planxty members Andy Irvine and Liam O'Flynn.

Moore is, quite simply, a great artist in his field. No one else sounds like him, and few would be foolhardy enough to try to emulate his brilliantly idiosyncratic but beautifully judged phrasing, or the inventive, tongue-twisting rush of his garrulous, semi-surreal poetic monologues about growing up in Catholic Ireland in the 1950s. He has a biting, dark-hued voice which is high on power but limited in range, and his style is inherently intense and dramatic.

Moore's championing of the ordinary person, the underprivileged and the oppressed went hand in hand with a passionate and uncompromising engagement with political and social issues in songs such as his version of Woody Guthrie's 'The Ludlow Massacre', on *Prosperous*, Eamon O' Doherty's 'Joe McCann' on *The Iron Behind The Velvet* (Tara, 1978), Johnny Duhan's 'El Salvador' and Bobby Sands's 'Back Home In Derry' on *Ride On* (WEA Ireland, 1984).

At the same time, Moore is a moving interpreter of a poignantly beautiful ballad like 'Nancy Spain' from *The Time Has Come* (WEA Ireland, 1983). Much of his material has a humorous and often satirical bent, epitomised in his version of Christy Hennessey's plaint on behalf of the Irish navvy, 'Don't Forget Your Shovel', on *The Time Has Come*, or his later annexation of Shane McGowan's 'Fairy Tale Of New York' on *Smoke & Strong Whiskey* (Newberry, 1991), with a colourful introduction added. The free-wheeling verbal inspiration of blackly comic hallucinatory tales like his own 'Delirium Tremens' or Colm Gallagher's 'The Reel In The Flickering Light', both on *Ordinary Man* (WEA Ireland, 1985), is hugely entertaining, and also belongs in a distinguished line of Irish literary endeavours.

Moore concentrated on his own career after leaving the Moving Hearts group in 1978, and increasingly performed solo, accompanying himself only on guitar or bodhrán. He is a fine songwriter, and his own songs came to play an increasing

role in his repertoire – although he told me in an interview in 1996 that "in a funny way, I would say I still feel more connected to the old songs than I do to the stuff I write". His 20 or so records form a substantial legacy, but his music came fully alive in performance in a way that is not quite captured on disc (even in live recordings). This made his reported decision to retire from performing in 1998 all the more disappointing.

Moore's colleague in Planxty, **Andy Irvine**, also carved out a significant solo career, but has done so while continuing his work in bands, including a reformed Planxty, the pan-European outfit Mosaic, and Patrick Street. Irvine was born in London to Scottish-Irish parents but moved to Ireland in 1962 where he played with Luke Kelly and Ronnie Drew of The Dubliners, and formed Sweeney's Men with Johnny Moynihan and Joe Dolan. The band was commemorated on Irvine's 'My Heart's Tonight In Ireland', a nostalgic reminiscence of adventures on the road set "in the days of Sweeney / In the sweet County Clare". Another of Irvine's best known songs, 'Never Tire Of The Road', also extols the virtues and vagaries of life as a touring musician. Irvine and Moynihan were pioneers in bringing the distinctive but at least distantly related sounds and rhythms of Balkan music into

■ Christy Moore at the Royal Lyceum Theatre in Edinburgh, 1994.

13

the Irish scene in the wake of Irvine's two-year spell in that part of Europe in 1968-70. It is a place where the Celts had historical roots, and it has remained part of his music.

Irvine's songwriting talents are well represented on *Rude Awakening* (Green Linnet, 1991), but while his bittersweet voice and distinctive delivery work well enough in a solo context, he generally benefits further from collaboration. Working with others seems to bring out his best, whether in a band setting with Planxty and Patrick Street or with another strong artist, as in his eponymous duo album with Paul Brady (Mulligan, 1976) and his work with Dick Gaughan on *Parallel Lines* (Green Linnet, 1983) and Davy Spillane on *East Wind* (Tara, 1991).

Paul Brady's music became more rock-oriented following his initial spell in Planxty and the release of his first traditionally-oriented solo album, *Welcome Here Kind Stranger* (Mulligan, 1978). The shift was signalled with the release of the more electric *Hard Station* (Polygram, 1981) which contained two of his best known songs, 'Crazy Dreams' and 'Nothing But The Same Old Story'.

While Brady is a fine, expressive singer, it is his songs that have proved more successful, and they have been covered by Tina Turner among others. His popular standing has never quite kept pace with his artistic credibility. But songs like 'The Island', given a simple but effective acoustic treatment on *Back To The Centre* (Mercury, 1986), have maintained his reputation as a writer of real intelligence and quality, while the release of *Spirits Colliding* (Mercury, 1995) marked a return to a more acoustic ambience.

Luka Bloom, a persona adopted by singer Barry Moore, the younger brother of Christy Moore, followed a similar trajectory from traditional folk to rock on records like *Riverside* (Reprise, 1989), *The Acoustic Motorbike* (Reprise, 1992) and *Turf* (Reprise, 1994). So did the excellent **Mary Coughlan**, although her traditional roots were already well intertwined with pop and jazz by the time of her highly-regarded debut, *Tired And Emotional* (WEA Ireland, 1987). It was to prove a well-travelled road for Irish music in the 1990s – and it would be the women singers, led by **Mary Black**, who were the most successful in the wider mass-market which beckoned. Black came from an impeccable traditional

■ *Albums (below, left to far right) by: Christy Moore; Various (A Woman's Heart); Mary Black; Dolores Keane & John Faulkner; Andy Irvine & Paul Brady; Maighread Ní Dhomhnaill; Enya; The Chieftains with Van Morrison.*

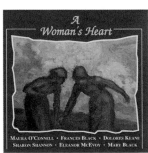

background. Brought up in a musical household in Dublin – and family lineage is a recurring theme in the annals of Irish music – she sang with her sister and three brothers as The Black Family, later joining De Dannan for a three-year spell in 1983. She had recorded her debut solo album the previous year, and by the end of the decade was widely regarded as Ireland's leading female singer.

International audiences began to take more notice of Black with the release of albums such as *No Frontiers* (Gifthorse, 1989), *Babes In The Woods* (Gifthorse, 1991) and *The Holy Ground* (Gifthorse, 1993), all cast in a more contemporary vein. But her traditional origins became less obvious as the decade progressed, especially when she replaced her long time producer Declan Sinnott with the more rock-inclined Larry Klein for Shine (Curb, 1997).

Both Mary and her sister Frances Black, whose career has followed a similar pattern, were featured on *A Woman's Heart* (Dara, 1992), a hugely successful compilation disc which helped to establish the popularity of several Irish women artists, including singers Dolores Keane and Maura O'Connell, accordionist Sharon Shannon, as well as new singers Eleanor McEvoy and, on the inevitable second volume, Sinéad Lohan. *A Woman's Heart 2* also found room for a Gaelic contribution from Maighread Ní Dhomhnaill, and a song from the controversial pop singer Sinéad O'Connor. These albums were emblematic of the drift away from traditional music in the work of the major Irish singers of the decade, whether toward sophisticated pop and rock or the country styles pursued by **Maura O'Connell** after her move to Nashville in 1987. She has recorded several albums since, and *Western Highway* (Third Floor, 1994) provides a good representation of her work.

At her best, **Dolores Keane** has few peers among Irish singers. A near-neighbour of fiddler Frankie Gavin in County Galway, she sang on De Dannan's first album (and rejoined the band later) before taking a solo career, most often in collaboration with her husband, guitarist John Faulkner.

Keane's best work is found on the albums she cut in the late 1970s and early 1980s, such as *There Was A Maid* (Claddagh, 1978), *Farewell To Eirinn* (Gael-Linn, 1981) or *Sail Óg Rua* (Gael-Linn, 1984) which includes the lovely 'Jimmy Mo

■ *Dolores Keane in 1990.*

Mhíle Stór' and a gem of an unaccompanied vocal duet with her sister, Sarah Keane, on the traditional title track. *The Best Of Dolores Keane* (Dara, 1997) offered a strong selection, including duets with Emmylou Harris and singer-songwriter Mick Hanly. Keane's brother Seán (not the great fiddler) is also a fine singer and flautist with several good albums to his credit, including the country- and rock-inflected *The Man I Am* (Grapevine, 2000).

Mary Black, Dolores Keane and Maura O'Connell all sang with De Dannan, and that great Galway band launched a fine fourth female singer onto the Irish scene: **Eleanor Shanley**. With a rich and powerful voice which belied her tiny stature, Shanley has gone on to make her own mark on albums such as *Eleanor Shanley* (Grapevine, 1995) and *Desert Heart* (Grapevine, 1997), although without quite matching the impact of her work with the band. Her successor with De Dannan, the powerful **Tommy Fleming** from Sligo, unfortunately suffered serious injuries in a car crash during 1998, and this was just at the time when his solo career was taking off. But Fleming was back in action to greet the new century with *The Contender* (Dara, 2000).

Frances Black and Naimh Parsons both sang with Arcady before embarking on solo careers. Black also cut a couple of records with singer Kieran Goss before releasing her own breakthrough album, *Talk To Me* (Dara, 1994), and has made several more as her reputation has grown. **Naimh Parsons** is another strong and adaptable singer who has used traditional roots in more commercial music on

Loosely Connected (Greentrax, 1995) and *Loosen Up* (Green Linnet, 1997), although *Blackbirds And Thrushes* (Green Linnet, 1999) saw Parsons returning to a more traditional style.

Rita Connolly has made her most impressive contributions on Shaun Davey's epic symphonic compositions *Granuaile*, *The Pilgrim* and *The Relief of Derry Symphony*, but her focus has been a little more diffuse in her own records.

The move away from traditional roots has been even more marked in the work of the two Brennan sisters from the hugely successful family band Clannad. Both Enya and Máire Brennan employed an ethereal, soft-focus, new age sound on their solo projects, with conspicuous success in the case of **Enya**'s 'Orinoco Flow (Sail Away)', a massive worldwide hit from her album *Watermark* (WEA, 1989). The same Donegal village is also home to **Aiofe**, a singer in a remarkably similar mould to the Brennans if one is to judge by her vocal contribution to Phil Coulter's *Highland Cathedral* (RCA Victor, 2000), the latest in a succession of popular Celtic "mood music" albums from the pop songwriter and producer who has now turned to arranging.

Tommy Sands, a member of The Sands Family as well as a solo singer, is best known for his attempts to reconcile Ireland's factions in songs like 'There Were Roses', a powerful but understated commemoration of the deaths of two friends, one Catholic and one Protestant, which was featured on *Singing Of The Times* (Green Linnet, 1989), or the more recent 'The Music Of Healing' on *The Heart's A Wonder* (Green Linnet, 1995). However, it should be noted that his repertoire does extend beyond these themes.

Mick Hanly, briefly the vocalist in Moving Hearts, is best known as a songwriter, but is also a fine performer, as he demonstrates on albums like *A Kiss In The Morning Early* (Green Linnet, 1977), *All I Remember* (Ringsend Road, 1989), which featured his own version of 'Past The Point Of Rescue', a hit for both Mary Black and country star Hal Ketchum, and *Warts And All* (Round Tower, 1993).

Kieran Halpin is another singer-songwriter who has not quite achieved the anticipated commercial breakthrough. Much the same might be said of the powerful and expressive singing of **Seán Tyrrell**, although that is partly his own doing. He has been singing since the 1960s, and recorded and toured with Davy Spillane, but did not get around to releasing his first solo album, the excellent *Cry Of A Dreamer* (Rykodisc), until 1994. By that time he had also written a successful music-theatre adaptation of a famous (or infamous) 18th-century Irish poem, Brian Merriman's *The Midnight Court*. Its advocacy of sexual forthrightness for women had not made it popular with the church – and historically the church in Ireland has done little to foster native music, often opposing or attempting to suppress it – but Tyrrell's adaptation, in which he was joined by the traditional singer Rosie Stewart from Fermanagh, among others, was enthusiastically received at its premiere in Galway in 1992. If anyone still needed convincing, *Cry Of A Dreamer* confirmed that Tyrrell is a singer of rare quality.

Mairéad Ní Mhaonaigh is a wonderful singer and virtuoso fiddler with the great Donegal band Altan, and has done most of her best work in the band context. That is also true of **Tríona Ní Dhomhnaill**, whose credits are impressive, including stints in Touchstone, The Bothy Band, and Relativity. She joined Nightnoise in 1986, a band formed three years earlier by her brother, guitarist and keyboard player Mícheál Ó Domhnaill, and violinist Billy Oskay (who was replaced in 1990 by John Cunningham).

Nightnoise's classical- and jazz-tinged music proved well suited to Ní Dhomhnaill's voice, and while their new-age-style treatments of Irish music will not be to everyone's liking, it is well represented on *Shadow Of Time* (Windham Hill, 1993). The family connection also extends to include Tríona's sister, **Maighread Ní Dhomnhaill**, a great exponent of the Donegal tradition who works with Donal Lunny on occasion and is heard in fine voice on her own *Gan Dhá Phingin Spré/No Dowry* (Gael Linn, 1991).

Finally, a number of pop and rock singers have dabbled in traditional music, sometimes drawing on an early background in the music. This is the case with Liam Ó Maonlai of Hothouse Flowers, an accomplished sean-nós singer. **Van Morrison**'s music has always carried a Celtic strain amid its soul and R&B leanings, and he made that connection in its most explicit form when he teamed up with The Chieftains on *Celtic Heartbeat* (Mercury, 1988).

Others who have ventured into (or close to) traditional music while retaining their own distinctive style include Mike Scott, a Scottish singer who lived in Ireland for a time in the late 1980s with his band The Waterboys. There's also Shane McGowan, the raggle-taggle frontman of The Pogues and The Popes, Ron Kavana, Sinéad O'Connor, Dolores Ó Riordan (of The Cranberries), Brian Kennedy, Andy White, and even Bono of U2. However, traditionalists drew the line when they heard Kate Bush performing in phonetically-learned Irish on Donal Lunny's crossover project *Common Ground* (EMI, 1996).

It remains to be seen how well "pure" traditional singing will survive the kind of rampant eclecticism which this brief survey has charted. The same arguments hold in instrumental music, and hinge on a continuing debate on the nature of the tradition itself. Even those who view it as an evolving entity which has always borrowed and assimilated from outside must be at least a little alarmed by the number of external influences now flooding into the music at an apparently accelerated pace. Paradoxically, however, while the community life which once sustained traditional music has now changed beyond recall, awareness of the music has reached new and unprecedented heights, and so seems quite likely to survive the search for new fusions and wider audiences.

RECOMMENDED RECORDS

MARY BLACK THE COLLECTION *(Grapevine, 1992) Mary Black was spreading her wings at the turn of the 1990s, and this well chosen compilation captures her in peak form.*
PAUL BRADY WELCOME HERE KIND STRANGER *(Mulligan, 1978) Brady is captured in his most traditional mode prior to the rock explorations of later albums like Hard Station.*
ANDY IRVINE AND PAUL BRADY ANDY IRVINE/PAUL BRADY *(Mulligan, 1976) A wonderful collaboration between two of the greats, this album includes Brady's classic interpretation of 'Arthur McBride And The Sergeant' among its many gems.*
DOLORES KEANE SAIL ÓG RUA *(Gael-Linn, 1984) The early 1980s were a vintage period for Dolores Keane, and this album with her husband, guitarist John Faulkner, is a perfect illustration of her greatness.*
CHRISTY MOORE LIVE AT THE POINT *(Grapevine, 1994) All of Moore's many albums are more or less essential listening, but this live set offers a characteristic mix of heartfelt political songs, beautiful ballads and satirical jibes.*
VAN MORRISON AND THE CHIEFTAINS CELTIC HEARTBEAT *(Mercury, 1988) Van The Man sets aside his soul and R&B leanings to delve into a highly enjoyable set of traditional and contemporary tunes with the band.*
VARIOUS ARTISTS A WOMAN'S HEART *(Dara, 1992) This disc (and its follow-up) confirmed that Irish women singers were big news, and its success brought new listeners for the likes of Mary Black, Dolores Keane and Maura O'Connell.*

IRELAND: FIDDLE

The fiddle, or violin, is the instrument which most directly reflects the many regional variations in Irish traditional music. Although the specific local nuances of these regional styles are becoming increasingly diffuse, there are strong stylistic traditions associated with many areas of Ireland, the best known of which are Donegal, Sligo, Clare, and the Sliabh Luachra area on the border of Kerry and Cork. Regional divisions were a product of isolated development, and have been eroded by easier travel, the power of radio, and the wider availability of recordings. Individual players, too, added further stylistic diversity, as did groupings of players from particular areas. The whole subject is complex, but occasional reference will still be made here to aspects of regional styles.

Other than the slow airs, most of the well-known Irish tune forms have their origins in dance music. They include reels, jigs, slides, hornpipes, polkas, mazurkas, barn dances, and the "highlands" and strathspeys of Donegal, among others.

Many Irish tunes follow a common structure in which two different "strains" of eight bars in length are each played through twice, and then the whole 32-bar sequence is repeated from the top. Tunes are generally played in "sets" of two, three or more tunes with no breaks between them. In playing for dancers, a rock-

■ *Eileen Ivers.*

steady rhythm rather than virtuoso execution was the essential constituent of the music, which could be played either by a single musician or by a small group (and later, with the rise of the céilí band, by a larger ensemble).

Melodic variation is a governing principle in Irish traditional music. The player embellishes, ornaments and otherwise alters the melody in small ways with each playing. The same tune is never the same twice, and a printed version is only one possibility among many. As the music developed for listening on record or in the concert hall rather than as an accompaniment to dance, the complexity and dexterity of the elaborations grew.

"Sessions", the quintessential Irish medium, are a fairly recent development. Traditionally, music was made in the home or at dances, including the outdoor "crossroads" dances, at weddings, and at other communal occasions. Music sessions in pubs originated among Irish musicians working in London after World War Two, and did not arrive in Dublin until the 1960s.

Sessions are now widespread in Ireland and well beyond, often targeted at the tourist market, and have evolved their own etiquette and lore, involving legendary after-hours stints and, of course, the "craic" (or crack) – roughly translatable as good conversation and fun. In practice, like the jam session in jazz, they are often routine affairs masquerading under a cloak of romantic associations. But if you are lucky enough to come across a good one you will understand how the sessions achieved their reputation. The fast, virtuosic, highly-ornamented Sligo style came to particular prominence in modern fiddling through the influence of several American-based fiddlers with origins in the region, led by Michael Coleman, Paddy Killoran, James Morrison and James 'Lad' O'Beirne, as well as the Cavan-born Ed Reavy, and Hugh Gillespie, a Donegal native. The music they recorded in the United States during the three decades prior to the 1950s found its way back to Ireland on 78rpm records, and became enormously influential. Also influential was the increasing availability of the recorded music itself, by way of the broadcast media as well as on disc.

Back home, the current generation of fiddlers was preceded by a rich crop of players. From Clare came Junior Crehan, Paddy Canny, Bobby Casey, Jack Mulcaire, John Kelly, Patrick Kelly, Peadar O'Loughlin, P. Joe Hayes and Frank Custy. Custy is a revered teacher whose daughter, Mary, is a leading light in the new wave of fiddlers.

Sligo fiddlers included Andrew Davey, Kathleen Harrington, Fred Finn, and Martin Wynne, while Donegal had John Doherty, Seán Reid, Néillidh Boyle, and Proinsias Ó Maonaigh. Pádraig O'Keefe, Julia Clifford and Seamus Creagh offer fine examples of the Sliabh Luachra style.

Galway's Paddy Fahy, Lucy Farr and Martin Byrnes, Des Donnelly from Tyrone, John Dwyer from Cork, Mick Hoy of Fermanagh, Joe Liddy and the Lennon family of Leitrim, Antoin MacGabhann of Cavan, Tommy Potts of Dublin, Brendan McGlinchey of Armagh, Eugene O'Donnell of Derry, Seán Maguire of Belfast, and American-born players such as Johnny McGreevy and Andy McGann all hold prominent places in the history of Irish traditional music, but there are very many more who have made a significant contribution.

The current generation reflects the influence of many of their predecessors, often through a direct family connection. **Martin Hayes**, for example, is the son of P. Joe Hayes, and was playing alongside his father in the celebrated Tulla Céilí Band at the age of 14. The experience of playing with the Tulla in the US led to his move there, and he eventually settled in Seattle. He dabbled with rock, then returned to traditional music but with a distinctive contemporary twist. He teamed up with the Chicagoan guitarist **Dennis Cahill** to form the most compelling duo at present in Irish music.

In an age when virtuoso fiddlers have pushed Irish music to turbo-charged extremes, Hayes flies in the face of fashion, and does so with breathtaking brilliance. His playing is rooted in the Clare style, with its gloriously flowing melodies and slower tempos, played with magisterial authority and absolute emotional expressiveness.

Hayes has strong technical ability, but his more measured approach allows the music to blossom, with notes and phrases flowing elegantly rather than tumbling over one another at a pace which can sacrifice expressive quality in the wrong hands. However, Hayes makes this work because he is a great musician with a strongly developed feel for the music he plays. Guitarist Cahill provides an equally musical and inventive counter-balance in their explorations, and the mounting, almost trance-like intensity which they build in their instrumental sets is completely gripping.

Their first studio album *The Lonesome Touch* (Green Linnet, 1997) is among the handful of essential Irish records of the 1990s, as is the magnificent *Under The Moon* (Green Linnet, 1995) which predates the fiddler's association with Cahill but features guitarists Randall Bays and Steve Cooney, with guest contributions from accordionist John Williams and the fiddler's father, P. Joe Hayes. Oddly, given the glories of their live performances, Hayes and Cahill's *Live In Seattle* (Green Linnet, 1999) was marginally less compelling on disc than the studio recording, although it does include one of the most extended instrumental sets you are likely to hear, clocking in at just under 28 minutes. Hayes also recorded with guitarist Bays on his fine debut album, *Martin Hayes* (Green Linnet, 1993).

The best known current exponents of the Donegal style are the twin fiddle team of Mairéad Ní Mhaonaigh and Ciarán Tourish, of Altan (see later Bands section). The regional taste for a sharp, staccato bowing style and the use of crisply executed triplets as a principal ornamentation is well illustrated in the playing of **Tommy Peoples**. Brought up in east Donegal, he moved to Dublin where he became involved in the city's traditional music scene. He flirted with fame for a time in the 1970s, notably as a founder member of The Bothy Band, but ultimately preferred the quiet life in Clare.

Peoples's playing on The Bothy Band's classic first album remains an exemplary sample of his work, and proved hugely influential. He recorded several albums under his own name, including a now rare debut for Comhaltas Ceoltóirí Éireann in 1976. *The High Part Of The Road* (Shanachie, 1976) and *The Iron Man* (Shanachie, 1985) are both fine records, although his eponymous album with Matt Molloy and Paul Brady (Mulligan, 1976) is probably the best of all.

Paddy Glackin hails from Dungloe in Donegal. His father, Tom Glackin, was a great fiddler and teacher, and his brothers, Kevin and Séamus, are also excellent fiddlers. Paddy was also briefly a member of The Bothy Band in its early days, and as an administrator and broadcaster as well as a player has done a great deal to promote traditional music. He can be heard on several discs under his own name, including the glorious *Rabharta Ceoil/In Full Spate* (Gael Linn, 1995) with his brothers, and *The Whirlwind* (Gael-Linn, 1995) with piper Robbie Hannan.

Galway's most famous fiddler today is **Frankie Gavin**, best known as the founder and subsequent heartbeat of the great De Dannan. Gavin also came from a musical family, and cultivated a style among the most exhilarating in Irish music.

Cherish The Ladies on-stage.

His playing is genuinely electrifying, both in terms of his dazzling and imaginative ornamentation and the fearsome tempos which he favours in the fast tunes. But even those who fear an excess of these qualities in Gavin's work must acknowledge his musicality and control. He flows where others might flounder, and while his best work is heard with De Dannan, his solo albums are worth seeking out. They include *Traditional Music Of Ireland* (Shanachie, 1977), *Omós Do Joe Cooley* (Gael Linn, 1986) in which the fiddler relaxes his usual high-octane approach, *Frankie Goes To Town* (Bees Knees, 1989), and *Irlande* (Ocoro, 1994). There are also collaborations with Stephane Grappelli and with the RTÉ Concert Orchestra. On *Croch Suas É* (Gael-Linn, 1983) he concentrates mainly but not exclusively on his second instrument, the flute.

Seán Keane is best known as a long standing member of The Chieftains and has committed most of his energies to that band since joining in the mid 1960s. But the Dublin-born fiddler has also recorded several albums under his own name. His debut, *Gusty's Frolicks* (Claddagh, 1975), featured unaccompanied traditional playing with a distinct Clare flavour and a marked debt to piping ornaments. He collaborated with his brother, the great accordion player James Keane, on *Roll Away The Reel World* (Green Linnet, 1980), and with fellow Chieftain Matt Molloy on both *Contentment Is Wealth* (Green Linnet, 1985) and *The Fire Aflame* (Claddagh, 1992), with Liam O'Flynn on board for the latter set.

Kevin Burke was born in London but his parents were from Sligo, and was raised on the recordings of Michael Coleman, Paddy Killoran and James Morrison. Burke took over from Tommy Peoples in The Bothy Band in 1976, and is currently part of Patrick Street as well as his own Open House. Burke's Sligo roots mingled with a variety of influences in London to produce an individual style which is heard to great effect on one of the classic Irish fiddle albums, *If The Cap Fits* (Mulligan, 1978), which has retained its freshness and appeal. Burke augments the accompaniment by overdubbing fiddle in places, a technique he uses at several points on the album's tour de force, an extended set of 13 tunes which formed one full side of the original vinyl LP.

Burke's two duet albums with Micheál Ó Domhnaill, *Promenade* (Mulligan, 1979) and *Portland* (Green Linnet, 1982), are gentler affairs, while his duets with accordionist Jackie Daly on *Eavesdropper* (Mulligan, 1981) and guitarist Gerry O'Beirne on *Up Close* (Green Linnet, 1984) are both recommended. His contribution to the classic *Andy Irvine/Paul Brady* (Mulligan, 1977) should not be ignored, and he also recorded with Arlo Guthrie on *Last Of The Brooklyn Cowboys* (Warner Brothers, 1973) where he has two brief instrumental features. Burke is also heard alongside fiddlers Johnny Cunningham and Christian Lemaître on *The Celtic Fiddle Festival* (Green Linnet, 1993) and *Encore* (Green Linnet, 1998).

Nollaig Casey from Cork is another fine Irish fiddler of the current generation. She trained as a classical player and spent several years in the RTÉ Symphony Orchestra, but contradicts the belief that classical technique is inimical to the development of a genuine traditional feel. Her work with her husband, guitarist Arty McGlynn, is heard on *Lead The Knave* (Ringsend Road, 1989) and *Causeway* (Tara, 1995), and she is featured in Donal Lunny's Coolfin.

Márie Breathnach also has a classical background, and spent a decade teaching at the College Of Music in Dublin before emerging as an in-demand player featuring on a wide range of albums, and as part of the *Riverdance* cast. Her own recordings include *Angels Candles* (Gift Horse, 1993), the disappointingly diffuse *Voyage Of Bran* (Celtic Heartbeat, 1994), which drew on a rather romanticised Celtic and pagan mythology, and *Celtic Lovers* (Blix Street, 1997).

The active Irish music scene in North America has produced many fine players, but the two outstanding fiddlers are **Eileen Ivers** and Liz Carroll. Ivers was born in New York to parents from Mayo, and studied as a teenager with Martin Mulvihill, a renowned fiddler and teacher from Limerick. Like so many Irish musicians, she came through the competition circuit as a teenager before launching a professional career.

Ivers played with several groups in the US including The Green Fields Of America, an Irish-American group formed by Mick Moloney, and Cherish The Ladies, as well as the New York-based Celtic rap/rock outfit Paddy A Go Go. But she is best known for her work under her own name, and for her contribution to *Riverdance* where she replaced Márie Breathnach. She has also toured with the American soul-rock stars Hall & Oates, as well as guesting with others including Hothouse Flowers and Patti Smith – and meanwhile has shown no inhibitions in extending her traditional roots.

She recorded *First Takes* (Green Linnet, 1987), a duet album with button-accordionist John Whelan, prior to her own debut album, simply entitled *Eileen Ivers* (Green Linnet, 1994). It bore the subtitle *Traditional Irish Music* on the sleeve, and substantiated the claim in an exciting way, although there were some indications of the eclecticism to be heard on her subsequent recordings. These include *Wild Blue* (Green Linnet, 1996), named for her striking blue electric violin, and *Crossing The Bridge* (Sony, 1999), both with diverse echoes of jazz, rock, rap and much ethnic music. *So Far: The Eileen Ivers Collection* (Green Linnet, 1997) is a good introduction to her work, and *Back To Titanic* (Sony, 1999) featured music from or inspired by the *Titanic* movie.

Liz Carroll was born in Chicago and became involved in the active Irish music scene there, learning from senior players such as fiddler John McGreevy and piper Joe Shannon. Like Ivers, Carroll has been a member of both Cherish The Ladies and Green Fields Of America. Later she formed the three-piece band Trian with accordionist Billy McComiskey and guitarist Dáithí Sproule. The albums that they released – *Trian* (Flying Fish, 1991) and *Trian II* (Green Linnet, 1995) – are both good, and well worth hearing.

Carroll recorded *Kiss Me Kate* (Shanachie, 1977) with accordion player Tommy Maguire, then made her solo debut with *A Friend Indeed* (Shanachie, 1979), but has staggered her subsequent recordings at decade-long intervals. *Liz Carroll* (Green Linnet, 1988) fulfilled the promise of her initial releases, but she surpassed even those with *Lost In The Loop* (Green Linnet, 2000), a superb album that featured a fine supporting cast of Irish-American collaborators including another accomplished fiddler, Winifred Horan from the group Solas.

Good fiddlers are something of an Irish speciality, and they continue to emerge, often as part of a group. Among those worth listening for are Matt Cranitch, Cathal Hayden and Paul Shaughnessy, as well as newer names such as Mary Custy, Dezi Donnelly and Liz Doherty.

RECOMMENDED RECORDS

KEVIN BURKE IF THE CAP FITS *(Mulligan, 1978) Burke is best known for his work in The Bothy Band and Patrick Street, but this is one of the essential Irish fiddle albums.*

LIZ CARROLL LOST IN THE LOOP *(Green Linnet, 2000) Carroll does not make many albums under her own name, but when she does go into the studio the results are well worth the wait.*

FRANKIE GAVIN FRANKIE GOES TO TOWN *(Bees Knees, 1989) De Dannan's frontman is in inspired fettle on this dazzling outing on traditional Irish dance tunes, accompanied by the ever-present Alec Finn on bouzouki and pianist Charlie Lennon.*

PADDY GLACKIN RABHARTA CEOIL/IN FULL SPATE *(Gael Linn, 1991) Few albums have been as appropriately named as this breathtaking display of the fiddler's art from Paddy Glackin, aided by his brothers.*

MARTIN HAYES AND DENNIS CAHILL THE LONESOME TOUCH *(Green Linnet, 1997) The combination of Hayes's Clare-rooted fiddling and Cahill's empathic guitar work makes this one of the key Irish albums of the 1990s.*

EILEEN IVERS EILEEN IVERS *(Green Linnet, 1994)*
A powerful album predating both Riverdance and her later more experimental work. Here Ivers focuses instead on the traditional aspects of her electrifying playing.

IRELAND: PIPES AND WHISTLE

Remarkably enough given the current popularity of almost anything associated with Irish traditional music, the uilleann pipes were perilously close to extinction as recently as the 1960s. But the subsequent revival of the instrument means that it is now more widely played than at any time in its history.

The uilleann pipes (pronounced "ill-yun") are among the most complex members of the bagpipe family, since they possess not only a chanter with a double reed, a two-octave range for fingering the melody, and three single reed drones for continuous accompaniment, but also an optional set of three pipes with double reeds and keys known as regulators. These can be used to supply a simple chordal harmony or rhythmic accompaniment – assuming that the piper has the dexterity

and musical ability to cope. The musician plays the uilleann pipes in a sitting position, and they are not so much held as worn. The end of the chanter is positioned against a leather "popping strap" on the player's thigh, although it is raised to play certain notes and to create the characteristic ornament known as "popping". As in the Northumbrian pipes and the Scottish cauld wind pipes, air is supplied by a bellows strapped under the player's right arm and depressed with the elbow. The air is then fed to the chanter from a bag under the left arm, also controlled by the elbow. The instrument takes its name from the Irish word for elbow, uille, although some still argue that the proper name is union pipes, after the "union" of chanter and regulators.

The instrument has its own repertoire of special fingering techniques and particular methods of ornamenting and embellishing the melody. This process is fundamental in traditional music, where melody and rhythm are paramount. While a greater degree of experiment with more extended harmony has become fashionable in recent times, this was never at the core of the music. As in Scottish music, many piping ornaments are also adapted for use on the fiddle, flute, accordion and other instruments, and this has led some musicians and observers to suggest that the pipes are the quintessential instrument of Irish music.

The uilleann pipes probably evolved from an early mouth-blown instrument similar to the Scottish Highland pipes, and have been around in their present form since the early 19th century. The pipes were a society instrument for some of that period, but were also played in farms and rural communities wherever ordinary people could afford a set, and more recently have become inextricably linked with traditional music.

There was a long-standing tradition of itinerant pipers, such as the legendary **John Cash** of Wicklow, who would tour the country playing at fairs, sporting events and crossroads dances, a tradition that disappeared only comparatively recently. **Johnny Doran**, a flamboyant stylist who died in 1950, is a famous example of that hardy breed. His brother, **Felix Doran**, carried on the family piping tradition until his death in 1972, and Felix's son is also a piper. Many other distinguished pipers have contributed to the development of the instrument in the

■ *Albums (below, far left to right) by: Martin Hayes & Dennis Cahill; Eileen Ivers; Liz Carroll; Frankie Gavin; Kevin Burke; Arty McGlynn; Paddy Glackin; and Trian.*

present century, but three players – Leo Rowsome, Séamus Ennis, and Willy Clancy – came to dominate uilleann piping prior to the current revival which began in the 1960s. All were distinctive stylists and left recorded legacies of their work.

Leo Rowsome belonged to a family with a long tradition of piping and pipe-making, and was also a distinguished teacher. He adopted a refined style of playing designed to show off the uilleann pipes as a serious and respectable instrument, and was fond – some would say overly fond – of the regulators. Rowsome's playing can be heard on many recordings, of which *Rí Na bPíobarí/King Of The Pipers* (Claddagh, reissued Shanachie) is a fine example.

Séamus Ennis was a virtuoso player who laid the foundations of the modern piping style, emphasising fleet, energised execution and cleanly articulated melody lines, never allowing the tune to be overwhelmed by its ornamentation. Ennis was an important collector of tunes and a broadcaster, and was famous for the beauty of his slow airs, as well as his much-quoted opinion that the bodhrán, the Irish hand drum, was best played with a knife. *The Return From Fingal* (RTE, 1996) is a fine example of his playing.

Like Ennis, **Willie Clancy** was influenced by the fire and flair of Johnny Doran's piping, but balanced that liveliness and his own irrepressible sense of fun with a seriousness of purpose that he may have acquired from one of his teachers, Leo Rowsome. In addition to his recordings, which include two individual volumes of the excellent *The Pipering Of Willie Clancy* (Claddagh), his substantial legacy is commemorated in the annual Willie Clancy Summer School that takes place in his hometown of Miltown Malbay, County Clare. It has now become one of Ireland's most famous musical events.

The revival of the uilleann pipes began in the 1960s, with Paddy Moloney of The Chieftains one of the first of the new generation to make his mark. A number of leading pipers formed their own organisation, Na Píobairí Uilleann (which simply means "the uilleann pipers"). It is open only to players and dedicated to the promotion and preservation of the instrument and its music. Rowsome and Ennis were its first patrons, with Breandán Breathnach, the collector, researcher and writer on Irish music, its chairman. It is still active today, though now operates in changed surroundings. A new breed of pipers and a new level of worldwide interest in the music have combined not only to establish the instrument at the centre of Irish music but to give it an almost iconic status. **Liam O'Flynn** has done as much as anyone, and more than most, to that end.

A native of County Kildare, O'Flynn took up pipes at the age of 11, and studied with Leo Rowsome in a relationship he has likened to that of master and apprentice. This has long been the way in which piping skills are passed down from player to player, both across and within the generations. O'Flynn has acknowledged the important influence of the two other members of the great

■ *Davy Spillane pictured in 1991.*

■ *Members of The Bothy Band.*

triumvirate, Willie Clancy and Séamus Ennis, and has a set of "flat" pipes given to him by Ennis. (Flat pipes are pitched lower than the standard instrument and have a more mellow sonority.)

O'Flynn came to wider notice as a founder member of Planxty in 1972, and remained with the band for a decade. He made the instrument's emotive combination of haunting poignancy and abandoned vitality a trademark sound in

Planxty, and the influence of the band had a powerful effect across a whole range of Irish music. The uilleann pipes, an instrument threatened with oblivion only a decade before, was now firmly back at the centre of the music.

O'Flynn's success with Planxty took him in several different musical directions in the ensuing decades. For the purest example of his piping in a traditional context, look no further than *The Fine Art Of Piping* (Celtic Music, 1991), a masterly exhibition of his artistry in a setting unadorned by additional instrumentation or extraneous borrowings. Even in the most virtuosic excursions his command of the sets of reels, jigs and hornpipes maintain both a structural integrity and an unhurried feel – always the mark of a true master. Notable too are O'Flynn's lovely treatments of slow airs, as heard for example in 'A Stóir mo Chrói' or in the Scottish tune 'Dark Lochnagar'.

Such an unambiguously traditional setting is rare in O'Flynn's recorded output, a significant portion of which is represented by his work with the Belfast-born composer Shaun Davey. Davey took the instrument into a formal orchestral setting with his great work for uilleann pipes and chamber orchestra, *The Brendan Voyage* (Tara, 1980). It was inspired by Tim Severin's reconstruction of the fabled navigation by Brendan and his monks from Ireland to America in a leather boat during the 6th century.

Irish traditional music had been orchestrated before, but Davey added a traditional musician, an often overlooked element. O'Flynn was placed at centre stage as the soloist, and made a great success, featuring in several subsequent large-scale works by Davey. These include *Granuaile* (Tara, 1985), *The Relief Of Derry Symphony* (Tara, 1990) and *The Pilgrim* (Tara, 1994). The latter was originally performed at Le Festival Interceltique de Lorient in Brittany in 1983, and was subsequently revised for a performance in Glasgow in 1990, which is the version that was released on CD in 1994.

O'Flynn has also worked with Bill Whelan, the creator of *Riverdance*, and has made more diverse explorations with his own band on excellent albums such as *Out To An Other Side* (Tara, 1993), which featured a version of Séamus Ennis's famously graphic epic 'The Fox Chase' with added string orchestra. Also noteworthy is *The Given Note* (Tara, 1995) and the blander *Piper's Call* (Tara, 1998).

His earlier records, including *Celtic Folkweave* (Polydor, 1974), a now rare album with Mick Hanly and Mícheál Ó Domhnaill, and his eponymous debut album in 1988, both produced by Donal Lunny, are more traditional in flavour, as is his superb collaboration with Matt Molloy, fiddler Séan Keane and Arty McGlynn on *The Fire Aflame* (Claddagh, 1992). O'Flynn has worked with musicians from many genres, from Mark Knopfler and Kate Bush to Elmer Bernstein and John Cage, not to mention poet Seamus Heaney. But whatever the context, his playing remains impressively poised and inventive.

Finbar Furey is a close contemporary of O'Flynn, and is best known as a member of the successful Irish ballad group The Fureys. Finbar's singing is an acquired taste -– his voice seems not so much to have rough edges as to be made up of them – and his choice of songs is decidedly and unapologetically sentimental. However, his music moves into a different area altogether when he takes up the uilleann pipes. His playing has always stood out for its fire and virtuosity amid the otherwise homely approach of The Fureys, and his dexterity and musicality on both pipes and whistles should not be underestimated. This becomes more obvious when he performs outside the group, and is probably most evident if you are lucky enough to catch him in an informal session.

For many knowledgeable judges, though, the most incendiary piper of his generation is **Paddy Keenan**. He is probably best known for the work he did with the other seminal Irish band of the 1970s, The Bothy Band, but in fact he is a dazzling virtuoso in any context, employing a level of spontaneous invention worthy of a jazz improviser.

Despite his pyrotechnics, Keenan is also an unfailingly musical player – and while these are two qualities that do not always go well together, the pipes have a way of bringing out the exhibitionist in many players. Keenan was brought up in a musical travelling family from County Meath, his father a fine piper, his mother an accordionist. He moved from whistle to pipes as a child, and as a teenager played with Finbar Furey before spending time playing blues in London and Europe. Irish music reclaimed him, however, and he became a member of Seachtair, which metamorphosed into The Bothy Band in 1974.

Keenan did not seek out another band after the demise of that group, but lived in Brittany and in Ireland before moving to the United States in 1991, where he is based today, in Boston. He has not sought fame, and has recorded all too rarely in his own right, but always to great effect. Notable examples are *Paddy Keenan* (Gael-Linn, 1978), on which he is accompanied by fiddler Paddy Glackin and his two brothers, John and Thomas Keenan, and *Poirt An Phiobaire* (Gael-Linn, 1983) with Arty McGlynn, as well as a duo album with Paddy Glackin, *Doublin* (Tara, 1979). Keenan re-emerged on his own label with *Ná Keen Affair* (Hot Conya, 1996) featuring fiddlers Tommy Peoples and Séamus Creagh, revealing his creativity intact despite occasionally indifferent recording.

Peter Browne has made many programmes as a radio producer, including a tribute to Paddy Keenan, but he is an accomplished uilleann piper in his own right. Browne was taught by Rowsome, Ennis and Clancy, an unimpeachable pedigree. He has been steeped in traditional music since his childhood, and while his own recordings are not numerous, they are of uniformly high quality. He can be heard in grand fettle on records such as Kevin Burke's *If The Cap Fits* (Mulligan, 1978) or the Paris segment of The Bothy Band's *Live In Concert*

(Windsong, 1994), recorded in 1976. The album also features a remarkable solo set comprising 'Garret Barry's' and 'The Bucks Of Oranmore' from Paddy Keenan, recorded in Kilburn, London, in 1978.

Davy Spillane is arguably the most widely recognised exponent of the uilleann pipes. His music reached an even bigger audience when he was a featured soloist in the phenomenally successful *Riverdance*, which featured music by composer Bill Whelan to accompany its exciting if ersatz modernisation of Irish step dance. Like the show and everything else related to it, the album was a bestseller. All who heard Spillane's emotive playing on uilleann pipes and low whistle (also known as the Overton whistle, after its original maker) on tunes such as 'Reel Around The Sun' or the lament 'Caoineadh cú Chulainn' were struck by the power and expressiveness of both player and instruments. Those who had followed the Irish music scene in the 1980s were already well acquainted with those qualities through Spillane's own bands and his contribution to the peerless Moving Hearts, still a benchmark group in the contemporary development of Irish music.

Spillane started out playing tin whistle as a child, then took up pipes at school, and began playing in competitions. He travelled around Ireland playing traditional music for a time before joining Moving Hearts as a founder member. The band built on the example of Planxty and The Bothy Band, but added electric instruments and a rock feel when the dominating trend was for small, often informal acoustic groups. Spillane explained that it was a move into electric music rather than into rock. "It wasn't predominantly a rock band, but it wasn't a folk band either," he said. "I suppose the best way to put it might be that it was a more modern approach to folk music."

He formed his own Davy Spillane Band after Moving Hearts split in 1986, taking further the use of electric instruments and rock influences. The line-up featured electric guitar and bass, keyboards and drums alongside his pipes and low whistle. Spillane produced a wide-ranging musical mix with diverse collaborators, although his own playing always seemed rooted in Irish idioms whatever the ostensible genre of the material to hand.

He recorded four albums, including the excellent *Atlantic Bridge* (Tara, 1987), *Out Of The Air* (Tara, 1988), which featured a longer version of the classic Moving Hearts track 'The Storm', and *Shadow Hunter* (Tara, 1990), before signing to Columbia Records for *A Place Among The Stones* (1994). Spillane is clearly willing to embrace a variety of idioms, ranging from Balkan folk – as in his collaboration with Andy Irvine on *East Wind* (Tara, 1991) – through to rock, country, and blues. This certainly brought his music to a much wider audience, but anyone inclined to wonder about his traditional-music credentials should listen to the unaccompanied 'Tribute To Johnny Doran' on *Atlantic Bridge*.

Spillane has been particularly successful in creating hauntingly atmospheric settings from which his pipes and whistle can soar. This quality was exploited to the full in Bill Whelan's *Riverdance* (Celtic Heartbeat, 1996) and the subsequent *Roots Of Riverdance* (Celtic Heartbeat, 1997), as well as in his contribution as a soloist with orchestra to Whelan's *The Seville Suite* (Uptown/Universal, 1997), which also featured Liam O' Flynn.

Ever versatile, Spillane has appeared on albums by Kate Bush, Van Morrison, Elvis Costello, Enya, Steve Winwood and Chris Rea among others. He established his own studio in the West of Ireland to work on film soundtracks (his credits include *Rob Roy* and *Michael Collins*). He also produces recordings and makes uilleann pipes. His experiments with new genres and lavish arrangements have not always been well received by musical traditionalists, but he has widened the audience for both the music and his instrument, of which he is a great exponent.

If these are the major figures in the pipes' post-1960s revival, they are but a few among an ever increasing number of players. There are, for example, over 800 members in the worldwide community of uilleann pipers. Musicians such as Christy O'Leary, Tommy Keane, Ronan Browne, Declan Masterson, Tomás Lynch, John McSherry, Steafan Hannigan, Michael McGoldrick and, on the other side of the Atlantic, Eric Rigler and Jerry O'Sullivan, have all made significant marks or are in the process of proving their worth by continuing the tradition and by moving it in new directions.

While many pipers – as well as flute players, fiddlers and others – also double on tin whistle or the more recent introduction, the low whistle, a small number have concentrated on whistle as their main instrument. They are led by the inimitable **Micho Russell** whose vast repertoire included an endless store of colourful tales about the tunes he played. Born in Doolin, County Clare, he played flute too, but became known for the whistle. He took his music around the world until his death in 1994.

■ *Albums (below, left to far right) by: Shaun Davey; Liam O'Flynn; Davy Spillane; Máire Ní Chathasaigh & Chris Newman; Sharon Shannon; Noel Hill & Tony Linnane; Mícheál Ó Súilleabháin; Cathal McConnell.*

Mary Bergin is another wonderful player who chooses to concentrate on the whistle, as she demonstrates with the band Dordan and on her own albums, including *Feadóga Stain* (Gael-Linn, 1979) and *Feadóga Stain 2* (Gael-Linn, 1993).

The whistle is often perceived as a beginner's instrument, but in the hands of these masters it stands alongside any of the core instruments of Irish music as a vehicle for feeling as well as virtuosity.

RECOMMENDED RECORDS

SHAUN DAVEY THE BRENDAN VOYAGE *(Tara, 1980) The most successful of Davey's fusions of traditional music with an orchestra, this epic recording features a leading role for Liam O'Flynn.*

PADDY KEENAN NÁ KEEN AFFAIR *(Hot Conya, 1996) Keenan's self-produced album is one of the most exhilarating contemporary uilleann pipe recordings of the 1990s.*

LIAM O'FLYNN THE FINE ART OF PIPING *(Celtic Music, 1991) A masterly demonstration of the piper's art in an unadorned traditional setting, at the same time underlining O'Flynn's virtuosity and expressiveness.*

DAVY SPILLANE ATLANTIC BRIDGE *(Tara, 1987) A classic album from Ireland's best known uilleann piper, giving a powerful taste of his straightforward traditional music as well as more fusion-oriented styles.*

IRELAND: HARP

The harp is among the oldest instruments used in Irish music, and provides the country's national emblem. The earliest surviving depiction of the instrument in Ireland dates from the late 11th century, and a harp from the late 14th century is preserved in Dublin. But the continuity of the tradition was severely disrupted at the end of the 1700s, and the instrument has been subject to many attempts at revival. Despite that historical legacy and the still popular music of harpists such as **Turlough Ó Carolan** (1670-1738), the harp has not assumed a central role in contemporary Irish music, although there are in evidence a number of significant performers.

The most important harpist is **Máire Ní Chathasaigh** whose work as a teacher as well as a player has been influential and invaluable, building on the

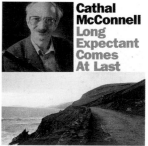

efforts of Grainne Yeats in the previous generation. Chathasaigh comes from a Cork family steeped in traditional music – her sister is the fiddler Nollaig Casey.

Chathasaigh's solo album *The New Strung Harp* (Temple Records, 1985) broke new ground by applying the instrument to traditional music and dance rhythms rather than soft-focus pseudo-Celtic mysticism. *The Carolan Album* (Old Bridge, 1994) was devoted to the music of Turlough Ó Carolan. Chathasaigh is married to the great English guitarist Chris Newman, and their duo provides a sparkling context for her work on albums like *Out Of Court* (Old Bridge, 1995) and *Live In The Highlands* (Old Bridge, 1995).

Derek Bell of The Chieftains has also been a major force in focusing attention on the harp in a traditional context, while singer and harpist Mary O'Hara has helped popularise the instrument. Many harpists, including Antoinette McKenna and Aine Minogue, are also singers. Laoise Kelly, a member of The Bumblebees, is the most significant of the younger talents emerging on the instrument.

IRELAND: FREE REEDS

This is the biggest and most significant group of "other instruments' in modern Irish music. They produce sound by vibrating a reed (now made of metal) which is fixed at one end but "free" to move at the other when air is passed across it. The air may be produced by blowing directly, as with a harmonica, or by a system of keys or buttons and a bellows action, as with the accordion family and the concertina. The current star of the accordion is the prodigiously gifted **Sharon Shannon**. She is also a superb fiddler. In a familiar pattern fundamental to the transmission of traditional music, Shannon grew up in a family steeped in music and dance, in Clare. She began on whistle, then switched to accordion, improving her skills by playing for dancers at céilís run by Frank Custy.

While still at school, Shannon played in a recording of Clare music organised by Gearóid Ó hAllmhuráin, the concertina player, academic and writer. The record also featured her brother Gary, a fine flute player, and sister Mary, a fiddler who plays in Sharon's band and in The Bumblebees. Sharon Shannon's reputation continued to grow, and she worked with Arcady and Christy Moore, and then reached an even wider audience when she toured and recorded with The Waterboys during their Celtic-influenced phase. This association led to her own debut album.

The accordionist's dazzling playing is straight out of the tradition on *Sharon Shannon* (Philo, 1991), most notably in its rhythmic qualities, although even here there are traces of wider influences at work which would flourish on her subsequent records. *Out The Gap* (Solid/Grapevine, 1994) threw open the doors to all manner of influences, taking in folk tunes from Finland, Quebec and the US, as well as a tribute to the calypso singer known as The Mighty Sparrow. The album was produced by Dennis Bovell, best known for dub reggae rather than Irish traditional. Shannon's playing provided the unifying factor in an overly eclectic mix.

She pulled these diverse strains together in even more convincing fashion on *Each Little Thing* (Green Linnet, 1997), aided by Donal Lunny's production. The album featured a couple of South American tunes this time, including a version of 'Libertango' with the late Kirsty MacColl as guest vocalist, as well as Shannon's sizzling fiddle duet with Mary Custy in the 'Bag Of Cats' set. *Spellbound: The Best Of Sharon Shannon* (Green Linnet, 1999) offered a good introduction to the work of a major talent.

The accordion arrived in Ireland in the second half of the 19th century and became widespread, particularly in its ten-key form, popularly known as the melodeon. It gradually usurped the more expensive and more intransigent pipes as an instrument to accompany dance. Early recordings were made by **John Kimmel** and, in the US, **Peter Conlon**, and the full chromatic version of the instrument became more common.

The instrument comes in several forms, principally the melodeon, with a single row of buttons, the two-row button accordion, which is the most popular in traditional music, and the piano accordion, which has piano-like keys rather than buttons. The melodeon is a diatonic instrument, while the button and piano accordions are chromatic.

■ *Sharon Shannon.*

There are alternative styles of playing the accordion, the most familiar of which in traditional music is the so-called "push and draw" method. This was championed by the most famous accordionist of his generation, **Joe Cooley**. A native of Galway, his playing can be heard on his only record, *Cooley* (Gael-Linn, 1975).

From the US comes the so-called "outside in" system which uses the two rows of buttons in a different way to create notes and rhythms. The "outside in" system is also known as the "B/C style" because of the pitching of the two rows of buttons, which in the "push and draw" method are tuned to C-sharp and D.

The "outside in" system was championed by **Joe Derrane**, and can be heard on a number of his records including *Return To Inis Mór* (Green Linnet, 1996) and *The Ties That Bind* (Shanachie, 1998). Several players in Ireland use the method, notably **Paddy O'Brien** of Tipperary, while **Joe Burke** is its best known exponent – and indeed one of the great Irish musicians, regardless of instrument.

Born and raised in Galway, Burke also plays fiddle, flute and pipes, and lived in America for a time in the early 1960s. His virtuoso command of the accordion is allied to a deep understanding and affinity with the music, which he plays with authority and a mischievous sense of fun that keeps his accompanists alert. His most regular on-stage partner is his wife, guitarist Anne Conroy.

Burke made his recording debut in 1971 and has cut numerous albums since, including the classic *Traditional Music Of Ireland* (Green Linnet, 1973) with pianist Charlie Lennon, *The Tailor's Choice* (Green Linnet, 1983), *Happy To Meet And Sorry To Part* (Green Linnet, 1986) and *The Bucks Of Oranmore* (Green Linnet, 1996). His *Tribute To Michael Coleman*, reissued by Green Linnet in 1994, featured fiddler Andy McGann and pianist Felix Dolan.

Jackie Daly is the best of the many distinguished "push and draw" players. Born in County Cork, he started by playing harmonica and his father's melodeon. He now also plays concertina, but is best know for his mastery of the button accordion. He is a leading exponent of the rhythmic Sliabh Luachra style, and his first solo album, *Music From Sliabh Luachra* (Topic/Green Linnet, 1977) remains one of the essential Irish recordings.

Daly recorded a great eponymous duo album with the undervalued fiddler Séamus Creagh (Gael-Linn, 1979) which also explored the Sliabh Luachra style and repertoire. He has also been a member of some seminal bands, including De Dannan, Patrick Street, Buttons And Bows (with fiddlers Séamus and Manus McGuire) and Arcady. His playing with all these groups is liberally represented on record. He has also recorded with fiddler Kevin Burke on *Eavesdropper* (Mulligan, 1981) and released a second solo album, *Many's A Wild Night* (Gael-Linn, 1995).

Tony MacMahon of Clare is a fine player, especially in the art of the slow air which he developed under the tutelage of Séamus Ennis. **Paul Brock** of Westmeath played tribute to Joe Cooley on a disc with Frankie Gavin, *Omós Do Joe Cooley* (Gael-Linn, 1986), and was a founder member of the band The Moving Cloud, with whom he has made several records.

James Keane, brother of fiddler Seán Keane, is a fine exponent of the B/C accordion method, and is well served on records such as *That's The Spirit* (Green Linnet, 1994) and the stellar *With Friends Like These* (Shanachie, 1998). **Máirtín O'Connor** is from Galway, and has been a member of both De Dannan and Skylark, among other bands, and was featured in the original production of *Riverdance*. His own records include *Perpetual Motion* (Claddagh, 1990) and *Chatterbox* (Dara, 1993).

Séamus and Breandán Begley are both fine players from a musical family in Kerry, while Dermot Byrne of Altan is an increasingly significant presence. American exponents of the accordion include Billy McComiskey who with fiddler Liz Carroll is a member of Trian.

Players who favour the smaller concertina rather than the accordion have included Elizabeth Crotty, a distinguished champion of the instrument from Clare. She died in 1960. Clare has been a stronghold of the instrument, and **Noel Hill** is widely regarded as the greatest of the contemporary players. *I gCnoc Na Graí* (Gael-Linn, 1985), recorded in a pub session in Cork with Tony MacMahon and set dancers from Clare, is one of the most immediate evocations of a real "session" ever captured on disc (and was reissued as *In Knocknagree* by Shanachie in 1992).

Hill's solo album *The Irish Concertina* (Claddagh, 1988) is a definitive exploration of the instrument's possibilities in Irish music. His earlier duo disc with fiddler Tony Linnane, *Noel Hill And Tony Linnane* (Tara, 1979) also featured Matt Molloy on flute, while Hill recorded with Tony MacMahon and singer Iarla Ó Lionaird on *Aislingí Ceoil* (Gael-Linn, 1995). Other eminent concertina players of the current generation include Josephine Marsh and Mary MacNamara, whose *Traditional Music From East Clare* (Claddagh, 1994) includes duets with Martin Hayes.

The harmonica is considered to be the junior member of the free-reed family, in much the same way as the whistle is to pipes, but the instrument has its own lineage. The best known harmonica players in Irish music are **Eddie Clarke**, a native of Cavan, and **Brendan Power**, the current star of the instrument, who was born in New Zealand. Power has a remarkable range and facility on both diatonic and chromatic harmonicas, and works with influences from all manner of music, including blues, jazz and various ethnic strains. *New Irish Harmonica* (Green Linnet, 1995) and *Plays The Music From Riverdance* (Greentrax, 1997) provide a good showcase for his expertise.

IRELAND: FLUTE

The flute is a popular instrument in Ireland, and is featured in settings that range from marching bands to the classical music of James Galway. In fact, Galway learned to play in a marching band, so the two are not unconnected. The instrument plays a significant role in traditional music, especially in more recent decades when the number of players has grown significantly. The type most used for traditional music, though not exclusively, is the so-called "simple system" wooden flute rather then the Böehm system instrument favoured in classical music, which has more complex keys.

The current performers include a number of distinguished elder statesmen, like John McKenna of Leitrim and Paddy Taylor of Limerick, plus more recent players such as Paddy Carty, Séamus Cooley and Vincent Broderick of Galway and Séamus Mac Mathúna and Michael Tubridy of Clare. The best known and most influential player is **Matt Molloy** of Roscommon. He was part of the active Dublin scene in the early 1970s and helped form The Bothy Band in 1974.

He was sidelined for a time by tuberculosis in 1977, but recovered to join Planxty briefly, and then joined The Chieftains in 1979. Molloy is a virtuosic, uninhibited but highly musical player in any setting, and is featured on many albums with The Chieftains as well as his own records, which include his seminal debut, *Matt Molloy* (Green Linnet, 1976), *Stony Steps* (Green Linnet, 1987) and *Shadows On Stone* (Real World, 1996), as well as significant collaborations on *Matt Molloy, Paul Brady, Tommy Peoples* (Green Linnet, 1977), *Contentment Is Wealth* (Green Linnet, 1985) with Seán Keane and Arty McGlynn, and *Matt Molloy, Seán Keane, Liam O'Flynn* (Claddagh, 1992).

Two other notable flute players from Ulster are mainly associated with the work they have done in their respective bands. **Cathal McConnell** of Fermanagh is a founder member of The Boys of The Lough, a band which began life as a trio in Belfast before shifting its base to Scotland to take on a pan-Celtic line-up. McConnell's singular sense of humour and rambling introductions are legendary, and both his playing and his engaging singing are featured on the group's many albums as well as on occasional recordings under his own name, including *Long Expectant Comes At Last* (Compass, 2000).

The early death from cancer of **Frankie Kennedy**, the Belfast-born flute player with the Donegal band Altan, robbed Irish music of one of its brightest talents on the instrument. Kennedy, who was married to the band's singer and fiddle player, Mairéad Ní Mhaonaigh, left a powerful legacy in his contribution to Altan's early albums.

Kevin Crawford was born in Birmingham, England, but his family are from Clare, where he later settled. He has emerged as a significant performer on flute in the course of his association with bands like Grianin, The Moving Cloud, and Raise The Rafters. He made a powerful debut solo album, *D Flute* (Green Linnet, 1994), while *The Moving Cloud* (Green Linnet, 1995) is a good example of his work with that group, which also features fiddlers Maeve Donnelly and Manus McGuire, accordionist Paul Brock, and pianist Carl Hession.

Brian Finnegan has also led his own band, and is a key member of the English outfit Flook!. As a footnote before leaving this instrument, we might note that dancer Michael Flatley, now world-famous as the star of *Riverdance* and *Lord Of The Dance*, is also an excellent player of the traditional flute.

IRELAND: GUITAR, PIANO AND PERCUSSION

Irish traditional music has always been based on melody and playing in unison, with largely rhythmic accompaniment. Recent developments have seen a growth of interest in the addition of more complex harmonies to the music, and with it a growing use of instruments capable of providing such harmonies. These include guitar and piano, plus various related instruments such as the now common bouzouki. This stringed instrument of Greek origin has become widespread in Irish music through the advocacy of players such as Johnny Moynihan, who is credited with its introduction, De Dannan's Alec Finn, who was also featured on his own *Blue Shamrock* (Celtic Heartbeat, 1994), and **Donal Lunny**.

Lunny is a key figure in Irish music, as much for his work as an arranger, record producer and general catalyst as for his skills on guitar and bouzouki. He has been the instigator of many of the more experimental directions in Irish music in the last three decades – for which he will be praised or damned according to taste – and his contribution to bands like Planxty, Moving Hearts and his own Coolfin represent only a small part of his achievements.

Arty McGlynn is the seminal figure when it comes to playing complex melodies on guitar in the context of Irish traditional music. He is from County Tyrone, and counts the great jazz guitarists as his earliest influences. That sophistication is evident in everything he plays, whether spinning out melody lines or cycling through hugely imaginative chordal and rhythmic accompaniments. McGlynn's only available album under his own name is *Lead The Knave* (Ringsend Road, 1989), made with his wife, fiddler Nollaig Casey, who takes first billing on their second duo album, *Causeway* (Tara, 1995).

But his work can be heard on countless recordings with artists ranging from Tommy Makem to Enya, as well as with bands such as The Chieftains, De Dannan, Patrick Street, and Four Men And A Dog.

The original role of the piano in Irish music was in the céilí bands where it was regarded as an integral part of the group. These outfits fostered many significant piano players including the likes of Kitty Linnane of the famous Kilfenora Band, and Charlie Lennon, a significant composer whose work includes some of the earliest attempts to marry Irish music with orchestral accompaniment.

That association of piano and composition has a strong presence in modern Irish music, stemming from the groundbreaking work of **Seán Ó Riada** whose music spanned both the Irish and classical traditions. He was a leading player in the revival of interest in Irish music in the 1960s, through his own music, including film and theatre scores, and the group Ceoltóirí Chualann, which helped to nurture the musicians who formed the most influential of the first wave of new Irish groups, The Chieftains. Ó Riada played harpsichord as well as piano in Irish settings, and his work with traditional music and orchestra paved the way for subsequent experiments by composers such as Charlie Lennon, Shaun Davey, Bill Whelan and **Mícheál Ó Súilleabháin**.

Ó Súilleabháin is a brilliant pianist and composer, and credits Ó Riada with converting him to traditional music when a student at the University College Of Cork in the early 1970s. He set about developing an appropriate piano style for Irish music which came to fruition in the magnificent *The Dolphin's Way* (Virgin Venture, 1987). Essentially a solo piano record with some traditional percussion from Colm Murphy on bodhrán and Mel Mercier on bones, it was fresh, radical and hugely enjoyable, clearly coming from within the tradition but arranged and played with a renewing vigour.

That record built on Ó Súilleabháin's earlier experiments on three keyboard-based albums for the Gael-Linn label which not only took on board the structures and practices of traditional music but filled them with techniques and musical influences from classical and jazz sources. Subsequent records such as *Oileán/Island* (Venture, 1989), *Casadh/Turning* (Venture, 1990), *Gaiseadh/Flowing* (Venture, 1992) and *Becoming* (Virgin, 1998) reveal still more ambitious extensions of his musical language, often incorporating orchestral accompaniment.

Outside of the céilí bands, piano was rare in traditional music, where melody instruments were paramount. There were also the obvious practicalities: pianos were both expensive and cumbersome, and therefore scarce. The more portable hammered dulcimer gained a foothold, especially in Antrim, but was not widespread; its best known Irish exponent was **John Rea**. Meanwhile, the growth of commercial recordings in recent decades has fostered the extensive use of pianos or electric equivalents in Irish music, and this is an area in which Donal Lunny has again given the lead.

The percussion instrument most associated with the tradition is the bodhrán, a frame drum made of cured goatskin stretched over a circular frame and played with either the hand or a beater. Percussion can be a mixed blessing in traditional music where flexibility and rhythm is often more important than a rigid pulse, but a really good bodhrán player such as Johnny "Ringo" McDonagh, Tommy Hayes or Mel Mercier is a priceless asset. Mercier is also a great exponent of the primitive "bones", literally the rib bones of an animal held between the fingers and brought rapidly together, in the same way that spoons or castanets are played. Once again the growth of more commercial forms of Irish music has led to the increasing use of standard kit drums, while ethnic percussion instruments such as congas are also more commonly heard today.

RECOMMENDED RECORDS

JACKIE DALY MUSIC FROM SLIABH LUACHRA *(Topic, 1977) Accordion maestro Daly's joyful celebration of the music of this region, one of the absolute masterpieces of Irish traditional music.*
NOEL HILL NOEL HILL AND TONY LINNANE *(Tara, 1979) Hill has few peers on the concertina, and this collaboration with fiddler Tony Linnane is a wonderful if all too rare example of his artistry.*
MÁIRE NÍ CHATHASAIGH & CHRIS NEWMAN LIVE IN THE HIGHLANDS *(Old Bridge, 1995) Harpist Máire Ní Chathasaigh is captured in scintillating form on this atmospheric live disc with her husband, the great guitarist Chris Newman.*

MÍCHEÁL Ó SÚILLEABHÁIN THE DOLPHIN'S WAY *(Virgin Venture, 1987) The pianist and composer is best known for larger-scale work, but broke new ground in the improvisatory brilliance of this solo album.*

SHARON SHANNON SHARON SHANNON *(Philo, 1991) The most traditional of the accordionist's dazzling albums, especially impressive in rhythmic terms, but with traces of the eclecticism to come.*

BILL WHELAN RIVERDANCE *(Celtic Heartbeat, 1996) Whatever you make of Riverdance there is no question that it was the Irish music phenomenon of the 1990s, bringing a vast new audience to the music as well as the dance of Ireland.*

IRELAND: BANDS

The growth of formally constituted bands in Irish music is a recent phenomenon, although there are antecedents in the céilí bands. The Kilfenora, Tulla and Aughrim Slopes bands are among the most famous of the hundreds of céilí outfits in Ireland and North America, both amateur and professional, regular and occasional, with a history going back into the late 19th century. They played for céilí dances, and provided an apprenticeship or a living for many excellent musicians.

The folk music revival of the 1960s started the growth of the Irish band as we now know it, sparked by the academic but still exciting and inspirational example set by Seán Ó Riada's Ceoltóirí Chualann, and the popular success of "ballad groups" such as The Clancy Brothers (generally known simply as The Clancys), The Dubliners, The Johnstons, The Sands Family and The Fureys.

The Clancys made their initial breakthrough in the US in the early 1960s with a robust, earthy sincerity and boisterously good-humoured performances. They provided the template for a wave of vocal groups, including **The Dubliners** who are still active despite the departures of their two most charismatic members, Luke Kelly (who died in 1984) and Ronnie Drew.

Ó Riada's **Ceoltóirí Chualann** focused on instrumental music and gave rise to the most influential of the first wave of new Irish groups, **The Chieftains**. The group came together when uilleann piper Paddy Moloney was asked to record an album for Claddagh Records in 1963 and recruited three of his fellow members of Ó Riada's group for the occasion.

Moloney has been an ever-present member of a band which has won an unprecedented worldwide following and featured some of the major names in Irish music, including flute players Michael Tubridy and Matt Molloy, harpist Derek Bell, fiddlers Martin Fay and Seán Keane, and bodhrán players Peadar Mercier and Kevin Conneff. The Chieftains remain a hugely entertaining live band, in concerts that usually also feature step dancers, and have recorded around 50 albums. Chieftains records range from early classics on Claddagh through to crossover

■ *Members of the group Clannad, including Máire Brennan (centre).*

recordings like *Another Country* (RCA Victor, 1992) with country stars such as Emmylou Harris and Willie Nelson, and *The Long Black Veil* (RCA Victor, 1995) which featured the likes of Mick Jagger, Sting and Van Morrison. They have also collaborated with musicians from Brittany, Galicia and Cape Breton. *Water From The Well* (RCA Victor, 2000) returned to an Irish traditional context after some more wide-ranging projects. The Irish tradition of family groups is well established, and includes The Black Family, formed in Dublin in 1965, and **Clannad**, the name chosen by the Brennan family for their now globally successful group. Clannad formed in 1970, playing at a family-owned bar in Gweedore, Donegal, and quickly established an international reputation for their soft-focus approach to Irish musical conventions, tinged with a fashionable veil of Celtic mysticism.

The success of Clannad's theme for the television series *Harry's Game*, featured on the album *Magical Ring* (Tara, 1983), gave them still greater fame and has left an indelible impression of the sound of Clannad's music. But there is more to it than simply ethereal vocals and shimmering synthesisers. They have made the most of their commercial hybrid of Irish music, and if their polished approach and slick visual presentation is not to the taste of purists, they can still be a compelling band, especially in live performance.

The Boys Of The Lough formed in 1967 in Belfast as a trio featuring Robin Morton on concertina, Cathal McConnell on flute, and Tommy Gunn on fiddle, with all three singing. Shetland fiddler Aly Bain replaced Gunn in 1968 and the band uprooted to Scotland where multi-instrumentalist Dave Richardson joined in 1973. Morton left in 1979 and concentrated on managing the Battlefield Band and running his Temple Records label, while The Boys coalesced around the trio of Bain, McConnell and Richardson with considerable success. (See also the Scotland section, which starts on page 54.)

Sweeney's Men, led by Andy Irvine and Johnny Moynihan, recorded only two albums, later reissued almost in their entirety on a single CD as *Time Was Never Here 1968-69* (Transatlantic). The band was formed in Galway in 1966. While they only lasted three years, Sweeney's Men were an important precursor of largely instrumental Irish groups which began with the formation of Planxty in 1972.

Planxty grew from a group of musicians who had contributed to Christy Moore's *Prosperous* album: Moore himself, plus piper Liam O'Flynn, Andy Irvine and Donal Lunny. Their debut album *Planxty* (Polydor, 1973) carried a starkly dramatic monochrome cover shot of the band on stage, a departure which itself signalled a new development in Irish music: this was an album aimed beyond the usual confines of the traditional music scene or the productions of the ballad groups. Planxty's crucial setting of traditional tunes and songs in a more

■ *Albums (below, left to far right) by: The Chieftains; The Black Family; Clannad; The Boys Of The Lough; Planxty; The Bothy Band; Moving Hearts; Donal Lunny's Coolfin.*

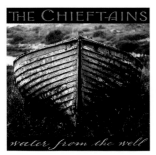

contemporary but still acoustic context was the catalyst for a great deal that followed. The band cut two more albums, *The Well Below The Valley* (Polydor, 1973) and *Cold Blow And The Rainy Night* (Polydor, 1974), the latter featuring Johnny Moynihan in place of Lunny, before their initial break-up. (Moore also left after this album and was replaced by Paul Brady in a line-up which remained unrecorded.) Those records were enough to ensure immortality, but the group reformed with the original line-up plus Matt Molloy on flute in 1979 and released the excellent *After The Break* (Tara, 1979) and *The Woman I Loved So Well* (Tara, 1980). Their final album *Words And Music* (WEA Ireland, 1983) featured a larger band but is not as strong as its predecessors.

Planxty helped to create a large new audience for Irish music, a process carried further by **The Bothy Band**. It was formed in 1974 out of a group originally named Seachtair (meaning seven) and convened for a one-off concert in Dublin. Five of those musicians – Donal Lunny, Paddy Keenan, Matt Molloy, Mícheál Ó Domhnaill and Tríona Ní Dhomhnaill – decided to continue as a band and added the great Donegal fiddler Tommy Peoples for their epochal debut album, *The Bothy Band* (Mulligan, 1974). Peoples left after that album, and was replaced for the rest of the band's existence by Kevin Burke.

The impact of The Bothy Band's debut album, with its tight-knit, virtuoso ensemble playing and supercharged Irish (and occasionally Scottish) tunes and songs had a galvanising effect on Irish musicians. Their subsequent albums – *Old Hag You Have Killed Me* (Mulligan, 1976), *Out Of The Wind Into The Sun* (Mulligan 1977) and the live *After Hours* (Mulligan, 1978) – formed a classic legacy prior to their break-up in 1979, later augmented by the release of *Live In Concert* (Windsong, 1994) featuring tapes made by the BBC in the late 1970s (with Peter Browne deputising for Paddy Keenan).

The split of The Bothy Band quickly provided much talent for a new generation of bands. Matt Molloy went off to The Chieftains by way of a stint in the reformed Planxty, but the rest started new projects, all of which made significant contributions to Irish music. Lunny, having already been in the two most important Irish groups of the 1970s, turned his attention to a signature band of the

■ *Gino Lupari of Four Men
And A Dog.*

1980s, **Moving Hearts**. This was the most radical departure to date, combining traditional tunes and instruments – Davy Spillane's uilleann pipes, Christy Moore's vocals and bodhrán – with saxophone, drums, keyboards and electric guitar and bass in a potent fusion of traditional music, plus contemporary and often politically controversial songs, and folk, rock and jazz.

Moving Hearts made two fine albums with the original line-up: *Moving Hearts* (WEA Ireland, 1981) and *The Dark End Of The Street* (WEA Ireland, 1982), and a third, *Live Hearts* (Green Linnet, 1983), with Mick Hanly replacing Moore. Ironically, the quintessential Moving Hearts album, the magnificent, purely instrumental *The Storm* (Tara, 1985), was not released until after the band had broken up. But they have occasionally reformed around Davy Spillane for concert appearances, which remain exhilarating occasions. The band opened up new areas of exploration in Irish music, and their work has not yet been surpassed.

The Domnaills from The Bothy Band teamed up for an Irish-Scottish family alliance with the virtuoso Cunningham brothers, John (fiddle) and Phil (accordion), to form **Relativity**, another exploratory group which released two fine albums. The first of these was *Relativity* (Green Linnet, 1985), followed by *Gathering Pace* (Green Linnet, 1987).

Paddy Keenan concentrated on his own projects, while Kevin Burke teamed up with Andy Irvine, Jackie Daly and Arty McGlynn (later replaced by Ged Foley) to form in 1986 another of the Irish music scene's finest bands, **Patrick Street**. This outfit combined to great effect Irvine's evocative singing and politically aware songs with the virtuoso wizardry of the instrumentalists. Their group playing has been honed to a level rarely equalled. The debut album *Patrick Street* (Green Linnet, 1986) announced their arrival in style and was followed by *No. 2 Patrick Street* (Green Linnet, 1988). *Irish Times* (Green Linnet, 1990), which featured four additional musicians, is arguably their best album, but *All In Good Time* (Green Linnet, 1993), *Corner Boys* (Green Linnet, 1995), their first disc with Foley on board, and *Made In Cork* (Green Linnet, 1997) maintained their high standards, while *Live From Patrick Street* (Green Linnet, 1999) captured a typical live set in highly enjoyable fashion.

De Dannan formed out of pub sessions in Spiddal, Galway, in 1974, and quickly established themselves as a major presence in Irish music, on a level comparable with that of The Bothy Band or Planxty. The original band featured fiddler Frankie Gavin and bouzouki player Alec Finn, and these two have remained at the core of the group's distinctive sound ever since. Johnny McDonough, Charlie Piggott and singer Dolores Keane were also members of the line-up that made the band's eponymous debut album in 1975, and they have maintained a full-throttle assault in the vanguard of Irish traditional music ever since.

Despite regular changes in personnel, De Dannan have retained a trademark acoustic sound, often with the effective if rather non-traditional addition of cello, and have not chosen to venture very far into the kind of crossover territory staked out by other groups. However, *1/2 Set In Harlem* (Celtic Music, 1991) did explore connections with gospel music. They have also worked their own exploratory magic on less than traditional tunes such as The Beatles' 'Hey Jude' on *The Star-Spangled Molly* (Shanachie, 1989), 'Let It Be' on *Anthem* (Dara, 1985) and 'Eleanor Rigby' on *A Jacket Of Batteries* (Harmac, 1988), their irresistible adaptation of Handel in 'Arrival Of The Queen Of Sheba (In Galway)' on *Song For Ireland* (Sugar Hill, 1990), or a virtuoso version of Queen's 'Bohemian Rhapsody' on *Hibernian Rhapsody* (The Bees Knees, 1995).

The band's other albums include *The Mist Covered Mountain* (Gael-Linn, 1980) and *Ballroom* (Green Linnet, 1987), and they have featured such eminent musicians as accordionists Jackie Daly, Máirtín O'Connor, Aiden Coffey and Derek Hickey, guitarist Arty McGlynn, bodhrán player Colm Murphy, and a handful of the best singers in Irish music, most recently the highly promising Cara Dillon. Mary Black's rendition of the title song on *Song For Ireland* is a classic moment of modern Irish music, while their breathtaking treatments of reels, jigs, hornpipes and polkas are delivered with unfailing vitality, expressiveness and ensemble precision. Like Clannad, **Altan** hail from Donegal, but they focused much more directly on the Scottish-influenced traditional music of the area, at least until the late 1990s. The band began as a duo when the husband and wife team of Frankie Kennedy (flute) and Mairéad Ní Mhaonaigh (vocal, fiddle) released *Ceol Aduaidh* (Gael-Linn, 1983). They formed Altan in 1987, and remained at the heart of the band until Kennedy's tragic death from cancer in 1994. First Paul O'Shaughnessy and later Cíarán Tourish formed their distinctive twin-fiddle attack with Ní Mhaonaigh, often playing unison lines in octaves for extra depth.

All three were in the band for a time in the early 1990s and contributed in that form to their strongest album, *Harvest Storm* (Green Linnet, 1992). Its predecessors, *Altan* (Green Linnet, 1987), the excellent *Horse With A Heart* (Green Linnet, 1989), *The Red Crow* (Green Linnet, 1990) and the subsequent *Island Angel* (Green Linnet, 1993) all featured Kennedy, and together they constitute Altan's most impressive recorded work.

Altan opted to continue after their flute player's death and recruited accordionist Dermot Byrne alongside the band's three guitar and bouzouki players, Cíaran Curran, Mark Kelly and Dáithí Sproule. Subsequent records such as *Blackwater* (Virgin, 1996), *Runaway Sunday* (Virgin, 1997) and *Another Sky* (Virgin, 2000) have diluted the traditional focus of the music, foregrounding Ní Mhaonaigh's lovely vocals in more commercial settings at the expense of the thrilling instrumental playing which made them such an exhilarating attraction on stage.

Arcady were formed by bodhrán maestro Johnny McDonagh with pianist Patsy Broderick in 1988, and although they have made only two albums, both were among the most significant Irish releases of the 1990s. Their debut *After The Ball* (Dara, 1991) featured Jackie Daly on accordion, Breton guitarist Nicolas Quemenar, fiddler Brendan Larrissey and singer Frances Black on a mixture of Irish tunes, Breton reels and contemporary songs. Their second album *Many Happy Returns* (Dara, 1996) was even better. It focused on Irish material, most of it traditional in origin, with Conor Keane replacing Daly on accordion and Niamh Parsons as the principal singer alongside a number of guests – including The Voice Squad who provide a stirring harmony chorus behind Parsons on evocative versions of 'The Rambling Irishman' and 'The Banks Of The Lee'. A number of other bands have been musically and commercially significant. **Stockton's Wing**

■ *Albums (below, left to far right) by: Patrick Street; Open House; De Dannan (two); Altan; Arcady; Four Men And A Dog; and Deiseal.*

featured the fine fiddle playing of Maurice Lennon and for a time the great bodhrán player Tommy Hayes. They enjoyed some crossover success with *Light In The Western Sky* (Tara, 1982) although they reverted to a more acoustic format on albums such as *The Crooked Rose* (Tara, 1992) and *Letting Go* (Tara, 1995).

Four Men And A Dog, fronted by bodhrán player and general showman Gino Lupari and featuring fiddlers Cathal Hayden and Gerry O'Connor indulged in eclectic tendencies on albums like *Barking Mad* (Green Linnet, 1991) and *Doctor A's Secret Remedies* (Transatlantic, 1995). They were a popular festival draw.

Kevin Burke's **Open House** forged a productive alliance between the great fiddler and American musicians Mark Graham and Paul Kotapish on *Open House* (Green Linnet, 1992), *Second Story* (Green Linnet, 1994) and *Hoof And Mouth* (Green Linnet, 1997). The latter album features what can only be described as the "foot percussion" of dancer Sandy Silva. Donal Lunny maintained his imposing presence as leader as well as producer on the dazzling *Coolfin* (Metro Blue, 1998) with his band of the same name.

Other good bands include **Déanta**, from Antrim, who made three fine albums before disbanding in 1998, culminating with *Whisper Of A Secret* (Green Linnet, 1997), and **Dervish**, a strong Sligo band well represented on *Harmony Hill* (Whirling Discs, 1993) and *At The End Of The Day* (Whirling Discs, 1996).

Deiseal made a feature of Cormac Breatnach's flute and whistle playing on the imaginative *The Long Long Note* (Starc, 1992), while whistle specialist Mary Bergin led the always intriguing Irish-baroque explorations of **Dordan** on records such as the self-explanatory *Irish Traditional And Baroque* (Shanachie, 1991) and *Jigs To The Moon* (Gael-Linn, 1994).

The Voice Squad and Anúna, a choir led by Michael McGlynn which came to prominence when featured in *Riverdance*, took different approaches to ensemble vocal music with roots in the tradition, while bands such as After Hours, Craobh Rua, Grianán, Cran, Nomos, La Lugh, Reeltime, Bohinta, Lia Luachra, Danú, Anam, Sine É and several more all made (or are making) notable contributions. More recently, Lunasa have emerged as a potential major force, and The Bumblebees have cultivated an infectious and unpretentious appeal.

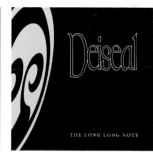

■ *Members of Stockton's Wing (left to right): Davey McNevin, Maurice Lennon and Paul Roche, on-stage during the early 1990s.*

The most significant of the American-Irish bands include the new-age-inclined Nightnoise, flute player Séamus Egan's **Solas**, and Cherish The Ladies.

Solas have the ability to play with a muscular energy, as in evidence on *Solas* (Shanachie, 1996), *Sunny Spells And Scattered Showers* (Shanachie, 1997) and *The Words That Remain* (Shanachie, 1998), with Egan's flute and Winifred Horan's energised fiddle well to the fore – with half a dozen other instruments – alongside Karan Casey's evocative vocals.

Cherish The Ladies, led by flute player Joanie Madden, adopt a more knockabout approach at times, especially on stage, but their exuberant interpretations of Irish tunes and songs are generally well played. The band grew out of a festival in New York in 1983 and has undergone numerous changes of personnel over the years, but is heard to advantage on *The Back Door* (Green Linnet, 1992) and *New Day Dawning* (Green Linnet, 1996).

The surge in interest in Irish music since the 1960s has also been reflected in the work of a number of rock and pop bands who have drawn on traditional as well as folk influences. The process began with the folk-rock band Horslips, in the 1970s, not to mention Thin Lizzy's strong chart success with their single 'Whiskey In The Jar'. Subsequent borrowings from the sources have been made by outfits such as The Waterboys, The Pogues, Hothouse Flowers, The Saw Doctors, Alias Ron Kavana, Goats Don't Shave, and The Corrs.

RECOMMENDED RECORDS

ALTAN HARVEST STORM *(Green Linnet, 1992) The Donegal band's trademark twin-fiddle sound is actually tripled on this classic album, which features the flute playing of the late Frankie Kennedy.*

ARCADY MANY HAPPY RETURNS *(Dara, 1996)*
One of only two albums made by the band, but both are among the best of the decade, and on this outing the focus is very much on Irish material.

THE BOTHY BAND OLD HAG YOU HAVE KILLED ME *(Mulligan, 1976) The band's second album established their most familiar line-up, with Kevin Burke taking the place of Tommy Peoples. It remains a classic.*

THE CHIEFTAINS WATER FROM THE WELL *(RCA Victor, 2000) An institution in Irish music, The Chieftains on this album returned to where they began, with supreme Irish traditional music.*

CLANNAD MAGICAL RING *(Tara, 1983) The group made ethereal Celtic mysticism their trademark, and this fine album marked their breakthrough to a wider audience.*

DE DANNAN SONG FOR IRELAND *(Sugar Hill, 1990) Frankie Gavin and Alec Finn have been at the core of these Galway greats since the outset, and this album is one of the band's best moments.*

DONAL LUNNY COOLFIN *(Metro Blue, 1998) Lunny has been a central figure in Irish music for three decades, and this stunning group album proved that his inspiration remains as strong as ever.*

MOVING HEARTS THE STORM *(Tara, 1985) The group brought a new electric sound to Irish music as well as rock and jazz influences, but had already disbanded by the time this definitive instrumental album was released.*

PATRICK STREET IRISH TIMES *(Green Linnet, 1990) The latest in a distinguished line of great Irish bands when they formed, Patrick Street have added longevity to their obvious musical qualities.*

PLANXTY THE WELL BELOW THE VALLEY *(Polydor, 1973) Planxty launched a revolution in Irish music in the 1970s with their debut album, and followed it with this even stronger outing.*

SCOTLAND

BY JIM GILCHRIST

Another great stronghold of Celtic tradition, Scotland is alive with a vigorous new music scene that takes in piping and harping as much as fiddling and singing. This extensive survey charts the growth of new singers and instrumentalists and their involvement in duos and bands, and at the same time sketches in some of the history behind the latest developments.

SCOTLAND: VOICE

Sheena Wellington delivered a spellbinding, unaccompanied rendition of 'A Man's A Man' at the state opening of the Scottish Parliament, resumed in the summer of 1999 after almost three centuries. The singing of Robert Burns's egalitarian anthem at such an event – and in the presence of the monarch, no less – not only marked a turning point in history, but was a recognition of the renewed worth in which Scottish folk song was held at the end of the 20th century.

At the beginning of that century, things had been looking rather different. Collectors of folk songs had been amassing material, but often with the elegiac approach that presumed the songs were on their way out. One such was the industrious Buchan schoolteacher Gavin Greig who, in collaboration with the Reverend James Duncan, gathered 3,000 or more folk song texts in north-east Scotland alone, but was moved to entitle those he published as the *Last Leaves Of Traditional Ballads And Ballad Airs*.

Yet within a mere half-century collectors such as Hamish Henderson and Calum McLean from the newly formed School Of Scottish Studies, joined by the American musicologist Alan Lomax, had embarked on their own field collecting, lugging cumbersome tape recorders about these same Aberdeenshire farmlands. At times, Henderson said later, it was "like holding a bucket underneath a waterfall". Everything from big, powerful ballads – the "muckle sangs" – to the pawkie songs of the bothy workers were found alive and very much kicking. Likewise, a rich heritage of Gaelic song was revealed which an ecstatic Lomax was moved to describe as "the flower of western Europe".

Members of Old Blind Dogs (opposite, left to right): Jonny Hardie, Buzzby McMillan and Ian F. Benzie.

Henderson and company were "discovering" the likes of **Jeannie Robertson**, the magnificent traveller singer whom he brought to sing at the seminal People's Festival of 1951 in Edinburgh. At the same time the Scottish folk revival was underway, based on an unlikely melting pot of American "Wobblies" anthems, anti-Polaris protest songs and the skiffle boom, as well as the new interpretations of that neglected tradition.

If much inspiration was coming from across the Atlantic and the likes of Woody Guthrie, Pete Seeger and The Weavers, would-be Scots folk singers were finding on home ground plenty of stimulation, inspiration and native repertoire. Apart from protest songs and politically-driven urban folk songs, Hamish Henderson, Ewan MacColl and others were revealing the immense musical treasure house of travellers, the much victimised "tinkers", such as Jeannie Robertson, the Stewarts of Blair, and Betsy Whyte. They were tapping into other rich sources from across the country: from the singing Hebrides to Border fastnesses such as Liddesdale, where the indefatigable shepherd Willie Scott was found to be singing material which more than a century before an earlier ballad enthusiast, Sir Walter Scott, would have regarded as verging on extinction.

Some of the singers, songwriters and activists of those heady early days may have since departed to join the great celestial ceilidh, but the songs go on. In recent years, however, the instrumental explosion has threatened to relegate singers to filling the interludes between the tunes. There are signs of recovery, but with some distinguished exceptions it is the women who are doing the serious singing these

■ *Karen Matheson of Capercaillie.*

days, in some cases with a return to minimal accompaniment or none at all.

Ask **Archie Fisher**, one man who has been singing his way through the revival, and he'll tell you he's beginning to feel like an endangered species. He claims to be "internationally deleted -– that's official", although this mellow-voiced singer and broadcaster has an album titled *The River And The Road* due for release, while certainly available is his *Sunsets I've Galloped Into* (Greentrax, 1992). Other survivors include the ebullient vocal trio **The McCalmans**, who made their first album in 1968 and whose 1999 release, *Keepers*, is on Greentrax, while **Adam MacNaughton**, composer of children's songs, droll ditties and classics such as 'Yellow On The Broom', has a compilation *The Words That I Used To Know* that came out in 2000 on the same label.

Best known of all the earlier revival figures were **The Corries**, formed as a trio with Paddy Bell in 1961 but for most of their existence performing as the duo of Roy Williamson and **Ronnie Browne**. Their commercial success brought the inevitable sniffy accusation that they had become entertainers rather than "real" folk singers. But they were widely influential. Williamson, composer of the much used and abused 'Flower Of Scotland', died in 1990. Browne continues to sing, and a 1987 Corries compilation, *Compact Collection*, is on Lismor. Meandering genially and idiosyncratically between the fey 1960s, the tradition and the new age is former Incredible String Band leader **Robin Williamson**, still singing, telling tales and playing the clarsach, or Celtic harp. His 1997 album, *Celtic Harp Airs & Dance Tunes*, was released on Greentrax.

From a more recent generation is the rich-voiced **Rod Paterson**, often described as the best interpreter of Burns songs in Scotland. He's currently vocalist with the group Ceolbeg who can do justice to everything from the big ballads to Cole Porter. A combination of his two solo albums is due from Greentrax, who in 2000 issued his *Songs From The Bottom Drawer* devoted to the Burns repertoire.

The laidback **James Malcolm** is another sweet-voiced exponent of both the tradition and contemporary material, including his own. He is currently fronting the north-east band Old Blind Dogs (see the later Bands section here) and his current solo album is *Resonance* (Beltane, 2000). Still lingering in the song-rich north-east, **Jim Reid** sings with the renowned Arbroath Foundry Bar Band and is also a popular performer in his own right: *I Saw The Wild Geese Flee* (Springthyme, 1996) includes his settings of the Angus poets Violet Jacob and Helen Cruickshank. On the same label is the sprightly **Jock Duncan**, master of the bothy ballad, who cut his first album, *Ye Shine Whar Ye Stan!* (Springthyme, 1996) when he was all of 70.

To discover some of what Hamish Henderson and his fellow collectors were encountering, you can hear the late Jeannie Robertson along with several other important source singers on 1992's *The Muckle Sangs*, one of the Greentrax reissues of the School Of Scottish Studies' *Scottish Tradition* archive series. One of its contributors, Sheila Stewart, recently made *From The Heart Of The Tradition* (Topic, 2000).

Andy Hunter was active in the early days of the revival, both as a singer and songwriter, and was greatly influenced in his style by Jeannie Robertson. He has an album available on cassette only from the Glasgow-based Scotsoun label, but for a rare experience of very early Scots balladry listen to Hunter's 18-minute extract from the medieval Scots epic 'Greysteil'. The piece appears on an album of the same name (Dorian Discovery, 1997), where Hunter is heard in the company of lutenist Rob MacKillop and harpist William Taylor.

Another useful cross-section of fine traditional singing is Greentrax's *Folk Songs Of North-East Scotland* based on a 1995 Edinburgh Festival concert series featuring material from the copious Greig-Duncan song collection. It is performed by some of the artists already dealt with here as well as other distinguished ballad singers such as Aileen Carr (of the a cappella group Palaver), Gordeanna McCulloch, Arthur Watson, Isla St Clair and Brian Miller. Also included is **Sheena Wellington**, who opened this chapter and the Scottish Parliament, and who can be heard on her own *Strong Women* (Greentrax, 1995).

While on the subject of grand events, Scots folk duo The Cast mixed it with the Clintons at the 1999 CBS Kennedy Center Honors, a showbiz fling in Washington celebrating the contribution of Sean Connery and others. Cast singer and fiddler **Mairi Campbell** and her guitarist husband Dave Francis were whisked across the Atlantic to perform the beautifully poised rendition of 'Auld Lang Syne' that can be heard on their album *The Winnowing* (Culburnie, 1994).

Other fine Scottish women singers currently to the fore include Elspeth Cowie, who delivers mainly unaccompanied on *Naked Voice* (Scotfolk, 2000), and Christine Kydd, whose *Dark Pearls* also returns very much to the ballad tradition. Kydd and Cowie join in rich a cappella harmony with singer and harpist Corrina Hewat in the jazz-inflected trio Chantan on *Primary Colours* (Culburnie, 1998).

A further acclaimed interpreter of the big ballads is Ayrshire's **Heather Heywood** on *By Yon Castle Wa'* (Greentrax, 1993), while a recent arrival who has proved herself with muckle sang is **Karine Polwart** of the group Malinky (their debut album is ironically titled *Last Leaves*), and now also singing with Battlefield Band. Inclining more toward contemporary blues and soul inflections is the fine Glasgow singer-songwriter Carol Laula.

Dougie MacLean is one of the best known of the singer-songwriters. The Perthshire-based former Tannahill Weavers fiddler first established his reputation for songwriting with the widely covered 'Caledonia' and has gone on to record a clutch of song albums, as well as writing music for theatre and film, for example *The Last*

■ *Albums (below, left to far right) by: The Cast; Elspeth Cowie; Various (Robert Burns Complete Songs); Flora MacNeil; Various (Gaelic Women); Dick Gaughan; Karen Matheson; Dougie MacLean.*

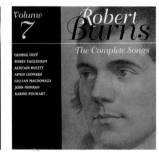

Of The Mohicans. His current albums are *Riof* (Dunkeld, 1997) and a suite for traditional instruments plus strings, *Perthshire Amber* (Dunkeld, 1999). Another Scot whose songs are covered by many other artists is **Eric Bogle**, long resident in Australia and composer of the hugely popular 'And the Band Played Waltzing Matilda' and 'No Man's Land'. The latter is an anti-war song so potent that *The Times* once reported that its writer had died during World War I.

Michael Marra's world-weary, coarse-grained tones and often surreal observations are in a category of their own. He sits at the piano and delivers his inspired cameo songs like a lugubrious Dundonian Randy Newman. When it comes to casting a percipient eye and excoriating pen over the Scottish condition, few can rival **Brian McNeill**, another songwriting fiddler, who sings his own muse on *No Gods* (Greentrax, 1995).

A formidable interpreter of the songs of McNeill and others is **Dick Gaughan**, who is perhaps Scotland's best known and certainly the country's most impassioned singer of political song. Gaughan's album *Sail On* (Greentrax, 1996) includes the song which has become the Scottish "internationale", the 'Freedom Come-All-Ye', written by that presiding and pervasive genius of the revival, poet and folklorist Hamish Henderson.

All the singers mentioned so far work either in English or in Lowland Scots, or both. But in recent years there has been a wonderful burgeoning of Gaelic singing – again, largely among women. For many years Gaelic song, in its public face at any rate, had been subject to the strictures set by the judging committees of the Mod, the annual Gaelic language and music festival, and by the lingering Victorian-drawing-room prettification of Gaelic songs by Marjorie Kennedy Fraser. One of the first to go against the grain and sing resolutely unaccompanied was **Flora MacNeil**, now in her 70s, who recently made her first album in 20 years, *Orain Floraidh* (Temple, 2000).

In the two decades between MacNeil's two albums many outstanding singers have emerged, including Christine Primrose, Ishbel MacAskill, Kenna Campbell, Mairi MacInnes and Margaret Stewart, as well as newer voices like Anna Murray and Alyth McCormack. All are performers of persuasive power who transcend any

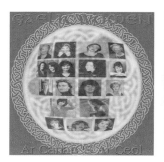   

language barrier with their keen voices and the often irresistible melodic quality of their repertoire, from rhythmic waulking songs to heart-stopping laments. Probably the most travelled of these voices is that of **Karen Matheson**, singer with Capercaillie. She can also be heard, in Gaelic and English, amid some thoughtful contemporary settings on her own album, *The Dreaming Sea* (Survival, 1996).

Closer to the tradition are the pure, lingering tones of **Ishbel MacAskill**, as heard on *Essentially Ishbel* (IMC, 2000), while the accomplished piper and singer **Anna Murray** exudes both delicacy and zest on *Tri Nithean: Three Things* (Lochshore, 1999). You can hear all of these and others on the 1999 Greentrax compilation *Gaelic Women: Ar Canan 's Ar Ceòl*, an excellent introduction to Gaelic song. It should not be forgotten, however, that there are fine male Gaelic singers too, such as **Arthur Cormack** and former Runrig frontman Donnie Munro.

Cormack has also featured in the ranks of two important Gaelic groups. In Mac-Talla he was joined by Alison Kinnaird on clarsach and Blair Douglas adding more contemporary touches on electric keyboards. For the six-piece Cliar, Cormack worked in the vocal trio alongside Maggie MacDonald and Mary Ann Kennedy, both for Gaelic songs and puirt-a-beul, the non-verbal "mouth music" of the Highland tradition. (Mouth Music was also the name of a briefly popular Celtic fusion band of the early 1990s.)

It is impossible to consider Scottish song without reference to one of the greatest collectors of all, Robert Burns. Even if he had never written a single stanza of poetry, Burns would still merit our eternal gratitude for the 300 or more songs that he collected, polished or seamlessly stitched together, marrying collected words or his own to pre-existing folk tunes – and in the process Burns managed to save many of these tunes for posterity.

The Linn Records series *Robert Burns: The Complete Songs* is engaged in recording this tremendous corpus, and stands at volume seven as this book went to press. The series features the cream of Scottish singers and instrumentalists, including many already mentioned here, as well as Davy Steele, Bobby Eaglesham, Mick West, Wendy Weatherby, Mae McKenna and Ian Bruce. Bruce does in fact also have his own Burns CD, *Alloway Tales* (Linn, 2000), a fine batch of the Bard's best, partly drawn from the series.

On the Greentrax label are the seven volumes of a US-based collaboration between internationally renowned interpreter of Scottish song **Jean Redpath** and the late Serge Hovey. The intention was to record as many as possible of Hovey's often innovative settings of the songs. Redpath, meanwhile, has many consummate non-Burns albums, most recently *Summer Of My Dreams* (Greentrax, 2000).

It was Burns who said that the composing of a "Scotch song" was no trifling business. It is to our enrichment that, today, the business continues, while the old songs are still being sung, perhaps as never before.

RECOMMENDED RECORDS

THE CAST THE WINNOWING *(Culburnie, 1994) Beguiling vocals and skeely fiddling and guitar from the duo of Mairi Campbell and Dave Francis.*

ELSPETH COWIE NAKED VOICE *(Scotfolk, 2000) Cowie's dusky-toned traditional singing, including some of the great ballads, and largely unaccompanied -– with a view to others learning them.*

DICK GAUGHAN SAIL ON *(Greentrax, 1996) Characteristically fiery delivery from Gaughan but with unexpected delights such as 'Ruby Tuesday' and a beautifully lingering rendition of 'Farewell To Sicily'.*

DOUGIE MACLEAN RIOF *(Dunkeld, 1997) One of Scotland's most widely known singer-songwriters with a new batch, including the excellent 'Stepping Stones'.*

FLORA MACNEIL ORAIN FLORAIDH – THE SONGS OF FLORA MACNEIL *(Temple, 2000) Twenty years after MacNeil's first album, the elder stateswoman of Gaelic song sounds in fine voice.*

KAREN MATHESON THE DREAMING SEA *(Survival, 1996) Sophisticatedly contemporary but effective settings of songs in Gaelic and English from the Capercaillie singer.*

VARIOUS ARTISTS GAELIC WOMEN: AR CANAN 'S AR CEÒL (OUR LANGUAGE AND OUR CULTURE) *(Greentrax, 1999) The Gaelic Women compilation, with everything from mouth music to choirs and electric guitars.*

VARIOUS ARTISTS THE MUCKLE SANGS *(Greentrax, 1992) Recordings from the School Of Scottish Studies featuring source singers such as Lizzie Higgins, Willie Scott and the great Jeannie Robertson.*

VARIOUS ARTISTS ROBERT BURNS: THE COMPLETE SONGS *(Linn) The Glasgow label's ongoing project to record all 300-plus songs written or collected by the Bard, using the cream of Scotland's folk singers and musicians.*

SCOTLAND: FIDDLE

No instrument can be quite so akin to the human voice as the fiddle, no instrument so pliable, no instrument so emotively human. Listen to the shrill flourish as it throws itself into a torrent of reels. Try the carnaptious swagger of a strathspey – such an idiosyncratic mannerism that its distinctive short and long notes on the beat have entered the universal musical lexicon as the "Scotch snap". Or hear the sobbing plangency of a lament, tugging at the Millennial heart strings just as potently as when Niel Gow or Scott Skinner or some inspired unknown composed it a century or two past.

Through fads and fashions, singing with Lowland or Highland lyricism, tempered by Nordic rigour, rising to the Italianate extravagance of the baroque, the Scots fiddle retains an irresistible voice of its own, as well as its regional accents. There are the emphatic strathspey and aureate slow airs of the North-East, the driving,

Aly Bain in concert.

bagpipe-inflected style of the west Highlands, and the ringing-stringed Norse inheritance of the Shetlander.

The violin probably arrived in Scotland during the second half of the 17th century, during the period of the great Italian violin-makers, when the instrument was becoming popular throughout Europe. The first Scottish manuscript to mention the instrument by name was *Lessones For Ye Violin* from Newbattle Abbey in Midlothian, around 1680.

The 18th century is often regarded as the golden age of the Scots fiddle. In the dextrous hands of the likes of **Niel Gow** and **William Marshall** the instrument ruled the most fashionable dancefloors and sounded out in the humblest howff. Italian composers such as Corelli provided the fashionable art music of the day, but there was a cheerful degree of "Scots baroque" crossover as composers like William McGibbon, Charles McLean and James Oswald wrote intricate Italianate variations on Scots tunes and resident Italian violinists such as Francesco Barsanti enthused about the native Scots canon.

The fiddle has remained a mainstay of Scottish music and is now enjoying the attentions of probably more players than ever before. Much of this can be attributed to the signal success in recent years of ventures such as Edinburgh's Adult Learning Project, or the general proliferation of learning opportunities from workshops and summer schools across Scotland. There is also the continuing vigour of the established "box and fiddle" club scene, and in the Highlands the Feisan movement, or Gaelic music festivals.

The 20th century opened with the legendary "Strathspey King", **James Scott Skinner**, surely the first of the international Celtic music superstars. He used an old Stroh violin with its unwieldy gramophone-horn amplification system to make the first recordings of fiddle music. These early cylinder and later 78rpm records would prove a major influence on both sides of the Atlantic as players found access for the first time to music which otherwise would almost certainly have remained beyond their hearing.

One concern today is that the sheer ubiquity and accessibility of recorded music may be blurring the edges between styles, causing their distinctive regional colours to run into one another – the "cultural grey-out", as a musicologist might well describe it. On the other hand, of course, recordings do provide today an invaluable archive of bygone players.

Added to that is the recent "discovery" by Scottish musicians of the vibrant music of the dispersed Gaelic peoples in Cape Breton Island, Nova Scotia, whose piping, step dancing and (especially) fiddling traditions are seen as preserving the playing and dancing styles of pre-Clearance Highland Scotland. Thus Cape Breton fiddle luminaries such as Natalie MacMaster and Ashley MacIsaac now attract much interest back in the old country, even if an older generation – Jerry Holland, Scotty Fitzgerald, Buddy MacMaster and company – were impressing Scottish fiddle enthusiasts two decades ago with the Cape Breton Symphony touring group.

The early, heady days of the folk revival were largely about song, and the late **Bobby Campbell**, with The Exiles, was perhaps the first fiddler to insinuate his instrument into a vocal line-up. But the arrival of the young **Aly Bain** from Shetland in the late 1960s introduced a new virtuosity to the folk scene, combining speed and flair with sensitivity of tone. With his global touring and several television series, Bain has become something of an ambassador for Scottish fiddling. Apart from a lengthy string of recordings with the heavily Irish-accented Boys Of The Lough, he can also be heard on a couple of solo albums, including *Lonely Bird* (Whirlie, 1992) which combines the expected dazzling up-tempo material from Scotland, Shetland and America with some beautifully tender airs and waltzes.

Classy fiddlers exist in greater numbers today. Enjoying much acclaim on either side of the Atlantic is the Californian-based Scot **Alasdair Fraser** who combines a contemporary exploration of Scots music in his band Skyedance with some loving treatment of the fiddle tradition. The latter style can be heard from Fraser in a

Members of Skyedance (left to right): Chris Norman, Alasdair Fraser, Eric Rigler and Mick Linden.

beautifully-matched partnership with guitarist Tony McManus on *Return To Kintail* (Culburnie, 1999).

Another Shetland fiddler now making a name for herself is **Catriona MacDonald.** Like Bain she is a protégé of the late Tom Anderson, mentor to so many young Shetland players. MacDonald's collaboration with accordionist Ian Lowthian is heard on *Opus Blue* (Acoustic Radio, 1993), but her second album, *Bold* (Peerie Angel, 2000), finds her sounding out splendidly in some adventurously modern settings. A telling moment comes when a set of Shetland reels starts with the taped playing of an old and now departed Shetland fiddler, and then moves to MacDonald and cohorts joining in with panache.

But the Shetlanders by no means have it all their own way. Fiddling is burgeoning in the Highlands today. Listen to **Eilidh Shaw** from Taynuilt. She grew up in the dance-band tradition but plays in the band Keep It Up with concertina ace Simon Thoumire, among others, as well as in the jazz-folk crossover band John Rae's Celtic Feet, and released her own album *Heepirumbo* on Greentrax in 1997.

Other Highland or Highland-based fiddlers widely heard on the fiddle circuit these days include prolific tune-writer **Ian Hardie** (whose 1998 album *Spider's Web* with Andy Thorburn is on Greentrax) and the redoubtable Blazin' Fiddles line-up – featuring luminaries such as Catriona MacDonald, Aidan O'Rourke, Iain MacFarlane and Duncan Chisholm – with a first album, *Fire On!*, released on their own label in 2000. Then there is Charlie McKerron of Capercaillie, and **Duncan Chisholm**, fiddler with the folk-rock band Wolfstone. Chisholm's albums in duet with singer Ivan Drever, such as *The Lewis Blue* (Iona, 1998), contain breakneck sets as well as sweet, lingering airs.

An influence on many a young fiddler has been the famous left-handed Fort William player, Angus Grant, who can be heard on *Angus Grant – Highland Fiddle* (Springthyme, 1997). His son, Angus R Grant, is the hirsute mean fiddler in Shooglenifty. A fine female fiddle duo is CMC, consisting of Claire McLaughlin and Marianne Campbell, the two fiddlers with Deaf Shepherd whose duo album *Snap And Roll* (Snap, 2000) effervesces with bubbly Scots-Irish fiddle fusion. Sprightly Orcadian player Jennifer Wrigley plays with her sister, Hazel, in The Wrigley Sisters. They are joined by co-fiddlers Alan Henderson and Julia Legge, founder member of the Gaelic band Tannas, with guitarist Sandy Wright in a zesty selection of Highland and island material on *Birlin' Fiddles* (Foot Stompin', 1999).

For a taste of the rich and continuing Aberdeenshire tradition, listen to one of its up-and-coming young exponents, **Paul Anderson** of Tarland on 1997's *The Road Home* on the Ross label. (Tarland, incidentally, is a distinguished locale in fiddle lore as Peter Milne, the "Tarland Minstrel", was a teacher of Scott Skinner in the 19th century.) And for slow strathspeys and airs rendered with real soul, there is Douglas Lawrence's *As You'd Expect* (Champion, 2000).

Brian McNeill, long-time and ebullient frontman with Battlefield Band, is a high-profile player who slips with disconcerting ease on to several other instruments – and writes songs and novels as well – yet maintains a distinctive flair on his first instrument. McNeill's fiddle skills can be heard to rare effect on *To Answer The Peacock* (Greentrax, 1998) where the querulous title-track strathspey, a composition of his own, exemplifies his aggressive yet lyrical style.

McNeill's successor in Battlefield, John McCusker, is another eloquent player, and has a current solo album, *Yella Hoose* (Temple, 2000). Another former frontliner with a now legendary outfit, Silly Wizard, is Johnny Cunningham, brother of accordionist Phil. He is known from his Wizard days as a formidable speedster, but displays a mellow, elegiac side on his album *Fair Warning* (Green Linnet, 1983). Among the ranks of other renowned bands are John Martin, the quiet man who has served with distinction in The Tannahill Weavers, Ossian and The Easy Club, and his successor in the Tannahill outfit, Stuart Morison, composer of some skeely reels, who also figures in the reformed version of Ossian. Others worth hearing include

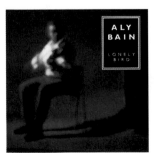 *Catriona MacDonald.*

Aidan O'Rourke, of Tabache, and Derek Hoy, as yet unrecorded in his own right, who plays alongside Ian Hardie in Jock Tamson's Bairns.

But what about the glory days in the 18th century when the fiddle was king? For a taste of them, catch **Pete Clark**'s celebration of the Gow repertoire in *Even Now* (Smiddymade, 1998). Clark played Niel Gow's old fiddle and made the recording in the great hall of Blair Castle, Perthshire, where the 18th-century master would have played for his patrons, the Duke and Duchess of Atholl. For a highly accessible introduction to the engaging Scots-baroque, composer James Oswald's acquaintance with fiddle music shines though his lovely 1995 album *Airs For The Seasons* (volume one of Altamira's *Scots Baroque* series), as played by violinist Jane Murdoch and accompanied by harpsichord, cello and double bass. Also well worth

Albums (below, left to far right) by: Aly Bain; Paul Anderson; Brian McNeill; Catriona MacDonald; Alasdair Fraser & Tony McManus; James Oswald; Pete Clark; Puirt a Baroque.

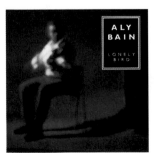

hearing is the elusive but richly rewarding *Fiddle Pibroch And Other Fancies* (cassette only, David Johnston Music, 1989) by the McGibbon Ensemble. It features violinist/fiddler **Edna Arthur** and includes sonatas by McGibbon and McLean as well as an example of that most contentious of genres, fiddle pibroch. (Pibroch is the "classical" music of the Highland bagpipe.) Taking the Scots baroque connection further – across the Atlantic, in fact – is American violinist/fiddler **David Greenberg** and his band Puirt a Baroque, whose excellent album *Return Of The Wanderer* (Marquis Classic, 1998) shows just how the sparks can fly when a classically-trained baroque specialist gets to grips with 18th-century Scotland and present-day Cape Breton Island.

However, to return to where it all came from, go to *The Fiddler And His Art* (Greentrax, 1993), first issued in the School Of Scottish Studies' *Scottish Tradition* series in the 1980s. These are Scotland's fiddling elders, many no longer with us, recorded at home in Orkney and Shetland, the west Highlands and Aberdeenshire – in one track you can hear a clock chiming behind the strains of the fiddle – and with rare spirit sounding tunes passed down though generations. There are "dancing springs" from Andrew Poleson on the island of Whalsay in Shetland, riveting bagpipe pastiche from Donald MacDonell, a strathspey and reel from John Reid, last of the old travelling fiddling and dancing masters, and a couple of sets by the illustrious Hector McAndrew, doyen of Aberdeenshire players and the man who passed on a few tips in strathspey bowing to Yehudi Menuhin.

And who better to sum up the plangent, emotive voice of the fiddle than Albert Stewart? He puts a sob into a Niel Gow air, and once remarked of the fiddle: "If ye canna mak' it greet, it's nae use ava."

RECOMMENDED RECORDS

PAUL ANDERSON THE ROAD HOME *(Ross, 1997) North-east fiddler Anderson in eloquent form, plus some vocal interludes from Jim Reid and Lucy Dale.*
ALY BAIN LONELY BIRD *(Whirlie, 1992) Scotland's fiddle ambassador sounds out in rare form, from Shetland reels and American hoedowns to rich-toned airs and waltzes.*

PETE CLARK EVEN NOW *(Smiddymade, 1998) Clark takes up the master's own fiddle in the great hall of Blair Castle to play the repertoire of the great Niel Gow and his family.*

ALASDAIR FRASER & TONY MCMANUS RETURN TO KINTAIL *(Culburnie, 1999) A beautiful collaboration in which fiddler Fraser and guitarist McManus play a variety of largely Highland material.*

DAVID GREENBERG RETURN OF THE WANDERER *(Marquis Classics, 1998) The American baroque violinist hooked on Scottish/Cape Breton music takes his group Puirt a Baroque through an engaging mixture of traditional strathspeys and reels and 18th-century Scots sonatas.*

BRIAN MCNEILL TO ANSWER THE PEACOCK *(Greentrax, 1998) Former Battlefield fiddler and songwriter McNeill plays with considerable flair on an album that also includes a reading from his novel of the same title.*

JANE MURDOCH AIRS FOR THE SEASONS *(Altamira, 1995) Murdoch gives a lyrical rendition of 18th-century Scots composer James Oswald's brilliant series of short sonatas.*

SCOTLAND: PIPES

And yesterday, and today, and forever
The bagpipes commit to the winds of Heaven
The deepest emotions of the Scotsman's heart
In joy and sorrow, in war and peace.

The poet Hugh MacDiarmid in his epic *Lament For The Great Music* was evoking the sound of the great Highland bagpipe, the pìob mhor (great pipe) of Scottish Gaeldom. This is the instrument which has become commonly identified throughout the world as *the* bagpipe. It spread largely on the back of British colonialism, having been taken up during the late 18th and 19th centuries by the Highland regiments of the British army.

Without getting bogged down in history, it's worth underlining the irony of the Highland pipe being adopted by the very agency that had tried so hard to destroy it in the grim wake of the 1745 Jacobite rebellion. Yet the British military's use of the pipes, along with the Victorian aristocracy's fashion for all things Highland, created a massive demand for the instrument. This ensured a complete turnaround in the decline of the pipe – and also created an environment in which the serious piper could make a living.

The focus on the Highland pipe was also partly the reason for a decline in the use of Scotland's other bagpipes: the largely bellows-blown small pipes, and the Lowland or Border pipes. The ubiquity of the Highland bagpipe has meant that there are perhaps no musical sounds more recognisable the world over than the strains of

a pipe band or the emotive calling of a lone piper. Yet beyond any clichéd and kitsch images of the tartaned piper strutting around, the reality is a vast and wonderful heritage of music, from the irresistibly spirited to the downright magisterial, as well as a thriving, continuing scene in which pipe music is ever developing.

▨ *Martyn Bennett on-stage.*

Both in mainstream piping circles and the folk scene, virtuoso soloists are steadily pushing forward, while pipe-band playing is an extremely popular activity. There are probably around 800 bands in Britain, with 400 registered as competing, and at least the same again elsewhere in the world, with the Scottish bands facing stiff competition from outfits based in former colonies such as Canada and Australia. It is an indication of the diversity that a record label which takes its piping seriously can offer military bands such as the Argyll & Sutherland Highlanders, near-legendary competition pipers like Donald MacPherson or Willie McCallum, and maverick young soloists such as **Fred Morrison**, who plays complete with bendy fingering, Irish-style reels and synthesised accompaniment.

It is the ceol beag, the "little music" of jigs and reels, marches, strathspeys and hornpipes, that brings audiences to their feet. But the ancient and indigenous music of the Highland pipe is ceol mor, the "big music", otherwise known as pibroch. Pibroch is often referred to as the classical music of the Highland bagpipe, and is an imperious, often stately, music form which many will tell you is an acquired taste. Certainly it is music that demands attention, but it has rewards of its own.

Pibroch consists of an "urlar" or theme, on which the piper plays a strictly delineated and increasingly complex series of variations. One of the great and unique moments in Scottish music, comparable perhaps to a good fiddler's subtle switch from strathspey to reel time, is that dramatic instant when the theme suddenly re-emerges naked and unadorned from the intense chatter of the "crunluath", the final and most complex of the variations.

The competition circuit still governs the leading bands' calendars on the thriving pipe-band scene, but a more musically adventurous approach has in recent years aimed to satisfy more than just the strictures of the judging panel. Scottish bands such as Shotts and Dykehead (world champions in 1997 and 1994 respectively), Vale of Atholl, and Dysart & Dundonald have led the way. But they have also found themselves seriously challenged by some of the "colonial" bands like the Simon Fraser University Pipe Band or 78th Fraser Highlanders, both from Canada, or the Victoria Police from Australia – all world champions, and all as innovative and entertaining in concert as they have been successful in the competition arena.

Solo piping, too, is often thought to have suffered from adoption by the military and from competition, where formidably honed and disciplined playing technique is combined with a straitjacketed approach. But piper and broadcaster Iain MacInnes argued in a recent lecture that the army helped these men breathe life into the music. "There was no contradiction, say, in playing 'The Cock Of The North' on the parade ground in the morning," said MacInnes, "and going home in the evening to compose a 'Jig Of Slurs' or a 'Little Cascade'."

■ Albums (below, left to far right) by: Ian Duncan & Robert MacLeod; Chris Armstrong; Fred Morrison; Gordon Duncan; Various (Great Highland Bagpipe); Iain MacInnes; Martyn Bennett; Gordon Mooney.

A major influence on the unbuttoning of Highland pipe music over the past few decades has been the folk revival. Folk groups have been reclaiming what is, despite some of the more aristocratic associations, a folk instrument. Twenty-five years ago

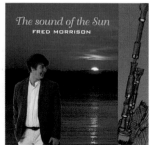

it would have been difficult to hear any of the newly-emerging groups of the Scottish folk revival boasting a bagpipe of any kind in its line-up. Today, the opposite is true. There is often clever deployment of the PA system to balance the powerful sound of the Highland pipes with other instruments, as well as an increased use of quieter bellows-blown pipes – of which more shortly. During the 1970s groups such as The Whistlebinkies, Alba and The Clutha experimented with bagpipes: Alba used Highland pipes alongside fiddle, flute and guitar; The Whistlebinkies employed a reconstructed set of Lowland or Border pipes; and The Clutha used both Highland pipes and small pipes.

A second wave of groups included The Tannahill Weavers, and Battlefield Band, who combined Highland pipes and fiddle with keyboards, while the earlier version of Ossian went for the Irish or uilleann pipes before taking up the Highland instrument later on. Not that there had been some sort of sanitary trench between pipers and other musicians: listen to the fiddle style of north-west Scotland and you will hear clear echoes of pipe music. But down among the more hide-bound elements of the piping establishment there were those who threw up their hands in horror, because they thought the "noble instrument" was being vulgarised to the level of a mere penny whistle.

The effect of the folk revival on Scottish piping in general would be profound. Pipers have become increasingly open to influences from Irish, Breton and Galician piping, while experimentation, questing reinterpretation and general reassessment have become more common. At the same time, the folk revival itself gained from the highly disciplined and formidably high standards of playing set by military and competitive use of the Highland pipes.

The folk revival has also brought a renaissance for Scotland's bellows-blown pipes. These are sometimes described generically by the old Scots name of the cauld-wind pipes, a reference to the bellows blowing cold, dry air into the pipe bag and over the reeds, as opposed to the warm, damp air of mouth-blown bagpipes. This important recent development in Scottish piping has seen the sweet-toned Scottish small pipes and the more strident Lowland or Border bagpipes enjoying new currency. They had been consigned to museums since the 18th and early 19th

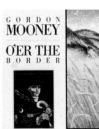

centuries when they were especially popular with Border minstrels and the municipal pipers of the Lowland Scots burghs.

The Highlands, too, had their small pipes and half-sized pipes – "reel pipes" – for dancing. They were made in mouth-blown or bellows-blown form, since pipe-makers were more flexible before the Highland pipe's widespread popularisation. Contemporary pioneers in this area have included players such as **Robert Wallace** with The Whistlebinkies, Hamish Moore, and Gordon Mooney, while recently Matt Seattle has done some important work in unearthing an important source manuscript of Border piping.

The Scottish piping scene is in thriving and dynamic form, with no shortage of historical reassessment and controversy, and a breathtaking degree of virtuosity. And there is no shortage of excellent recordings of all contemporary aspects of pipe music. The Glasgow-based Lismor label alone has a vast catalogue, including its Great Highland Bagpipe series of compilations. This is a good introduction to the instrument, and covers everything from pibroch to some of the more innovative work both from soloists and pipe-bands. The company's World's Greatest Pipers series covers individuals who have made their mark in competitions over the past few generations, and includes **Iain MacFadyen**, **Willie McCallum** and **Donald MacPherson**.

The Temple label has among its piping releases an excellent series of live recordings made during concerts at Glasgow's Piping Centre. They feature great piping elders such as **John D Burgess** as well as some of the fiery young players who have also become associated with the folk scene, including the breathtakingly accomplished **Gordon Duncan**. Greentrax, too, has made some fine concert recordings. One ideal entrance to pibroch is its *Ceòl Na Pìoba: Pìob Mhor* recording (Greentrax, 2000) of an important concert at the 1999 Edinburgh International Festival. It featured top-rate players such as Robert Wallace, **Roderick MacLeod** and **William MacDonald**.

Formidably accomplished pipers are emerging all the time, but some of those worth listening out for – in addition to the aforementioned Gordon Duncan – include Angus McColl, Pipe Major Robert Mathieson, currently of Shotts and Dykehead pipe band, and, among the youngest, Chris Armstrong. The three MacDonald brothers of Glenuig have made their presence felt on the piping scene: Dr Angus MacDonald delivers a fine store of tunes on *A' Sireadh Spors* (Temple, 1996); Iain MacDonald makes his reputation with the groups Ossian and Battlefield; and Allan MacDonald, meanwhile, is a piping researcher who investigates Gaelic culture, and also a performer who can be heard on the beautiful album he made with Margaret Stewart, *Fhuair Mi Pog* (Greentrax, 1998). There he put into action his theories on the links between pibroch and Gaelic song. Some pipers today are making their mark with both the Highland and bellows-blown pipes. Robert

Wallace, for instance, uses Lowland and small pipes with The Whistlebinkies but is also a respected figure on the Highland piping circuit. **Iain MacInnes**, too, uses both Highland and small pipes, as on his recent album *Tryst* (Greentrax, 1999). **Rory Campbell** (who also plays in the Deaf Shepherd and Old Blind Dogs folk groups) and **Fred Morrison** have recently adopted bellows-blown as well as Highland instruments. Listen to Campbell playing with Deaf Shepherd co-member **Malcolm Stitt** on *Field Of Bells* (Lochshore, 1999).

The inventive and eclectic **Martyn Bennett** is frequently called a "techno-piper" but this does less than full justice to his impressive musicianship. He lays down a fiery mix of Highland and small pipes as well as mean electric fiddle over hip-hop beats and samples. But for sheer high-spirited fun get hold of one of the recordings piper **Hamish Moore** made with clarinet/sax wizard Dick Lee, such as *The Bees Knees* (Harbourtown, 1990) or *Farewell To Decorum* (Greentrax, 1993). Finally, moving well south of the Highland line, bellows-pipes pioneer **Gordon Mooney**'s *O'er The Border* (Temple, 1989) is a landmark recording that celebrates the virtually lost piping repertoire of the Scottish Border country.

RECOMMENDED RECORDS

CHRIS ARMSTRONG QUANTUM LEAP *(Lochshore, 1999) Exuberant modern piping with some rock-ish accompaniments from one of the youngest of the young Turks presently working in the piping world.*

MARTYN BENNETT MARTYN BENNETT *(Eclectic, 1996) The recording with which the "techno piper" first made an impact, mixing formidable playing with electronic dance beats and samples. Listen for manic ravings from Harry Lauder. Or try his later Bothy Culture (Rykodisc, 1997).*

GORDON DUNCAN JUST FOR SEUMAS *(Greentrax, 1994) The album that set the seal on Duncan's reputation as a piper of dazzling ability: there are some straight sets played with panache, plus some characteristic fireworks.*

IAIN MACINNES TRYST *(Greentrax, 1999) The piper with the reformed Ossian and, formerly, with the Tannahill Weavers displays a light and considerate touch, mainly on small pipes and in the company of some fine fiddling and harping.*

GORDON MOONEY O'ER THE BORDER *(Temple, 1989) Mooney's important recording celebrates the little-heard music of the Border country. He plays Border pipes, small pipes and other instruments.*

FRED MORRISON THE SOUND OF THE SUN *(Lochshore, 1999) Morrison takes a maverick approach to Highland piping, using Border pipes in a flamboyant style that at times comes close to jazz.*

MARGARET STEWART & ALLAN MACDONALD FHUAIR MI POG *(Greentrax, 1998) Singer Stewart and piper MacDonald make an electrifying duo on this highly accessible* *exposition of MacDonald's theories on the links between Gaelic song and pibroch.*

VARIOUS ARTISTS CEÒL NA PÌOBA: PÌOB MHOR *(Greentrax, 2000) An ideal introduction to pibroch, with a wide range from some of piping's best, including Robert Wallace, Roderick McLeod and Barnaby Brown.*

VARIOUS ARTISTS THE GREAT HIGHLAND BAGPIPE: PIPING VARIATIONS *(Lismor, 2000) From Lismor's useful series of compilations, this featuring solos, duos and other groupings from leading bands.*

VARIOUS ARTISTS THE PIPING CENTRE: 1997 RECITAL SERIES *(Temple, 1997) One of the label's excellent series of recorded recitals at Glasgow's Piping Centre, this one featuring Ian Duncan and Roddy MacLeod, director of piping at the Centre.*

78TH FRASER HIGHLANDERS FLAME OF WRATH *(Lismor, 1998) Showing just what a world championship pipe-band can do in concert, with pibroch settings, augmented percussion, dancers… the works.*

SCOTLAND: ACCORDION

Despite its ubiquity in Scottish life since the 19th century the accordion has often been studiously ignored or peremptorily dismissed by "serious" commentators on Scottish music. It has been seen as an interloper among the "genuine" Scottish folk instruments, as a usurper of the fiddle and an accessory to Scottish kitsch.

Stuart Eydmann, concertina player and fiddler with The Whistlebinkies, is an industrious researcher into the history of Scottish popular music. Charting the widespread adoption of the accordion and other free-reed instruments in Scottish country dance bands as well as religious and temperance groups, Eydmann points to musicologist Frances Collinson's landmark work *The Traditional And National Music Of Scotland*, published in 1966. "It quite rightly devoted considerable space to the fiddle, bagpipe and harp traditions, but failed to mention the accordion even once," says Eydmann. "Other folklorists and commentators on Scottish music have been even more forthright in their dismissal of the instrument as a prop of 'tartanry', part of the 'haggis and heather' music against which the agenda of the post-war folk revival is set."

The accordion, whether of the piano or button-row type, has in recent years shed much of its negative image, partly because of the clearer importance of Scottish country dance bands, the template for which was largely set by the renowned **Jimmy Shand**. Musicians and activists of the Scottish folk revival tended to react against the "strict tempo" associated with the crisp but unvarying sound of the Shand-style country dance bands, and against the showbiz image of tartan-jacketed musicians. But the current revival of the ceilidh dance has helped musicians and dancers to appreciate how masterly the late Shand and his peers have been as players for dancing. Shand, of course, was not the only luminary, though he is

Phil Cunningham.

probably the best known. The late **Bobby MacLeod** of Tobermory, for instance, could really fly when he felt like it. Or listen to the reissue of *Island Heritage* (Springthyme, 1997) by **Iain McLachlan** of Benbecula. McLachlan, who died in 1995, was the composer of 'The Dark Island', a hackneyed but fine tune. He played in the company of fiddle and pipes, and you can hear the influence of those instruments in this lightsome yet earthy ceilidh music.

Early in the 20th century the melodeon, a humbler version of the button accordion, was the instrument of both farm bothy and miner's row. Melodeons and concertinas would find their way into countless impromptu "bothy bands" put together by farm workers. There remains a thriving "box and fiddle" scene in Scotland which until recently would not necessarily have identified itself with the folk scene, but whose players were nevertheless a strong part of the Scottish music tradition because of their ability to carry – and create – a tune.

Phil Cunningham is important in bringing a new attack to the instrument. His formidably nimble-fingered style on the piano accordion was a key component in the sound of the high-powered group Silly Wizard during the 1970s and 1980s, and

■ *Savourna Stevenson.*

later on within Relativity (in both cases alongside his fiddler brother John). Cunningham's sometimes outrageously fast playing was perceived as a reaction against the "strict tempo" school, although he has paid due credit to the importance of Shand as an influence. Cunningham hasn't issued an album of his own since *The Palomino Waltz* (Green Linnet, 1989) although at the time of writing he is working on a new project, and has made two discs that capture his inspired playing partnership with Shetland fiddler Aly Bain, *The Pearl* and *The Ruby* (Whirlie,

1994/1998). Another accordionist associated with the folk revival is **Freeland Barbour** whose outfit The Occasionals is well respected both as a folk band and a country-dance band (try *Live At The Music Hall, Aberdeen* on Greentrax, 1999), while Donald Shaw is a founder and mainstay of the one of the biggest names in Celtic music, Capercaillie.

A more recent arrival among accordion players is **Sandy Brechin**, a dynamic player who manages not only to issue his own albums like *Out Of His Box* (Brechin All, 1996) and *Out Of His Tree* (Greentrax, 1999), but fronts the bands Burach and Seelyhoo as well as in his own ceilidh band, The Sensational Jimmy Shandrix Experience – an affectionate tribute from the new wave to an old master.

The diminutive but sprightly concertina is another free-reed instrument once favoured by a wide range of musicians, from The Salvation Army to the little combos that used to play "doon the watter" excursions on the Clyde steamers. One fine player of long standing is **Norman Chalmers** of the groups Jock Tamson's Bairns and The Cauld Blast Orchestra.

Scotland's current young wizard of the concertina is **Simon Thoumire**, a player of idiosyncratic and sometimes manically inventive ability. He divides his time between playing in more or less traditional outfits like Keep It Up and composing and performing ambitious fusion works that draw on folk, jazz and classical influences, such as his rumbustious *Celtic Connections Suite* (Tartan Tapes, 1998).

SCOTLAND: HARP

In contrast to the accordion, the stilling, crystalline sound of the harp has been heard in Scotland for more than a thousand years, and it vies with the bagpipe as the national instrument of Scotland.

In fact the harp probably predates the bagpipe. Triangular harps appear on Pictish carvings dating from the 10th century, alongside musicians playing what appear to be some kind of bagless pipes. And there is speculation that pibroch, the "classical" music of the Highland bagpipe, may have evolved from early harp music. Harpists such as **Bill Taylor** and Anne Heymann today play pieces drawn from ancient sources like the Welsh *Ap Hyw* manuscript that are strikingly reminiscent of pibroch in their progression of variations. (Listen to **Anne Heymann**'s harp interpretation of a pibroch on her album *Queen Of Harps*, on Temple, 1994.)

The harp became the instrument of the Gaelic bards, of early Christian monks and of travelling minstrels. By the 18th century, however, it was defunct. There was an awakening of interest in the instrument in the 1890s, suffused with Victorian Celtic mist and associated with the arrangements of Marjory and Patuffa Kennedy-Fraser. Then, in 1931, the formation of the Clarsach Society provided the basis for what now exhibits all the hallmarks of a vigorous renaissance. Hundreds of players in Scotland and elsewhere are taking the instrument far beyond the Victorian drawing room. The term "clarsach" is generally applied today to the small Scots or Celtic harp, but really refers to the wire-strung harp of Gaelic Scotland which was played with the fingernails. (An established punishment for harpists unwise enough to offend a patron was to have their nails cut.) Meanwhile, "Scottish harp" defines the lighter-tensioned Lowlands gut-strung harp, played using the fingertips.

Today, most "clarsachs" tend to be gut- or nylon-strung. But in keeping with current research into the origins, the playing styles and the repertoire, there is now a burgeoning interest in the wire-strung instrument. Electro-harps, too, such as those made by Camac of Brittany, are expanding the instrument's capability in the studio and on the concert platform.

In the 1950s the redoubtable **Jean Campbell** of Edinburgh taught a handful of players, including **Isobel Mieras** who is herself now an energetic activist and teacher in the current revival, which has seen the appearance of many accomplished players. Some, such as **Alison Kinnaird** or early-music specialist **William Taylor**, are delving deep into the tradition. Others to a greater or lesser degree are taking on board the influences of jazz, rock and world music; they include Savourna Stevenson, Wendy Stewart, who also plays with the group Ceolbeg, and Patsy Seddon and Mary MacMaster, whose twin gut- and wire-strung harps drive the sound of Sileas.

An album that provides a useful cross-section of the clarsach revival is Greentrax's compilation based on the Scottish Harps season at the 1998 Edinburgh International Festival. Otherwise, good signposts to the Scottish harp's new directions include **Savourna Stevenson**'s *Touch Me Like The Sun* (Cooking Vinyl, 2000), **Wendy Stewart**'s *About Time 2* (Greentrax, 1997), Sileas's *Play On Light* (Greentrax, 1996), or *A Certain Smile* (Culburnie, 1999) by the fusion duo Bachué featuring harpist and singer **Corrina Hewat** and pianist Dave Milligan.

■ *Albums (below, left to far right) by: Sandy Brechin; Keep It Up; Iain McLachlan; Rob MacKillop; Savourna Stevenson; Various (Scottish Harps); Tony McManus; William Jackson.*

Scottish and Irish harping seem still to be largely the preserve of women, but a distinguished exception is composer, multi-instrumentalist and Ossian member **William Jackson**. He can be heard on solo albums or in various ensemble and orchestral settings, as in his album *Inchcolm* (Linn, 1994).

SCOTLAND: GUITAR

In every session, on every album, behind almost every fiddle, pipe, or accordion, you will find a guitar. In the earliest days of the revival the guitar was the folk singer's instrument of choice, picking out blues and hammering out protest songs or come-all-ye Jacobite anthems. Instrumental finesse wasn't a necessity.

Like the accordion, the guitar was regarded by some purists as a vulgar alien interloper. Yet it is worth bearing in mind that one of the earliest printed tutors for the guitar was published by Bremner in Edinburgh in 1758.

Attitudes are different today. The guitar, and sometimes the cittern and bouzouki, retain their driving power behind some high-flying frontliners, but are also shown off in their own right. The accompanists are stepping into the spotlight, too, as can be heard on the solo albums *Birlinn* (Greentrax, 1999) by mandolinist **Rod Paul** of The Iron Horse, and *Springwell* (Greentrax, 1999) by **Kevin Macleod** of The Occasionals. **Tony Cuffe**, a distinctive singer as well as a pioneer in transposing pipe tunes and other Scottish material to guitar, is now resident in America, but his "farewell" recording, *When First I Went To Caledonia* (Iona, 1994), is still available.

Two equally rewarding albums show two distinct directions in which the guitar is being taken in Scotland. First is **Tony McManus**, consummate guitarist and ubiquitous sessionman on many other artists' albums. His second album on Greentrax, 1998's *Pourquoi Quebec?*, glitters with nimble and expressive fingering of largely traditional tunes in the company of some excellent sidemen, including the Breton bassist Alain Genty. Second is **Rob MacKillop**, whose *Flowers Of The Forest* (Greentrax, 1998) is a beguiling introduction to Scottish lute and early guitar music, and resounding proof of the enduring appeal of even the most venerable tunes.

RECOMMENDED RECORDS

SANDY BRECHIN OUT OF HIS TREE *(Greentrax, 1999) Ubiquitous accordionist let loose on his second album with characteristically zesty stuff and titles such as 'Green Mutant Ninja Turtle Blood'.*

WILLIAM JACKSON INCHCOLM *(Linn, 1994) That rarity: a male harpist. This is a good*

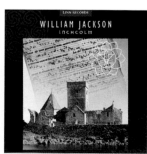

■ *Members of Sileas:*
Patsy Seddon (left) and
Mary MacMaster.

showcase of Jackson's ability both as a player and as a composer and arranger, in
collaboration with the Scottish Chamber Orchestra strings.

KEEP IT UP KEEP IT UP *(Tartan Tapes, 1998) Concertina wizard Simon Thoumire in more*
or less traditional mode with fiddler Eilidh Shaw, guitarist Kevin MacKenzie, and Malcolm
Stitt on bouzouki and pipes. Light, tight and springy.

ROB MACKILLOP FLOWERS OF THE FOREST *(Greentrax, 1998) Lutenist MacKillop's*
rare excursion through the surprisingly accessible realms of Scots lute and early guitar music
reveals fine tunes that have weathered the centuries.

IAIN MCLACHLAN AN ISLAND HERITAGE *(Springthyme, 1997) The late McLachlan of*
Benbecula here plays in the company of a fiddler and piper in a fine showcase of grass-roots
Hebridean music – including his own 'Dark Island'.

TONY MCMANUS POURQUOI QUEBEC? *(Greentrax, 1998) Masterly guitarist and*
ubiquitous sessionman McManus produces a showcase of mainly traditional material, with
lovely bass work from Breton Alain Genty.

SAVOURNA STEVENSON TOUCH ME LIKE THE SUN *(Cooking Vinyl, 2000) Stevenson*
is the daughter of composer Ronald Stevenson, and on this recording she lays down some quite
simply dazzling as well as innovative solo harp work. She is joined for the title track by singer
Eddi Reader.

VARIOUS ARTISTS SCOTTISH HARPS *(Greentrax, 1998) A fine introduction to the harp*
scene featuring participants at an Edinburgh Festival season and including Sileas, Savourna
Stevenson, Isobel Mieras, Wendy Stewart, and Alison Kinnaird.

SCOTLAND: BANDS

Whatever one might think of "Celtic music" as a catch-all phrase, perhaps its most enduring image is that of the folk group, Scots or Irish, providing a delicately fretted song setting, or in full flight, with fiddles, pipes, citterns and guitars birling out jigs and reels as if there were no tomorrow. But in Scotland recently it seemed for a while that the folk singer was almost becoming an endangered species as the traditional music scene was swept off in waves of instrumental fire.

Much of the impetus came initially from the Irish instrumental revolution, triggered by composer and musicologist Seán Ó Riada's formation in the 1960s of Ceoltóirí Chualann, the proto-Chieftains. They may have worn dinner jackets, but the Ceoltóirí showed just what could be done with an inventive ensemble using traditional instruments, plus Ó Riada's harpsichord.

Not that the Scottish tradition was devoid of ensemble playing: there were thriving if somewhat predictable strathspey and reel societies, country dance bands and, earlier, the bothy bands knocked together by farm labourers. And if you look back further, Scottish painters such as David Wilkie and David Allan captured bucolic scenes of Highland weddings at which pipers played for the dance, side by side with fiddlers and cellists.

With the Ceoltóirí and then The Chieftains, however, came the realisation that traditional music could be arranged for permutations of traditional – and non-traditional – instruments, with effective, elegant, driving results. More Irish bands such as Planxty and The Bothy Band followed on. Indeed there were times during the 1970s when, had you walked into any session pub in Glasgow or Edinburgh, you would have been hard put to hear a Scottish tune. The aspiring fiddlers would be faithfully reeling off tune after tune from the latest albums by The Chieftains, The Bothy Band, De Danaan and the rest.

But there was more going on. As the 1960s rolled toward the 1970s, **The Corries** were gaining wide popularity within and beyond the still largely song-based Scottish folk revival. Initially a trio with Paddy Bell, and then the duo of Ronnie Browne and the late Roy Williamson, The Corries between them deployed a bewildering array of instruments from assorted guitars and mandolins to Northumbrian pipes. Meanwhile in England the earliest versions of Fairport Convention were sowing the seeds of folk-rock, later to be grown north of the border by **The JSD Band** and **Contraband**. Gradually the concept of an acoustic, tradition-based, multi-instrumental line-up developed, initially in groups such as The Clutha, which combined the powerful ballad singing of Gordeanna McCulloch with fiddles and pipes. The early 1970s saw The Whistlebinkies taking shape. At first the band played a mix of Irish and American music but soon brought together fiddle, harp and the rediscovered bellows-blown Lowland pipes, while Alba installed Highland pipes within a string-driven, Planxty-like framework.

The Boys Of The Lough formed as a trio in Northern Ireland, and then re-rooted themselves in Edinburgh in the early 1970s. They would become the first group to embark on the gruelling routine of the international concert tour that has become the necessary lot of the professional Scottish folk band. Shetland fiddler Aly Bain, Ulster flautist Cathal McConnell and Northumbrian Dave Richards on mandolin, banjo and concertina have remained at the core of this much-loved Celtic string band. Their most recent album is *The West Of Ireland* (Lough, 1999) which also features Kerryman Brendan Begley on accordion and Scot Malcolm Stitt on guitar and bouzouki. The album is as Irish-weighted as its title suggests; for more of a Scots and Shetland spread, seek out their beautiful winter solstice celebration, *The Day Dawn* (Lough, 1994).

Battlefield Band are another group who soon took the globe-trotting troubadour's trail, playing in venues as far apart as Alaska and Singapore. They were the first to experiment by backing Highland pipes and fiddle with keyboards. The one remaining founder member, keyboardist Alan Reid, is currently joined by piper Mike Katz and fiddler John McCusker, while at the time of writing their singer, Davy Steele, was stepping down due to illness, to be replaced by Karine Polwart. Steele features, however, on their album *Leaving Friday Harbour* (Temple, 1999), the latest in a long line of recordings.

Another internationally popular outfit is the hard-driving **Tannahill Weavers**, whose ranks have nurtured a succession of fiery pipers and fiddlers. A good compilation is *Choice Cuts: 1987-96* (Green Linnet, 1997). **The Whistlebinkies**, a veteran group who have avoided the perpetual tour grind by continuing to play on a part-time basis, have a distinctive, all-acoustic sound that combines Lowland and small pipes, fiddles, concertina, clarsach, and pipe-band side-drum. The band includes a composer of "art music", Eddie McGuire, who plays flute, so a tune which features in his score for the ballet *Peter Pan* may quite unabashedly crop up during a Whistlebinkies set – and none the worse for the change of garb.

Back in the late 1970s, in a notable reversal of the usual process, the folk-rock band Contraband downed amps, took up clarsach, Irish and later Highland pipes, and became the widely acclaimed **Ossian**. A re-formed version with original members Billy Ross (vocals) and Billy Jackson (harp) joined by piper Iain MacInnes and fiddler Stuart Morison (both former Tannahills) can be heard on *The Carrying Stream* (Greentrax, 1997).

No revivals, however, for **Silly Wizard**, one of the fastest and fiercest Scottish groups of the 1970s and 1980s, although they also teased some winsome arrangements around the singing of Andy M Stewart. With brothers Johnny and

Capercaillie on-stage.

Phil Cunningham setting the pace on fiddle and accordion, the Wizard at their turbocharged best were a memorable experience. You can still find their recordings on the Green Linnet label. The 1980s saw the formation of what is now one of the most commercially successful Scottish folk bands, **Capercaillie**. The outfit that started as a modest ceilidh band in Taynuilt, near Oban, seems at ease as Celtic standard-bearers in the world music boom, having provided music for the movie *Rob Roy*. They also managed to put an ancient Hebridean waulking song, 'Coisich A Ruin', into the charts. The combination of the gorgeously poised Gaelic vocals of Karen Matheson and the fiddle-accordion-keyboard muscle of Charlie McKerron and Donald Shaw has been a winner, though in recent years they have been much augmented by percussion and assorted remixes. Their progress over the 1990s can be charted in *Dusk Till Dawn* (Survival, 1998).

The 1980s saw the development of "Scots swing" as the seminal group **Jock Tamson's Bairns** emerged from Edinburgh's Sandy Bell's pub sessions. The

Members of Shooglenifty: Angus Grant (left) and Conrad Ivitsky.

band were influenced by everything from pipe marches to the snappy jazz guitar style of the late Jimmy Eliot as well as swing stylists such as Eddie Lang and Joe Venuti. To that zesty, guitar-driven, twin-fiddle sound the Bairns added the delectable vocals of Rod Paterson, and before breaking up in 1983 recorded two fine albums, the bulk of which you can hear on *A' Jock Tamson's Bairns* (Greentrax, 1996).

Out of the Bairns came the even swinger, snappier **Easy Club**, with the formidable line-up of John Martin on fiddle, Rod Paterson on guitar and vocals, Jack Evans on guitar, and percussion ace Jim Sutherland on bodhrán. These constituent talents eventually went their own disparate ways, though you can hear the best of them on *Essential* (Eclectic, 1992).

Meanwhile the reformed Jock Tamson's Bairns are due to produce their first album in 20 years, though without the guitar of Jack Evans who is engaged with other projects – including his highly enjoyable swing- and 1960s-tinged collaboration with singer-fiddler Mairi Campbell and fiddler Jenny Gardner, *Once Upon A Time In The North* (Greentrax, 2000). Evans and Bairns sidekick Norman Chalmers were also involved in the powerfully inventive **Cauld Blast Orchestra** whose stylistic gamut from eccentric reels and tangos to full, rip-roaring big-band jazz is manifest on *Durgar's Feast* (Eclectic, 1994). Rod Paterson, meantime, sings in **Ceolbeg**. This is another hefty and at times anthemic-sounding band, but more traditionally centred. Paterson is in the company of piper Gary West, harpist Wendy Stewart, plus keyboards and drums, on *Cairnwater* (Greentrax, 2000).

A similarly muscular band is **Deaf Shepherd**, with a front row of Highland pipes plus two fiddles and a fine Lowland Scots singer in John Morran. Their music is heard in impressive fashion on *Synergy* (Greentrax, 1997), while the band's piper, Rory Campbell, also plays with the re-shuffled north-east band **Old Blind Dogs** along with singer Jim Malcolm. You can hear the new Dogs on *The World's Room* (Green Linnet, 2000). For an older incarnation with rumbustious Aberdeenshire vigour, juddering percussion from Davy Cattenach and the soft Doric vocals of Ian Benzie, get hold of *Old Blind Dogs Live* (Lochshore, 1999). Also to be found recording for the Lochshore label are the similarly popular and fiddle-driven **Iron Horse**.

Capercaillie's fiddler Charlie McKerron has projects of his own, notably the expansive pop and world music of **Big Sky** that features his cousin Laura McKerron on vocals, stirring in an ear-tweaking mix of electronic beats and samples with a cross-section of folk and jazz players from a currently heady fusion scene. Back in Gaeldom, but still with a cool, poppish sensibility, McKerron also crops up on *Suilean Dubh / Dark Eyes* (Lochshore, 1999) by **Tannas**. This is usually a duo of Amy Geddes (vocals and fiddle) and Sandra MacKay (vocals), but is bolstered here by McKerron, fellow-Capercaillie mainstay Donald Shaw and several others … which begs the idle question: when does a duo become a group?

The same may be asked of the accomplished and stylish jazz fusion of *A Certain Smile* by **Bachué** (Culburnie, 1999), the duo of harpist and singer Corrina Hewat and jazz pianist Dave Milligan. They are aided and abetted in confounding pigeon-holers by the likes of prime Scots jazzers Phil Bancroft on saxes and Brian Shiels on double bass. **Tabache**, too, are a fleet, Irish-orientated duo of fiddler Aidan O'Rourke and fiddler, flautist and singer Claire Mann, supported on their debut album *Waves Of Rush* (Lochshore, 1999) by Malcom Stitt, Donald Shaw and Rory Campbell. Another recent arrival, playing largely Shetland music with great panache, is the young band **Fiddlers' Bid**. They require no assistance from anybody, with four fiddles plus harp, guitar and bass, and an excellent second album in *Hamnataing* (Greentrax, 1998).

Further afield, fiddler Alasdair Fraser's American-based group **Skyedance** comes up with some rich and exhilarating playing that shifts seamlessly in and out of Scottish idioms on *Labyrinth* (Culburnie, 1999). Another group making a name for itself on the international touring circuit are the pan-Celtic **Anam** whose members are Irish, Cornish and Scots, including the fine Gaelic singer Fiona Mackenzie and fiddler Anna-Wendy Stevenson.

Burach, propelled by the forthright swirl of Sandy Brechin's accordion, veer toward the rockier end of folk-rock and are one of a string of younger groups such as Shetlanders Rock Salt & Nails who are melding traditional music with a rock'n'pop sensibility. Perhaps the most popular of these has been the hyper-syncopated **Shooglenifty**.

The band's 1999 album *A Whisky Kiss* provided the Greentrax label with its biggest seller yet. Shooglenifty's line-up includes Angus R Grant on fiddle, Iain MacLeod on mandolin and the dynamic Jim MacIntosh on drums. Their brand of unrelenting psychedelic ceilidh music has had audiences on their feet from Dingwall to Sydney Opera House, and encouraged numerous imitators of the style, including The Tartan Amoebas.

Sound collages rather than tune sets are the stuff of the *Nahoo 1*, *Nahoo 2* and *Nahoo 3* albums (Iona, 1994/1997/1999) produced by the Brazilian-based Scot **Paul Mounsey**. His method is to splice snatches of fiddle and pipes and Gaelic song with pounding beats and spun-in speech samples. Touching upon topics such as colonialism and identity, Mounsey's pieces may not be to everybody's taste, but they offer a unique take on the exile's view.

Still carrying the torch for good old fashioned folk-rock are **Wolfstone**, with beefy pipe and fiddle tunes. Constituting a cultural phenomenon in their own right are **Runrig**, usually referred to as "the Gaelic rock band" although the bulk of their songs have been in English.

Albums (below, left to far right) by: Shooglenifty; Battlefield Band; The Boys Of The Lough; Capercaillie; Deaf Shepherd; Fiddlers' Bid; Skyedance; The Whistlebinkies.

Donnie Munro, their eloquent-voiced singer of long standing, is now busying himself elsewhere – and Runrig may have passed the days when they could draw thousands to Edinburgh Castle Esplanade or Loch Lomondside. But you'll find the band still sounding in good heart, now with Nova Scotian singer Bruce

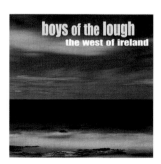

Guthro, on *In Search Of Angels* (Ridge, 1999). For a whiff of that heady period when the band seemed so emblematic of the upsurge in cultural confidence for both Gaeldom and Scotland as a whole, listen to the classic album *The Cutter And The Clan* (Chrysalis, 1987) with its moving, exuberant songs covering themes such as land, exile and resurgence.

RECOMMENDED RECORDS

BATTLEFIELD BAND LEAVING FRIDAY HARBOUR *(Temple, 1999) A popular outfit who put in more than their share of air miles, now taking on board singer Karine Polwart.*
THE BOYS OF THE LOUGH THE WEST OF IRELAND *(Lough, 1999) A heavily Irish-accented work from the first of the Celtic bands to establish themselves on the international touring circuit – and they still pull in the big audiences.*
CAPERCAILLIE DUSK TILL DAWN *(Survival, 1998) The best of Capercaillie over the 1990s, during which time they firmly established themselves as a major Celtic presence in world music.*
DEAF SHEPHERD SYNERGY *(Greentrax, 1997) The instrumental fire of the band's powerful sound – with pipes and twin fiddles – is tempered here by fine singing from John Morran.*
THE EASY CLUB ESSENTIAL *(Eclectic, 1992) Gone but not forgotten, The Easy Club showed how close the Scotch snap was to jazz swing. This is a comprehensive selection.*
FIDDLERS' BID HAMNATAING *(Greentrax, 1998) Multiple Shetland fiddles plus harp, guitar and bass from an accomplished young instrumental group.*
ALASDAIR FRASER'S SKYEDANCE LABYRINTH *(Culburnie, 1999) Master fiddler Fraser in the company of his American-based band wind their way through contemporary explorations of the Scots idiom.*
SHOOGLENIFTY A WHISKY KISS *(Greentrax, 1996) The band spin out hypnotically supercharged ceilidh music that has made this the label's best-seller.*
THE WHISTLEBINKIES TIMBER TIMBRE *(Greentrax, 1999) The distinctive and long-standing sound of Lowland pipes, fiddles, concertina, harp and side-drum, plus the influence of composer Eddie McGuire on flute.*

W A L E S
ISLE OF MAN AND ENGLAND

BY KENNY MATHIESON

Wales, the Isle of Man and Cornwall are the recognised homes of Celtic traditions within the United Kingdom. But the music from these areas – and especially that of the Isle of Man and Cornwall – has long been obscured by the considerable shadow cast by Ireland and Scotland, and even Brittany. Wales has a musical tradition that can be traced back at least as far as its larger counterparts, with the same story of persecution that threatened the eradication of oral folk traditions.

This threat was both political, with the Anglicising effect of the Act of Union, and religious, with the rise of a dour Methodist creed in the 18th and 19th centuries. As in Ireland and Scotland, the Welsh church saw music and dance of the oral traditional as the devil's work – though they were happy enough to steal his tunes for their hymns. More recently, and most especially during the period of the general post-

1960s Celtic revival which is the primary focus of this book, Welsh music has experienced a real resurgence, hand in hand with the even more remarkable revival of the Welsh language.

The stereotyped view of Welsh music is dominated by the male voice choir, still a strong institution even in the face of the collapse of the mining industry which traditionally sustained it, and the growth of mixed male and female choirs. Close-harmony singing by small groups is also a major component of Welsh music.

The second most famous institution is the Eisteddfod, great festive competitions which date back to the 12th century, providing Wales with the equivalent of the Mod in Scotland or the Irish Fleadh Cheoil. These remain important occasions, and have played an important part in preserving and handing down Welsh music and culture in less receptive times.

The key instruments in the Welsh tradition have been the voice and the harp, but the contemporary period has seen an important restoration of the bagpipe (pibe cwd), and the fiddle has moved to centre stage. If the best known singers from Wales are still Shirley Bassey and Tom Jones, the folk tradition has also thrown up its homegrown stars, the most established being **Dafydd Iwan**. He began singing during the folk revival of the 1960s and gradually moved from an American-influenced style to Welsh song and the nationalist movement. His earthy, open-hearted, directly expressive style is highly effective in both a solo context and in his collaborations with the band Ar Log. He remains a key figure in the Welsh revival, not least as the co-founder of the crucial Sain record label.

■ *Dafydd Iwan (opposite).*

Sain (meaning "sound") was set up by Iwan, Huw Jones (also a singer-songwriter) and Brian Morgan Edwards in Cardiff in 1969 amid the ferment of a Welsh nationalist revival. The label's initial focus was on folk singers, usually with a political message, but it quickly became a focal point for all kinds of Welsh music, and the catalogue grew to reflect that. Vocal and instrumental music in both traditional and modern styles was included, as well as many of the emerging folk and folk-rock bands of the late 1970s, easy-listening acts like the country duo John Ac Alun, male voice choirs, classical singers like the boy treble Aled Jones and the acclaimed Bryn Terfel, and contemporary rock acts such as Mike Peters, the lead singer with the stadium rock band The Alarm (the band also issued an album of songs in Welsh for the label), and Catatonia.

The arrival of the Fflach Tradd label in the late 1990s added another key outlet for the dissemination of Welsh music. The newcomer to this scene would do well to start with the various compilation albums issued by these labels. Both *Gorau Gwerin: The Best Of Welsh Folk Music* (Sain, 1992) and *Goreuon Canu Gwerin Newydd: The Best Of New Welsh Folk Music* (Sain, 1997) offer a strong representation of the most important names in modern Welsh folk. Also well worth investigating are Fflach Tradd's more thematic projects like *Ffidlil*, featuring 13 fiddlers, and *Daigan*, focusing on traditional singing, not exclusively from Wales. While much singing in Wales takes place in a group, a number of artists have succeeded in making names as soloists. Singer, harpist and pianist **Sián James** is one of the most important of the current generation of Welsh artists, and her haunting vocal style is well captured on the Welsh songs on discs such as *Distaw/Silent* (Sain, 1993), *Gweini Tymor/Serving Season* (Sain, 1996) and *Di-gwsg/Sleepless* (Sain, 1997).

Siswann George, a fine singer from the Rhondda, made her name as part of the group Mabsant, but is an excellent solo singer in her own right, as she demonstrated on *Traditional Songs Of Wales* (Saydisc, 1995). George has also been part of The Folk Divas, a group convened for the Celtic Connections Festival in Glasgow and which also featured Scotland's Sheena Wellington and Ishbel McAskill. Heather Jones, a Cardiff-based singer, is another fine solo voice, and is also part of the trio Hin Deg.

Meredydd Evans represents an older tradition of unaccompanied solo singing which he has done much to preserve. **Dafydd Iwan**'s style is heard to good effect on albums like *Cân Celt* (Sain, 1995) and *Caneunon Gwerin* (Sain, 1997) which feature both traditional Welsh folk songs and his own material. **Meic Stevens** is worth hearing, too, on *Michangel* (Sain, 1998).

Tudur Morgan takes a more contemporary approach on her exploration of the famous Welsh legend of the Mabinogi on *Branwen* (Sain, 1997), an album which features Donal Lunny as both player and producer. The duo of Huw and Tony Williams have also established a reputation for their fine folk singing, although they have concentrated on English-language material.

The harp (telyn) has undergone a strong revival. The Welsh triple harp is a complex chromatic version of the instrument, with three rows of strings, the middle row sounding sympathetically with the played notes in the two duplicated outer rows. It yields a lush, full-bodied sound. The instrument was introduced into Wales in the 17th century, but the modern revival was pioneered by **Nansi Richards**, and most famously by **Robin Huw Bowen**, known as a virtuoso performer and arranger on the instrument as well as for uncovering much forgotten music.

Bowen's solo playing is featured in both traditional and modern material on the excellent *Hen Aelwyd/Old Hearth* (Sain, 1999). He was a member of Mabsant, an important group in the development of modern Welsh music, and now works with Cusan Tân (with singers Ann Morgan-Jones and Sue Jones-Davies) and Crasdant (where he collaborates with fiddler Stephen Rees, guitarist Huw Williams and woodwind player Andy McLauchlin).

Another important exponent of the triple harp is **Llio Rhydderch**, as a solo harpist and in her group Telynwyr. Her explorations of traditional harp techniques as applied to both old and new arrangements of traditional melodies is heard on *Telyn* (Fflach Tradd, 1997). The triple harp is widely seen as the most characteristic of the harps associated with Wales, but the concert pedal harp is also widely played, notably

Siân James.

by **Elinor Bennett**. She explores the music of a famous 19th century harp virtuoso on *Alawon Cymeig, John Thomas* (Sain, 1998). Another popular type of instrument now is the Welsh version of the smaller Celtic harp, usually referred to as the knee or lap harp in Wales, and often found in groups. Some players have also experimented with an early Welsh instrument known as a crwth, a type of lute which can be either plucked or bowed.

The bagpipes have played a less central role in recent Welsh music than in the other Celtic regions, although their historical legacy is at least as old as the harp. They are often mentioned in the Bardic tradition, although there are no known surviving examples of native Welsh instruments in existence, partly as a result of deliberate destruction by religious zealots.

Ceri Rhys Matthews, the founder of the Fflach Tradd label, has spearheaded a revival in Welsh piping, which can be heard on *Pibau* (Flach Tradd, 1999), his duo album with musician and instrument-maker Jonathan Shorland. Shorland plays the bombo, a type of early oboe (and not at all related to the percussion instrument of that name from Galicia), and the pibgorn, an ancient Welsh reed instrument. Matthews is also a member of the group Fernhill. This grew out of his earlier band,

Saith Rhyfeddod, and features the piper with singer Julie Murphy and accordion player Andy Cutting.

The fiddle has appeared in many Welsh groups in the revival period, while some players have become established as soloists. **Sián Phillips** is one, a fifth-generation fiddler who released her debut album *Gramundus/Big World* (Fflach Tradd, 1998) with guitar accompaniment from John Rodge. She is also a member of Wild Welsh Women, formed in 1999 when they issued their self-released debut album, *Isle Of*

■ *Members of The Kilbrides (left to right): Bernard; Gerard; and Danny.*

Môn. Despite the name, half the group are men, but it's based on the mother and daughter team of Rozi Morris and Tamzin Powell.

The leaders on the Welsh fiddle scene are the Cardiff-based siblings **The Kilbrides**, a family group featuring Bernard and Gerard on fiddles and Daniel on guitar. They come from a musical family, and while their principal focus is the traditional acoustic music of South Wales their repertoire also includes tunes from Ireland, Scotland, Brittany and even further afield, as demonstrated on their album *Kilbride* (Fflach Tradd, 1997).

As in Ireland and Scotland, the revival has also launched a whole series of important groups on to the Welsh scene. Probably the best known is **Ar Log**, who formed in the late 1970s to play at the Festival Interceltique in Lorient and decided to stay together (their cheeky name means "for hire").

The group is built on the harping brothers Dayfdd (triple harp) and Gwyndaf Roberts (knee harp), blended with fiddles, accordion, flute, guitar, and voice. They collaborated with singer Dafydd Iwan on a couple of albums in the early 1980s, *Rhwng Hwyl A Thaith* and *Yma O Hyd*, later combined on a single CD (Sain, 1993), and have issued a number of records in their own right. *Ar Log IV* (Sain, 1996) is the most recent and the most contemporary in sound and production values. Material from its two immediate predecessors has also been issued on CD, as *O IV I V* (Sain, 1991). **The Hennesseys** remain a popular draw after three decades on the folk circuit with their uncomplicated trio style, while **Plethyn**, another band which formed during the 1970s, are still to be heard occasionally, with their three- and four-part harmony arrangements of Welsh songs.

Now defunct bands like **Climeri** and its successor, **Pedwar Yn Y Bar**, made highly influential contributions to the evolving Welsh music scene. Their direct influence is still evident in the music of **Gwerinos**, an exciting seven-piece band from Gwynnedd with a driving, Irish-style attack featured on the dance tunes on discs like *Seilam* (Sain, 1997) and *Lleuad Llawn* (Sain, 1999).

Calennig, a quartet from Glamorgan with Mick Tems's accordion and Patricia Carron-Smith's concertina at the heart of the band, also features Peter Davies on pipes. They have explored traditional Welsh music as well as seafaring songs associated with the sea ports of South Wales, which was the subject of their album *Trade Winds* (Sain, 1997).

A number of groups have succeeded in introducing more contemporary world-music flavours into a basic Welsh mix. They include **Aberjaber**, formed by saxophonist and piper Peter Stacey, the acclaimed harp player Delyn Evans, and Stevie Wishart, a classically-trained player who used the viol and hurdy-gurdy to add a distinctive flavouring to their mix of Welsh traditional, jazz and world music. Wishart was later replaced in a reformed version of the group by African percussionist Ben Assare. The band's album is *Y Bwced Perffaith* (Sain, 1997), while Evans also has a very active career as a solo harpist.

Carreg Lafar, a young band from Cardiff, have made a big impression with their fresh-sounding treatments of Welsh and Celtic tunes. Their name translates as Echo Stone, and their music does indeed carry an echo of a distant time within their contemporary ambience. The band uses the voices of singers Linda Owen Jones and Rhian Evan Jones as a highly effective focus for their music, but they are also excellent instrumentalists. Their fine debut album, *Ysbryd Y Werin* (Sain, 1995), was followed by the even more impressive *Hyn* (Sain, 1998).

The music of Cusan Tân is also built on close-harmony vocals, featuring Ann Morgan Jones and Sue Jones-Davies in often ethereal settings featuring the harp of Robin Huw Bowen. Pigyn Clust too have experimented with modern arrangements of Welsh traditional tunes, employing lusher, harp-led soundscapes, some of which have brought comparisons with the early work of Clannad.

Rock played a bigger part in the music of Bob Delyn a'r Ebillion where it intermingled in original and promiscuous fashion with Welsh and Breton influences. Rock influence also appears in the sound of bands like Moniars, an exuberant anything-goes folk-rock outfit from Anglesey, and Blue Horses, who mix twin fiddles with Hammond organ and electric guitars in what they call "Celtadclic roots-rock".

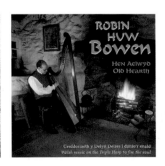
Julie Murphy of Fernhill.

ISLE OF MAN

If Welsh music has been sidelined by that of Ireland and Scotland, then the music of the Isle Of Man and Cornwall is an even bigger secret. Here are some starting points, but bear in mind that recordings may be hard to find.

Harpist and singer **Emma Christian** made an impact in the mid 1990s with her concerts and recordings rooted in Manx traditions. Her music can be heard on a couple of recent albums: *Beneath The Twilight* (Manx Celtic, 1994); and *Celtic Airs And Ballads* (Beautiful Jo, 1996).

The doyen of Manx music, however, is **Charles Guard**, a harpist who is also the administrator of the Manx Heritage Foundation. Guard's *Avenging And Bright* (Shanachie, 1991) features material from Ireland and Scotland as well as the Isle Of Man, while *The Secret Island* (Mananan, 1993) offered more contemporary arrangements, using synthesisers and electronic keyboards. **MacTullagh Vannin** are the island's leading band, but The Mollag Band and the younger Paitchyn Vannin have also made their mark.

Albums (below, left to far right) by: Various (Best Of Welsh Folk Music); Robin Huw Bowen; Various (Best Of New Welsh Folk Music); Ceri Rhys Matthews & Jonathan Shorland; Elinor Bennett; Various (Daigan); Llio Rhydderch; Various (Traditional Fiddle Music From Cardiff).

CORNWALL

Cornwall also boasts Celtic roots, and its music and dance is much influenced by Celtic cousins across the channel in Brittany. There are few Cornish artists, but the group **Anao Atao** are regarded as the foremost practitioners of the area's traditional music and dance. The group is a family band featuring the husband and wife team of Kyt and Soazig Le Nen Davey. They met in an earlier Cornish band, Bucca; their children, Sterenn and Maela, also feature in Anao Atao. The release of their debut album, *Esoteric Stones* (Kesson, 1994), brought enthusiastic reaction, as did the subsequent *Poll Lyfans* (Kesson, 1998). The family's other son, Neil Davey, is currently a member of the young Irish-Scottish group Anam.

The influence of Celtic music in England certainly extends beyond Cornwall. It turns up in all manner of places, but is arguably most strongly reflected where geography might lead us to expect it: in the north, and especially in the Northumbrian tradition. The work of musicians such as the brilliant Northumbrian pipers Kathryn Tickell and Pauline Cato, the fiddler Tom McConville, or the duo of accordionist Karen Tweed and guitarist Ian Carr all reveal at least a kinship with Celtic forms and moods.

RECOMMENDED RECORDS

FERNHILL CA NOS *(Beautiful Jo, 1996) Debut album from Anglo-Welsh band with piper Ceri Matthews alongside singer Julie Murphy and accordion player Andy Cutting.*
ROBIN HUW BOWEN HEN AELWYD / OLD HEARTH *(Sain, 1999) A fine example of Welsh harp music, both traditional and modern, from its leading practitioner.*
THE KILBRIDES KILBRIDE *(Fflach Tradd, 1997) This fiddle-based family trio are emerging as a major force in Welsh music.*
VARIOUS ARTISTS GORAU GWERIN: THE BEST OF WELSH FOLK MUSIC *(Sain, 1992) A good cross-section of the prime movers of the Welsh scene, featuring the likes of Ar Log, Cilmeri, Plethyn, Calennig, Aberjaber, Robin Huw Bowen, and Dafydd Iwan.*
VARIOUS ARTISTS THE BEST OF NEW WELSH FOLK MUSIC *(Sain, 1997) More from Sain including newer acts like Sián James, Bob Delyn a'r Ebillion, and Carreg Lafar.*

CAPE BRETON

BY KENNY MATHIESON

The music of the Celtic heartlands has travelled all over the world, following in the wake of colonial expansion and the forced migrations of the Scottish and Irish in particular. Celtic music enclaves exist all around the globe, but the music has made its most fundamental impact in North America. Often, the influences have been subsumed within a distinct new idiom, as in the adaptation of Scottish and Irish music to the so-called hillbilly and later country music of America, a connection widely explored in recent years on both sides of the Atlantic. Other musicians have preserved the music of their forefathers in a more undiluted fashion.

There is one area which has come to particular prominence in its own right in the course of the current Celtic revival, and where historic influences have remained intact. That area is the Canadian Maritimes on the eastern seaboard, including Newfoundland, Nova Scotia, Prince Edward Island, and notably Cape

Breton Island, which has a multi-layered musical history. The Island's native population was the Mi'qmaq tribe. The earliest white settlers were Scottish, although they were quickly supplanted by the French, known as the Acadians from a Mi'qmaq word meaning "abundance". In their search for a new home they eventually moved south to Louisiana, where the name became corrupted as the more familiar "Cajun".

The waves of Scottish and Irish emigration in the 18th and 19th centuries brought the Island its most decisive cultural stamp, with a Highland Scottish influence remaining dominant, reflected in place names such as Glencoe Station and Inverness County. There are those who feel that Scottish music and dance have been preserved in more pristine fashion in this distant enclave than they have in Scotland, and the debate continues to divide opinion.

What is not in doubt is that these things have survived in Cape Breton Island's culture. However, they are now being subjected to the same kind of commercial hybridisation as the music of Ireland and Scotland, with artists like The Rankin Family, Natalie MacMaster and Ashley MacIsaac bursting on to the world stage in spectacular fashion with new contemporary variations on the tradition and new crossovers. Cape Breton has become the focus for a remarkable upsurge of international attention in the past decade or so, and the effects will change its music irrevocably. But of course that is not to say that more traditional strains will be eradicated in the process.

■ *Ashley MacIsaac (opposite).*

For a time, however, the best known singer from Cape Breton was **Rita MacNeil**, an enormously successful mainstream popular singer whose background lay in the Island's Celtic community but whose music seldom reflected that heritage in any direct fashion. **Stan Rogers**, a popular singer-songwriter who died tragically in a fire in 1983, was born in Ontario, but came from a Nova Scotia family, and his *Fogarty's Cove* (Fogarty's Cove, 1977) celebrated the sea-going exploits of the Canadian Maritimes rather than its Celtic traditions.

Those traditions, while not in the wider public view until relatively recently, were very much alive in the kitchens (and later the festivals) of Cape Breton, as Sheldon MacInnes, the son of one of the Island's best known fiddlers Joe Dan MacInnes, describes in his book *A Journey In Celtic Music*. The fiddle was the dominant instrument in that tradition, often with piano accompaniment, but singing and piping also remained strong.

One of the first musicians to take the Celtic music of Cape Breton out onto a wider stage was singer, storyteller and guitarist **John Allen Cameron**, the son of a famously eccentric fiddler, Katie Ann Cameron. She in turn was the sister of the even more eccentric Dan Rory MacDonald, who is credited with having composed over 3,000 tunes. John Allen grew up in an environment which was passionately devoted to music, and celebrated that heritage in the course of numerous

■ *Natalie MacMaster in concert.*

recordings, from his debut album *Here Comes John Allen Cameron* (Apex, 1969) to *Glencoe Station* (Margaree Sound, 1996).

Singer-songwriter **Sarah McLachlan**, a native of Halifax, Nova Scotia, brought a hint of Celtic flavour to some of her music on albums such as *Solace* (Nettwerk, 1991) and *Fumbling Towards Ecstasy* (Nettwerk, 1993). But the most important solo singer of the newer generation of Cape Breton artists is **Mary Jane Lamond**. Although she grew up on mainland Canada she was a regular visitor to her grandparents' home in Cape Breton. A trip to a "milling frolic", the Cape Breton version of waulking the tweed, opened her ears to the potential of Gaelic song, and she set about learning the language, in which she now sings exclusively.

Lamond's vocal contribution to Ashley MacIsaac's hit single 'Sleepy Maggie' brought her to wider notice, and this continued with a major-label contract and festival appearances around the world. Her debut album *Bho Thir Nan Craobh* (B&R, 1994) trod a much stricter traditional path than its successor *Suas E!* (A&M, 1997) in which her pure, clear vocals were set in increasingly non-traditional contexts, using electronic instruments as well as rhythms and harmonies borrowed from pop and contemporary dance music. These updatings were handled with care and respect for the Gaelic melodies, and the subtly modernised settings were again evident on *Làn Dùil* (Wicklow, 2000) which included two songs with no instruments: a milling song for four female voices, and a song featuring a chorus of children.

Loreena McKennitt is from Manitoba rather than Nova Scotia, but she has made highly effective use of her own variation on the Celtic theme, successfully exploiting the more mystical aspects of the contemporary fascination with all things Celtic. She has her own Quinlan Road record label which is distributed worldwide through a deal with Warner Brothers. McKennitt may at times exude an ethereal, otherworldly air in her work, but she has planned and built her career in admirably business-like fashion. Albums like *The Visit* (Warner, 1992), *The Mask And The Mirror* (Warner, 1994) and *The Book Of Secrets* (Warner, 1997) sold in large quantities, and were supported by her imaginative concert staging. As with Enya, traditionalists fulminated but her public lapped it up.

The Island's music is still dominated by the fiddle, but a handful of musicians playing other instruments have also succeeded. The piano is a significant accompanying instrument in Cape Breton fiddle music, but some musicians have recorded in their own right, including **Doug MacPhee** on *Cape Breton Piano* (Rounder, 1990) and **Tracey Dares** who is best known for her work with Natalie MacMaster but is also represented on her own *Crooked Lake* (EMI Canada, 1994).

The bagpipes are another important part of the Cape Breton tradition and have undergone a recent resurgence of interest through the work of pipers such as Angus MacDonald, Barry Shears, Paul MacNeil and Jamie MacInnes, although no one has yet made a substantial impact on the wider stage to match that of either the fiddlers or the bands of the area.

Guitar is a popular instrument everywhere, and Cape Breton is no exception. Here it is mainly used in a group or as accompaniment. New York banjo player **Ken Perlman**'s *Island Boy* (Wizmak, 1996) is a stirring album of tunes from the Canadian Maritimes, principally Prince Edward Island.

Flute player **Chris Norman**, a Nova Scotian by birth, is best known for his work with bands like Helicon and Alasdair Fraser's Skyedance, but has also made a number of records under his own name, drawing on both his Celtic and classical backgrounds. The traditional vein is dominant on discs like *Man With The Wooden Flute* (Dorian, 1992) and *Beauty Of The North* (Dorian, 1994), while *Highlands* (Dorian, 1997) featured a collaboration with a small orchestra on Brian Packham's *Cape Breton Concerto*, one of a number of such works that include a similarly-named piece by Daniel Goode and Scott MacMillan's orchestral suite *Songs Of The Cape*.

Speak of Cape Breton music, however, and that most often means fiddle music. The Cape Breton fiddlers have their own distinctive style, intensely focused on the melody of the tune, with little of the variation and ornate embellishment that is commonplace in the Irish style. Cape Breton fiddlers also make their own characteristic use of certain technical stylistic features, primarily the cut, a way of playing a note in a series of smaller bow movements and regarded as a fundamental signature of the Cape Breton style.

The dominant influence in fiddle music is, again, Scottish. To say that a player "has the Gaelic" in his fiddling is a great compliment. Nonetheless there was also an

Irish presence on the Island, represented by players such as Joe Confiant and his nephews, Tommy Wilmot and Bobby Stubbert. The most famous fiddler of Irish descent, and perhaps the most famous Cape Breton fiddler of all, was **Winston "Scotty" Fitzgerald**. He was a highly influential figure in the development of modern Cape Breton fiddling, placing an emphasis on clarity of execution and rhythmic vitality – ideal for a music still very much intended for dancing.

Fitzgerald, who died in 1987, belonged to a pioneering generation of fiddlers who kept the music alive and thriving in Cape Breton and who succeeded in securing fame beyond the Island, often in the latter part of their lives. They include such great fiddlers as Angus Chisholm, Dan Joe MacInnes, Dan Hughie MacEachern, Donald Angus Beaton, Joe MacLean, Theresa MacLellan, Bill Lamey, Joe Cormier, Paddy LeBlanc, Alex Francis MacKay, and Buddy MacMaster, among many others. Some of these players recorded on local labels, and some were later recorded by the American folk label Rounder which began a valuable programme of Cape Breton issues in the early 1970s.

Buddy MacMaster is probably the best known of this group beyond Cape Breton, in part because of the success of his niece, Natalie. His career is typical of most of the players of his generation in that he was not a full-time professional musician. He worked for much of his life for the Canadian National Railway.

MacMaster was born in Ontario but as a child moved with his family to the Cape Breton community of Judique, in 1929. His father played fiddle, and Buddy took up the instrument at the age of 11, revealing an instant aptitude which saw him performing in an amateur contest within a year and playing his first dance at 14. He took a job with the railway company in 1943. His reputation was built playing for dances, house parties, weddings, and later concerts and festivals in Cape Breton. Although he was a legendary presence in Cape Breton music for four decades, it was only when he retired from his day job in 1988 that he made his debut recording, *Judique On the Floor* (Sea Cape, 1989), with piano accompaniment by the late John Morris Rankin. A second album, *Glencoe Hall* (self-issued, 1991), added guitarist Dave MacIsaac to the duo.

These players laid the foundations for the wider growth of interest in the music of Cape Breton, and the newer generation of musicians have profited from their example. **Jerry Holland** is the senior figure in that newer grouping, although he is not a Cape Breton native. Holland was born in 1955 across the US border in Boston, but his father – also Jerry, and also a fiddler – had fallen under the spell of the Cape Breton style and encouraged his son to pursue that music from an early age.

Holland recalls hearing Scotty Fitzgerald play at a house party in Halifax as a child in 1958, and took up fiddle himself at the age of five. Within five years he was sitting in at dances organised by another Boston-based Cape Breton great, Bill Lamey. Holland played guitar accompaniments for fiddler Angus Chisholm as a teenager, and moved to Cape Breton in 1976 with as strong a background in the Island's music and traditions as any native.

He made his debut recording *Jerry Holland* (Rounder, 1976) shortly after taking up residence on the Island, and followed it with several more recordings which had only a limited release outside Canada. These include his very influential *Master Cape Breton Fiddler* (Boot, 1982) and a number of cassette-only releases which provided material for *The Fiddlesticks Collection* (Green Linnet, 1995), a good introduction to his virtuoso fiddling and his prolific output as a composer of fiddle tunes. *Fiddler's Choice* (Fiddlesticks, 1999) provided a further excellent showcase for both aspects of his work, and included jigs, reels and strathspeys written for the unusual combination (for Cape Breton) of fiddle and uilleann pipes, the latter played by Kieran O'Hare.

Holland is also one of a number of illustrious Cape Breton musicians who travelled to Cork in 1993 for the Cork University Traditional Music Festival, the first time that the Island's music had been represented at the important event. A concert devoted to the music was issued as *Traditional Music From Cape Breton* (Nimbus, 1993) and subsequently included in the bargain-price four-CD set *From A Distant Shore: Irish And Cape Breton Traditional Music* (Nimbus, 1999) which is well worth tracking down. In addition to Holland, the Cape Breton disc features a fine cross-section of contemporary players that includes fiddlers John Morris Rankin, Howie MacDonald, Brenda Stubbert, Natalie MacMaster, Dougie MacDonald, Carl MacKenzie and Buddy MacMaster, as well as pipers Paul MacNeil and Jamie MacInnes, and accompanists Tracey Dares and Hilda Chiasson on piano and Dave MacIsaac on guitar. (The disc may still be available separately, but the Irish material is also well worth having.)

Natalie MacMaster is undoubtedly the most successful of contemporary Cape Breton fiddlers. Her breathtaking live performances that combine expressive, stunning, virtuoso fiddling with athletic step-dancing – simultaneously, that is – have made her a star on the international folk circuit. Jerry Holland is said to have been the first fiddler to introduce, in performance, simultaneous playing and step-dancing. This combination may seem a gimmick to some, but it serves to emphasise the close connection between music and dance in the Cape Breton tradition.

MacMaster came from a musical family: Buddy MacMaster is her uncle, and Ashley MacIsaac her cousin. She was given her first fiddle at the age of three, but took to the instrument seriously when she was nine. She made her debut cassette, *Four On The Floor* (1989), when she was only 16, and although it's now unavailable, *A Compilation* (MacMaster, 1998) gathers material from that release and its successor, *Road To The Isle* (1990). Her next album, *Fit As A Fiddle* (MacMaster, 1992), remains an impressive demonstration of her talents on traditional Cape Breton material, and by this time her performances were bringing serious attention well beyond the confines of her native locality. As MacMaster's international reputation burgeoned

■ *Cookie Rankin of The Rankin Family.*

her music took a more contemporary turn with the release of *No Boundaries* (Rounder/Greentrax, 1997). This combined further explorations of traditional Cape Breton material with a foray into bluegrass on 'Beaumont Rag', a funky band treatment of 'Reel Beatrice', and a couple of songs with guest vocalists Cookie Rankin and Bruce Guthro, the Cape Breton singer who would later replace Donnie Munro in Runrig. The album was dedicated to MacMaster's grandmother, Margaret Ann Beaton, who would sing the Gaelic lyrics of songs which Natalie was learning to play on the fiddle.

That formula was continued with *In My Hands* (Rounder/Greentrax, 1999) which featured a similar combination of tunes in a traditional style, although often in expanded contemporary band settings featuring electric instruments, a horn section and a string quartet. The songs this time had Alison Krauss as guest vocalist. The contrasts worked effectively on both discs, and MacMaster's playing remained true to the melodic integrity and expressive spirit of her Cape Breton roots, even where the settings departed from that model.

Those who wished to hear more of her in a strictly traditional context could turn to *My Roots Are Showing* (Rounder/Greentrax, 1998), a superb collection of traditional tunes in which the only concessions to non-traditional Cape Breton practices were the discreet use of bass, synth and snare drum on four tracks. Otherwise, it featured MacMaster's fiddle accompanied by piano and guitar, while the closing 'A Glencoe Dance Set' boasted the fiddle of Buddy MacMaster.

Natalie MacMaster is not the only young Cape Breton fiddle virtuoso to make a huge impression on international audiences. Her cousin **Ashley MacIsaac** has done so in more controversial fashion. Although he started out as a youngster playing (and also step-dancing) in a traditional style, he has radically extended those roots in contemporary directions.

The straighter side of his playing is reflected on MacIsaac's first album, *Close To The Floor* (A&M, 1992), but he was snapped up by a major label before he was 20 and his work took a quite different turn – although he has never lost hold of his Cape Breton roots amid the non-conformist experiments of his later discs (see New Directions, starting on page 176).

Richard Wood, a young fiddler from Prince Edward Island, seemed to be emerging as a potential rival to MacIsaac and one of the wilder representatives of the fusion of old and new in Maritimes music. This is notable on his third album, *The Celtic Touch* (Iona, 1997), but his intense, high-energy style in traditional tunes and rock-influenced material like his own 'Fire Dance' still lacked a developed sense of light and shade.

Wendy MacIsaac is a cousin of Ashley MacIsaac and a fine fiddler, pianist and step-dancer. Her music is heard on *The Reel Thing* (World, 1994) and *That's What You Get* (Lochshore, 1996), the latter featuring cousin Ashley on piano as well as the usual accomplished guitar accompaniments from two of Cape Breton's finest, Dave MacIsaac and Gordie Sampson. The album also featured the fiddle playing of the previously unrecorded veteran Willie Kennedy.

Brenda Stubbert is the daughter of fiddler Bobby Stubbert and, like most of these players, she grew up not just aware of the music but with many of its greatest exponents as regular house guests. She recorded two live albums, *Tameracker Down* (Celestial, 1987) and *House Sessions* (Celestial, 1992), before going into the studio for the first time to make the excellent In Jig Time (Celestial/Greentrax, 1995), a vibrant showcase for her work as fiddler and composer. Her accompanists are pianist Jackie Dunn and guitarist Gordie Sampson, while Bruce McPhee contributes on Scottish small pipes and Jerry Holland adds a second fiddle on one set. Her tunes on the record include dedications to two of her fiddling contemporaries, 'Ashley MacIsaac's Reel' and 'Stephanie Wills'. Wills is a fine young player from the Creignish area, heard on her album *Tradition Continued* (self-issued, 1994), and is a player to listen out for. Also in that category is Jennifer Roland. She made her debut with *Dedication* (self-issued, 1998) after a cameo appearance in the movie *Margaret's Museum* (1995).

J. P. Cormier has also established a sound reputation as a fine fiddler, although he plays several other instruments as well, notably guitar. He was born in Ontario of Cape Breton stock and lived in Texas before settling in his family's hometown of Cheticamp, where he married one of the Island's leading traditional pianists, Hilda Chaisson. His three albums include *Return To The Cape* (Borealis, 1995) and *Another Morning* (Iona, 1997).

If the fiddle is the hallmark of Cape Breton music, the principal agent in bringing the music to a wider international audience was the success of **The Rankin Family**, arguably more instrumental than Natalie MacMaster or Ashley MacIsaac in bringing Cape Breton music to wider attention. The band had already decided to quit after a couple of decades before the tragic death of John Morris Rankin in a driving accident early in 2000, but their impact on the development of Cape Breton music is unmatched.

The Rankin Family, who ultimately changed their name to simply The Rankins, was made up of five siblings from Inverness County: John Morris (fiddle and multi-instrumentalist), Jimmy (guitar, drums), and singers Heather, Carol Jean (better known as Cookie) and Raylene. Although there were no professional musicians in the family, their parents were both musical and encouraged them all to take an interest. They were exposed to traditional music at home from an early age, a very familiar pattern in Cape Breton music, and began to perform locally, adding vocal harmonies to the traditional songs with which they had grown up.

They made and released their first album, *The Rankin Family* (Rankins, 1989), on their own label. It included fresh arrangements of familiar songs such as 'Mairi's Wedding' as well as some tracks sung a cappella (without instrumental

accompaniment), including the haunting 'Lament Of The Irish Immigrant'. To the group's surprise, the album began to sell in considerable numbers, and quickly brought many engagements, launching them on a professional career.

Lucy MacNeil and Stewart MacNeil of the Barra MacNeils.

The group's sweet vocal harmonies and potent mixture of traditional tunes with an ever-increasing emphasis on contemporary songs clearly struck a powerful chord with listeners around the world, pushing each successive record to greater sales and establishing them as a major concert draw on the international festival and touring circuit. As they progressed commercially so the traditional content of their music also changed. But when I asked John Morris Rankin about that in an interview in 1996 he felt that the variation they were able to introduce was a major part of their success. "I think the versatility and the range of what we can do within the group has helped us enormously," said John. "If there is a cross-section of music happening, that helps broaden out your appeal, I guess. We have tried to keep the music fresh, as well. When you start making records, you face the risk of duplicating yourself, so we have tried to do something a bit different each time. As for being seen as a traditional band or not, we don't think a whole lot about that. We were brought up with traditional music, but also with modern pop and other stuff as well, and we see our own music in that context."

The band followed their debut with *Fare Thee Well Love* (Rankins, 1990) which proved an even greater success. Both albums were reissued when they signed to EMI, where they opened their account with the more pop-oriented flavours and syrupy synths of *North Country* (EMI, 1993). They reverted to something closer to a roots sound on *Endless Seasons* (EMI, 1996) and in a departure from their earlier records drafted in producer John Jennings, best known as both bass player and producer for the highly successful singer-songwriter Mary-Chapin Carpenter. Also, they cut the record in Nashville and Springfield rather than Canada, mainly for practical reasons. The more acoustic sound of the album worked well, contrasting its predecessor, and there was a generally more reflective, even introspective feel to the material. The band's final album was *Uprooted* (EMI, 1998), although the three women also issued *Do You Hear* (EMI, 1997), a Christmas record.

While The Rankins were the most successful group to emerge from the Celtic music scene in the Maritimes, they were by no means alone, or even first. **Figgy Duff**, a folk-rock band from nearby Newfoundland, was founded in 1974 by singer Pamela Morgan and drummer Noel Dinn, and went on to make several albums. At first they concentrated on the cover versions of Newfoundland folk tunes and ballads which made up their first two records, *Figgy Duff* (Hagdown, 1981) and *After The Tempest* (Celtic, 1984), but later incorporated original material written by Morgan and Dinn, starting this on the third of their four albums, *Weather Out The Storm* (Hypnotic, 1990). Traditional material had disappeared entirely by their final album, *Downstream* (Hypnotic, 1993). The death of Noel Dinn in 1993 brought the group to an end, but Morgan went on to record a fine seasonal album, *Amber Christmas* (Amber, 1997), and assembled a useful compilation of the band's music, *Figgy Duff: A Retrospective 1974-1993* (Amber, 1995).

More good recent Newfoundland bands are **The Irish Descendants** – whose albums include *Gypsies And Lovers* (Duckworth, 1994) and *Rollin' Home* (Duckworth, 1998) – and the rambunctious, rock-oriented **Great Big Sea**, heard on records such

Albums (left to right) by: Brenda Stubbert; Various (Cape Breton Connection); Various (From A Distant Shore); Alex Francis Mackay; Mary Jane Lamond; Natalie MacMaster (two).

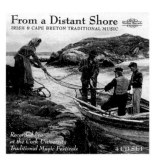

as their debut, *Great Big Sea* (self-issued, 1991), and *Play* (Warner, 1997). **Rawlins Cross**, another band from the Atlantic seaboard, have also issued several well regarded albums in Canada, including *Reel'N'Roll* (Groundswell, 1993) and *Celtic Instrumentals* (Groundswell, 1997), as have the well-established duo of **Kevin Evans & Brian Doherty** from Nova Scotia, including Shine On Brightly (self-issued, 1996) with special guest Liam Clancy of The Clancy Brothers

The Rankins are the best-known group to emerge from Cape Breton itself, but following closely is another family band, **The Barra MacNeils**, from Sydney Mines. The band comprised four siblings –- Sheumas, Kyle, Stewart, and Lucy MacNeil – each of whom sang and also played a variety of instruments. They too were encouraged to play as children, and were performing professionally during the holidays when still of school age. Lucy was only 16 when the band released their first album, *The Barra MacNeils* (Polydor, 1986), which focused on traditional music. In the course of seven subsequent discs they have explored a range of material, taking in more folk and traditional music alongside rock, pop, ethnic music and even a hint of jazz. While their first two albums achieved moderate success and set them on their way beyond their own locality, it was their third album, *Timeframe* (Polydor, 1992), which brought their breakthrough.

The success of that record resulted in a major label contract, and their subsequent releases have kept their audience guessing as to where they would go next. *Closer To Paradise* (Polydor, 1993) had a strong pop feel and featured a successful cover version of The Lovin' Spoonful's 'Darling Be Home Soon', while *The Question* (Mercury, 1995) is the most controversial of their recordings, an odd mish-mash of scrambled genres, touching on jazz and punk in the process. *Until Now* (Celtic Aire, 1997) was a sound compilation of their music, but their excellent *The Traditional Album* (Iona, 1994) is the pick of the bunch, an entirely instrumental selection of tunes that is designed to showcase their considerable capabilities as players rather than as singers.

Not content with producing one acclaimed band, the MacNeil family then launched a second, **Slàinte Mhath**, featuring two younger brothers, Ryan (keyboards) and Boyd (fiddle), alongside piper Bruce MacPhee, fiddler Breagh

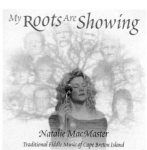

■ *Members of La Bottine Souriante (left to right): Yves Lambert, André Brunet and Jean Fréchette.*

MacDonald (later replaced by Lisa Gallant) and singer Stephanie Hardy. Their debut album, *Prophecy* (1996), was followed by the even better *Music For A Kilted Generation* (1998), both of which augur well for the band's future.

The growing interest in the music of Cape Breton also provided an opportunity for listeners in Europe to sample some of the other delights which Canada had to offer. The most spectacular example of that phenomenon has been **La Bottine Souriante** – which means roughly "the smiling boot", an appropriately surreal name for this outfit. With their delicious three- and four-part harmony singing and bewilderingly eclectic range of musical references, this nine-piece outfit are a pigeon-holer's nightmare. The French-Canadian music of their native Quebec is the heartbeat of their music, but they are equally likely to draw on Scottish and Irish influences, not to mention launching off into a reggae groove, a slice of vibrant Afrobeat, or a Cuban clave.

It is not so much a matter of puzzling over which genre they should be assigned to, more a case of wondering where each tune is about to go next. Their instrumentation is equally eclectic. A traditional tune on twin fiddles and accordion might suddenly burst into a full-scale band assault on the music, with the four-man horn section riffing like a jazz big-band, or a soul revue, or a Mexican mariachi band. Then there is Michel Bordeleau's show-stopping foot percussion solo, which – if you haven't seen him do it – is probably best described as a form of tap or step dancing, but performed while sitting down.

La Bottine Souriante's ability to communicate directly across linguistic and cultural barriers remains irresistible. They play some of the most exciting music you are likely to hear anywhere, and are great fun into the bargain. They are a band to catch live. While their recordings are good, they don't capture the full resonance and sheer physical exuberance of the band's music.

RECOMMENDED RECORDS

THE BARRA MACNEILS UNTIL NOW *(Celtic Aire, 1997) The MacNeil family explored so many different styles on their albums that picking just one is difficult, but this compilation gives a good overview.*

JERRY HOLLAND FIDDLER'S CHOICE *(Fiddlesticks, 1999) An excellent showcase for the playing and writing of this influential fiddler, including jigs, reels and strathspeys written for the unusual combination of fiddle and uilleann pipes.*

MARY JANE LAMOND LÀN DÙIL *(Wicklow, 2000) The most important solo singer to have emerged in the new wave of Cape Breton musicians, Lamond sings exclusively in Gaelic but with a contemporary feel to the instrumental accompaniments on this fine album.*

NATALIE MACMASTER MY ROOTS ARE SHOWING *(Greentrax, 1998) The star of the contemporary Cape Breton fiddle scene celebrates her roots in a strictly traditional set that features a rare duet with her illustrious uncle, Buddy MacMaster.*

NATALIE MACMASTER IN MY HANDS *(Greentrax, 1999) A more sophisticated, contemporary album, although still firmly rooted in the Cape Breton manner.*

THE RANKINS ENDLESS SEASONS *(EMI, 1996) The most successful Cape Breton band, drafting in country producer John Jennings for a fine set and reverting to a more acoustic sound after the pop-influenced North Country.*

BRENDA STUBBERT IN JIG TIME *(Celestial/Greentrax, 1995) Stubbert's first studio album is a vibrant example of the fiddler and the composer, with more than a hint of her Irish descent peeking through.*

VARIOUS ARTISTS FROM A DISTANT SHORE *(Nimbus, 1999) An indispensable four-CD set from a memorable gathering in Cork in 1993, with many important Cape Breton musicians on the final disc (as well as three excellent discs of Irish music).*

VARIOUS ARTISTS THE CAPE BRETON CONNECTION *(Lakewind, 1998) A useful compilation of contemporary Cape Breton music, with major names like Natalie MacMaster and The Barra MacNeils plus newer artists such as Stephanie Wills and Jennifer Roland.*

BRITTANY

BY STEPHEN D. WINICK

France is commonly called the Hexagon, a geometrical fiction that helps children draw maps in crayon and bureaucrats add syllables to their speeches. But look at the Hexagon's north-west corner and you will notice Brittany, jutting out from the rest of France like a hitchhiker's thumb. This led Jamie McMenamy, one-time singer for Battlefield Band and Kornog, to describe Brittany as "the bit that sticks out".

Brittany does stick out, not only physically but culturally. It was invaded and settled by British Celts, speakers of a Brythonic Celtic language, about 1,500 years ago. That Celtic language, now called Breton, is still spoken by about 300,000 people as a daily language in the western half of Brittany, called Basse-Bretagne in French and Breizh Izel in Breton. In eastern Brittany (Haute-Bretagne in French, Breizh-Uhel in Breton) people speak French or a distinctive French Romance dialect called Gallo. For many years – from the French Revolution until the 1970s – the French government tried to eradicate the distinctive Breton language and culture. This led to resentment and militant regionalism on the part of many Bretons. When World War II came to a close and French patriotism was at an all-time high these regionalists found that Breton nationalism was, as Paul Jegat described it, "decidedly no longer in the air". So they turned to folk culture.

While a Breton political consciousness was a subversive idea associated with fanaticism, researching quaint folk customs was seen as innocuous, even calming. Because the only outlet for people interested in any form of Breton consciousness, political or otherwise, was to research folk traditions, a vital movement began to emerge. People joined cultural organisations, among them the extant Cercles Celtiques. These were clubs of amateur musicians and dancers that met all over Brittany as well as wherever Bretons lived – as far away as Paris. These groups, as well as others, helped many people to become involved in music-making as a first step toward Breton pride.

These early revivalists led their children and grandchildren to take up old forms of music and remake them, fresh, for the contemporary world. Today, Brittany has one of the richest and most complex traditional music scenes anywhere. Brittany has also developed one of the strongest regional recording industries in Europe, and this ensures that music of all sorts – old and new, traditional and revival – is constantly released for public consumption.

An old engraving (opposite) of sonneurs, or folk musicians, in Brittany.

BRITTANY: VOICE

Brittany's foremost singing tradition is called kan ha diskan. It was one of the first traditional music styles to gain a widespread audience in Brittany and has always been a major part of the Breton folk revival. In kan ha diskan (roughly translated as call-and-response singing) two singers provide a lively sound, suitable for dancing.

Writer Jean-Michel Guilcher described the simple principle of kan ha diskan. "One of the executors, the kaner, reveals the first phrase," he said. "The second, or diskaner, sings the end of it with him, at least the very last notes, then repeats the entire phrase alone. The first singer joins him on the last notes, then continues the next phrase alone. Until the end of the song, each sings thus turn by turn, the ends of phrases always being said 'à deux'. The variations of impulse and intensity between the passages sung solo and those sung in unison, and the slight differences of melodic design between the two singers, make their alternation more than and better than the imitation of the first by the second."

Kan ha diskan songs can be about anything, from simple declarations of love to ballads about conscription. Any tale will do. However, the song must be rhythmically appropriate to one of the many line- and round-dances traditional to Brittany. Long refrains of nonsense words are often added to short lines of text, with "tra la la la le

Frères Morvan on-stage at Spézet, 1993.

lo" probably the most common stock phrase in this tradition. The vocal quality is notably nasal, sharp and loud; in the old days the singers had to be heard above the co-ordinated footfalls of a roomful of people, and without the benefit of amplifiers.

There's no better place to start listening than with **Les Soeurs Goadec** and **Les Frères Morvan**. These are to the Breton revival what source singers like Joe Heaney and Eddie Butcher were to the Irish folksong movement: older people from a rural labouring background who also happened to be brilliant singers with large repertoires of songs learned from aged grandmothers around the fire. They are the epitome of the "folk" from whom folk-songs could be collected.

Henri, Yvon and François Morvan worked on a family farm when neighbours asked them to sing for a dance in the late 1950s. In 1998 they celebrated their 40th year of public performing. Their tremendous and unusual repertoire of songs and lively singing have been indispensable at many, many dances over those decades.

Similarly, the Goadec sisters enjoyed great success from the 1960s through to the early 1980s, mostly at rural "night parties" in the region around Carhaix, but also on festival stages. When Maryvonne Goadec died in 1983 her two sisters stopped appearing in public. Anastasie Goadec died some years later, leaving Eugénie to sing only at home with her family. In 1994 Eugénie's daughter Louise Ebrel convinced her to come out of retirement, and she released *Gwriziou* (Arfolk, 1994) on which Ebrel served as diskaner. The album shows the deep connection made between older and younger practitioners in Breton music, and the influence of a deep-seated and living tradition on the revivalist generation.

For many young people in the 1960s and 1970s kan ha diskan had to be sought out and learned. Generally, the student-teacher relationship is validated when the younger singer becomes diskaner to his teacher. This special situation brings us many teams of older and younger men, the most famous of of whom are probably **Yann-Fanch Kemener** and **Marcel Guilloux**, who recorded several LPs in the 1970s. But the tradition continues. One recent CD features the teams of Manuel Kerjean and Alain Le Clere, and Bastien Guern and Jean-Claude Talec. All of these singers have strong voices and are highly skilled interpreters of their material. Teams like these make it clear that kan ha diskan will carry on among younger generations of Bretons.

Loeiz Ropars is the singer most directly responsible for kan ha diskan's continued vigour. In the 1950s he created a new type of social event for Breton music. It would be like the community-based outdoor fest-noz or "night party" from his rural background, but would unite people from all over Brittany rather than those from a single small area, and it would take place indoors. The new-style fest-noz is extremely popular today, making it easier for kan ha diskan to be passed on to the current generation of singers.

Beyond kan ha diskan there is in Brittany a whole tradition of solo unaccompanied singing. The traditional songs sung in this way are divided into two categories: the gwerzioù (singular "gwerz"), with gruesome or gloomy subject matter, and the sonnioù (singular "sôn"), with happier themes.

Jean Le Meut from the Vannes region is one of the best known of the older singers. For years he has performed with Ar Trouzerion, a singing group from his home region, and he also sings as a soloist. Like the Goadec sisters, he epitomises the perfect folklore informant. As the liner notes to his album *Pe Yuvankiz Kuhet* (Keltia, 1994) proclaim, his songs "are airs that he learned in his tenderest youth, on the knees of his grandmother, who, to put him to sleep, cradled him while singing 'Mandal' or 'Er Jouis'." This pastoral picture is borne out by his songs, most of which are sonnioù dealing with love and marriage in a rural setting.

Many younger singers are also taking up the art of unaccompanied singing. But while older singers epitomise "the folk", **Ifig Troadeg** and others of his generation are more like academic folklorists, as familiar with the library and the archive as they are with "the field" and with collecting.

The songs Troadeg performs are researched in books, and recorded orally by various fieldworkers from Dastum, Brittany's premiere archive of folklore and traditional music. Troadeg himself has collected for Dastum, and several of the songs he performs he personally recorded from the lips of rural singers. His singing has a calm beauty similar to that of Gregorian chant, despite the frequently shocking storylines of the gwerzioù he performs. He is a singer well worth hearing. Troadeg's generation continues to produce fine unaccompanied singers. Listen out for Mathieu Hamon, Patrick Marie, Marthe Vassalo and Klervi Rivière, all relative youngsters who will be singing for a long time. One who particularly deserves mention is **Annie Ebrel**, one of Brittany's best-loved solo singers. Her clear, piercing voice is a perfect instrument for Breton traditional singing, alone and as part of a kan ha diskan pair.

In the sleevenotes to *E Skeud Tosenn Vre*, Ifig Troadeg thanks **Yann-Fañch Kemener**, who, he says, brought about a new sense of respect for the heritage of Breton song. Kemener, an important singer of Breton songs since the 1970s, has recorded a number of solo and duo projects. The first on CD was *Chants Profonds De Bretagne, Vol. 1* (Arion, 1991) on which he was credited as Jean-François Quéméner. A compilation of tracks from several of Kemener's LPs for Arion, it is a fine recording on which his sharp voice, with its weightless quality and gentle quaver, shines through brightly.

Kemener's singing can also be heard on a CD of sacred and profane songs of Brittany with Anne Auffret, and two with the pianist Didier Squiban. The project with Auffret includes gruesome ballads alongside religious and ritual material, including hymns and Christmas carols. Most of the songs Kemener performs with Squiban tell of the hard lives of the fishing families and sailors who lived years ago on Brittany's rugged islands. Kemener also sang regularly with the group Barzaz, and his voice can be heard on all their recordings.

Two more notable singers are **Erik Marchand** and Arnaud Maisonneuve. Marchand has a powerful and nasal singing voice that sends a thrill up your spine. He's been the lead singer of the group Gwerz, but also leads his own trio in which he is joined by fellow Breton Thierry Robin and Moroccan percussionist Hameed Khan. While the accompaniment is exotic, Marchand's voice dominates as he sings powerful ballads and kan ha diskan songs with invited guests.

Arnaud Maisonneuve has a less stringent voice, but one that is quite engaging. He has two solo CDs available. *Eur Zon Hevez Ma Zantiment* (Ocora, 1989) contains a good deal of unaccompanied singing plus a few songs with the vocal ensemble Ar Trouzerion and a few accompanied by clarinet, violin and bagpipe. *Ouilet Men*

▧ *Albums (below, left to far right) by: Eugénie Goadec & Louise Ebrel; Les Frères Morvan; Taillevent; Yann-Fañch Kemener; Various (Voix De Bretagne); Brou-Hamon-Quimbert; Arnaud Maisonneuve.*

 Erik Marchand at Cardiff, 1998.

Deulagad (Keltia, 1996) is completely different, featuring Maisonneuve's passionately sung gwerzioù accompanied by his own country-blues guitar picking. Remarkably enough, the result is good.

Alongside the gwerz and the sôn there is the kantik (a religious song, hymn or carol), another important genre of Breton-language folksong. **Anne Auffret** has recorded a fine album of this material called *Sonj* (Keltia, 1991), on which her clear and pretty voice is accompanied by her own harp playing, by Jean Baron on the bombarde (see the later section on piping), and by Michel Ghesquiere on pipe organ, to beautiful effect. Similar albums have been recorded by the **Ensemble Choral du Bout du Monde** from Finisterre in western Brittany, featuring a full choir on vocals plus accompaniments on organ, flute, tin whistle, guitar and bagpipe. The result is a

Prigend and Maisonneuve at Brest, 1992.

very full and engaging sound. While it is true that the Breton-language song tradition has undergone the most thorough revival, there is also a healthy tradition of singing in the Pays Gallo, the area of Brittany where the Gallo dialect is spoken. **Yann Dour** is an excellent performer of Gallo songs who accompanies himself on accordion and plays with a cadre of experienced accompanists.

Another popular act, the Roland Brou-Mathieu Hamon-Charles Quimbert trio, has been described as the "quintessence of traditional singing" of the middle-aged generation, but is nonetheless quite magnificent. Several bands have a repertoire heavily laced with Gallo songs; the popular and long-lived band Tri Yann, for example, perform many traditional songs from the Pays Gallo. Another strong French-language tradition in Brittany comes from the towns along the coast. As merchant ports and strategic points-of-entry for the navy, Breton towns like Brest and St. Malo have been hotbeds of maritime culture, and here sea shanties and forebitters are the songs of choice.

Several individuals and groups specialise in chansons de marins, or sailor songs. The longest-standing and best known of these groups is **Cabestan**, who have been plying the sea-song trade for over 15 years. They perform ballads about shipwrecks and disasters, light-hearted songs about shipboard life and, above all, rousing sea shanties. Their lusty vocals are accompanied by fiddle, accordion and other instruments, and they also include on each of their five albums a few selections of dance music.

L'Echo is a group featuring Roland Brou singing chansons de marins. The group has a harmonically rich and rhythmically free sound based on clarinets, bagpipes, fiddles and accordions. **Taillevent** come from Sarzeau on the gulf of Morbihan and, despite being less polished performers than Cabestan or L'Echo, they convey an obvious love of singing and of maritime culture, belting out songs with great enthusiasm. Cabaret singer **Marc Ogeret** has recorded a CD of Breton sailor songs with creditable results. Other sea-music bands such as Djiboudjep, Shanghaïé, and the "sailor-songwriter" Michel Tonnere aren't as consistently good, but have made some good records.

Yet another trend in French-language song from Brittany is the chanteur engagé. The French meaning is something like "enraged singer", although "topical singer-songwriter" is a good compromise. Probably the best known chanteur engagé recording today is **Gilles Servat** whose song 'La Blanche Hermine' became a Breton anthem in the 1970s. A veteran of stage, studio and political demonstration, Servat still has fierce convictions and a magisterial singing voice. His recent recordings on CD are all worth hearing, and if you can find any of his old LPs so much the better.

The finest chanteur engagé of all time was probably the poet, philosopher and political maverick, **Glenmor**. He recorded 15 LPs, five singles and four CDs from 1958 to 1990, when he retired from performing. He died in 1996, but his declamatory poems and songs still make for compelling listening.

There is not necessarily a sharp distinction between the singer of traditional songs and the chanteur engagé. Not only can the chanteur engagé express his political views through traditional songs, but the very existence in today's oral tradition of political songs from times past is clear proof that these two types of singing have always existed together, one alongside the other. The writing and circulation of new songs on broadsides continued from at least the 17th century until the late 1960s, and the chanteur engagé can be seen as a continuation of that process, as another step on the path of tradition.

RECOMMENDED RECORDS

ANNE AUFFRET, JEAN BARON, MICHEL GHESQUIERE SONJ *(Keltia, 1991) A majestic sounding album that includes hymns, carols and praise songs with voice, harp, bombarde and organ.*

BROU-HAMON-QUIMBERT TROIS P'TITS OISEAUX IL Y A *(Coop Breizh, 1999) The trio's performances here of unaccompanied Gallo songs are impeccable, restrained and tasteful.*

CABESTAN TEMPÊTE POUR SORTIR *(Keltia, 1995) Brittany's premier crew of sea-shanty singers perform lively, upbeat material full of deep, resonant singing, singalong choruses and foot-tapping arrangements.*

EUGÉNIE GOADEC & LOUISE EBREL GWRIZIOÙ *(Arfolk, 1994) Goadec's return to recording features songs ranging from simple tales of courtship to gruesome ballads.*

AR C'HOAREZED GOADEC (THE GOADEC SISTERS) MOUEZIOU BRUDED A VREIZ *(Keltia, 1990) Originally released in 1975, this is one of the most historically significant releases of Breton vocal music. It is a superb example of old-style singing that includes gwerziwhere and kan ha diskan songs.*

YANN-FAÑCH KEMENER & DIDIER SQUIBAN ENEZ EUSSA *(L'Oz, 1995) Among sparse and moody piano arrangements, Squiban Kemener's sad voice floats gently like a spar on a peaceful sea.*

LOEIZ ROPARS KAN HA DISKAN *(Keltia, 1992) The excellent singing on this important archival release was recorded mostly live at dances between 1957 and 1992.*

GILLES SERVAT LES ALBUMS DE LA JEUNESSE *(Keltia, 1992) Contains songs from Servat's ten LPs, plus one new track. It's the ideal way to get acquainted with Servat before buying his more recent CDs.*

IFIG TROADEG E SKEUD TOSENN VRE *(Arfolk, undated but mid 1990s) Gloomy gwerziwhere and happy sonnioù of Tregor in northern Brittany, sung unaccompanied in Troadeg's easy, floating voice.*

VARIOUS ARTISTS VOIX DE BRETAGNE *(France 3 Ouest, 1993) Features original recordings of Erik Marchand, Annie Ebrel, Arnaud Maisonneuve, Jean le Meut and others: a great way to start exploring Breton singing.*

BRITTANY: PIPES

More than the vocal tradition, the instrumental music of Brittany is deeply influenced by sounds from the other Celtic countries. This can be heard most readily in the widespread adoption of Scottish bagpipes into Breton music. But the story of the pipes in Brittany does not begin with the Highland instrument, because Brittany has a tradition of piping back to the Middle Ages and two different native bagpipes, the veuze and the biniou.

The larger and older of the two bagpipes, the veuze, resembles the most common bagpipe in medieval western Europe. It has one chanter of conical bore fitted with a

double reed, and one drone fitted with a single reed, both attached to a bag which is inflated by mouth. The sound of the veuze is thus similar to that of other western-European bagpipes, including the Flemish pipes and the Galician gaita.

Youenn Le Bihan (left) and Patrick Molard at Spézet, 1992.

From the Middle Ages until the 19th century the veuze was a common instrument for festive music in Brittany, but the 20th century saw a steep decline. This was almost certainly due to the appearance of the diatonic accordion, for this came to be called veuze in Haute-Bretagne, stealing the name from the instrument it supplanted. The "real" veuze was recently brought back from the brink of extinction by revivalists, but according to Lois Kuter in his *Guide To Music In Brittany* there are only about 80 musicians playing it today. It does turn up now and again in bands – and these include outfits such as Strakal and L'Echo – but solo recordings of the instrument are very rare indeed.

The smaller and more recent biniou is far more popular than the veuze. Sometimes called the biniou-bihan (little biniou) or the biniou-koz (old biniou), this single-drone bagpipe was adapted from the veuze in the 19th century to play in a higher register; it has the smallest chanter and the highest pitch of any European

■ *Christian Anneix and Jean Baron pictured at Landerneau, 1998.*

bagpipe. The adaptation seems to have occurred when musicians sought an instrument with a loud, piercing sound to accompany the bombarde.

The bombarde is an oboe, a double-reeded pipe of conical bore, blown directly by the mouth. Unlike the orchestral oboe it has no complex system of keys to create a tempered scale; instead it has six open holes, plus a seventh hole that can be uncovered by means of a single key. The bombarde has been played in Brittany since at least the 15th century. There is evidence of bombarde-and-bagpipe duos from about the time of the French Revolution, but it was not until the development of the biniou in the 19th century that the two pipes could be played together systematically; the biniou sounds exactly one octave above the bombarde.

This pairing of a bombarde player and a biniou player, referred to collectively as sonneurs de couple, is one of the most important instrumental sounds in Brittany. (A "sonneur" is a folk musician.) Like kan ha diskan, it is primarily found in Basse-Bretagne as an accompaniment to dancing, and involves two performers playing alternate lines. The biniou plays continuously, while the bombarde is played either on every other line, or in a three-lines-on/one-line-off rotation.

One of the reasons why the "couple" is so much more popular than the veuze alone is that many people involved in the early revival judged the importance of a tradition by how different it was from French culture. Thus, the fiddle, veuze and hurdy-gurdy, being similar to French traditions, were under-emphasised, while the biniou and bombarde were highlighted and the Highland bagpipe and Celtic harp were imported. The creation of a system of championships on the bombarde, biniou and Highland bagpipe encouraged greater participation by young people and further helped the popularity of those instruments.

The foremost recording artists of biniou-bombarde music are **Jean Baron** and **Christian Anneix**, and they have won the couple championship numerous times. They play for dances throughout Basse-Bretagne and beyond, and also make up half of the band Gwenva. Their playing is spectacular, smooth-toned, rhythmically precise and melodically intricate, probably the best introduction to biniou-and-bombarde. Jean Baron is half of another championship "couple" with Georges Epinette; they won the championship in 1974 and again in 1994. Their music is another example of biniou-bombarde playing at its finest.

A third championship "couple", **Youenn Le Bihan** and **Patrick Molard**, have individually and together been at the forefront of the Breton folk revival in groups like The Alan Stivell Band, Gwerz, Skolvan, Den, Triptyque, Celtic Procession, Heritage des Celtes, and Pennoù Skoulm. They have been innovators and explorers of the music, yet are also capable of playing in a very traditional "couple" style, and have recordings to prove it.

Pierre Crépillon and **Laurent Bigot** can also play very traditional "couple" music, or they can venture into something different. Sometimes they play with Molard on Highland bagpipe, creating an interesting twist on the duos that prevail in the Breton piping tradition. Other "couples" to watch for include Gildas Moal and René Chaplain, Daniel Feon and Jil Lehart, and one of the younger teams, Teddy Molard and Yann Simon.

The Highland bagpipe is sometimes referred to in Breton as biniou-braz (big biniou) but is more often known simply as the bagpipe. It was first introduced to Brittany late in the 19th century and gained acceptance in the 1930s when, during a wave of militant Celticism, the biniou was judged by Roland Becker and Laure Le Gurun to be "less perfected, less prestigious, less martial, less Celtic". Since then, it has gained popularity as a solo instrument, as a part of bagpipe-bombarde pairs, and as a part of the Breton "bagad" pipe-band (or "bagadoù" in plural).

The idea for the pipe-band occurred to Breton musicians who visited Scotland during World Wars I and II. They soon imported Scottish bagpipes to Brittany and teamed them up with bombardes and drums. This was part of the more general cultural reawakening that followed World War II, when Loeiz Ropars revived kan ha diskan and from when the current revival of Breton music ultimately derives.

In general the bagadoù sound similar to their Scottish counterparts, but the bombarde gives the music a somewhat greater resonance than in the Scottish bands, and the bagadoù's melodies are often built on the model of sonneurs de couple. Early pipe-band recordings tend to be straightahead marches and martial-sounding dance tunes – not ideal for casual listening. Eventually, the bagadoù learned to add variety to their recordings. **Bagad Kemper**'s *Lip Ar Maout* (Keltia, 1995) includes guest musicians such as flute player Jean-Michel Veillon, from the bands Barzaz, Den, Pennoù Skoulm and Kornog, and guitarist Gilles Le Bigot, from Barzaz, Skolvan and Kornog. In addition to the usual Scottish and Breton marches and dances they include a set of Gallo music played on unusual C-minor bagpipes, a klezmer tune, and several Bulgarian dance tunes.

Ag An Douar d'Ar Mor (Arfolk, 1994) by the **Bagad Ronsed-Mor** features some marches and dance tunes in which the whole pipe-band plays, but it also features solo moments and collaborations between the band and organist Hervé Rivière. A Bulgarian dance and a march with African-style syncopated percussion contribute to the international flavour, and a baroque oboe piece lends a classical touch. Their 1996 follow-up album *Coeff.116* is even wilder, teaming them with a jazz ensemble, La Marmite Infernale.

One further type of bagpipe that is becoming more common in Brittany is the Irish uilleann pipes. They are used by Marc Pollier to play Irish music with a Breton twist, but also in Breton music proper by such pipers as Ronan Le Bars, Pascal Martin, Alan Cloatr and Patrick Molard. The bands Glaz and Celtic Procession have featured the playing of Le Bars, while Koun features Martin, and Tri Yann have invited Cloatr to appear on their albums. Several groups including Den, Pennou Skoulm, and Gwerz have centred on Patrick Molard and his uilleann pipes.

RECOMMENDED RECORDS

BAGAD KEMPER LIP AR MAOUT *(Keltia, 1995) A fabulous recording ranging from traditional Breton music to klezmer, played by a pipe-band with musical guests.*
BAGAD RONSED-MOR COEFF.116 *(Arfolk, 1996) Pipe-band joins brass-band for a suite of jazz-flavoured pipe music replete with resonant saxophones and buzzing pipes.*
JEAN BARON & CHRISTIAN ANNEIX DANSES DE BRETAGNE *(Keltia, 1988) The best CD available to introduce biniou-bombarde music. The notes contain descriptions of the instruments, a history of Breton dance, and dancing instructions.*

■ *Albums (left to right) by: Various (Fest Deiz); Various (Sonneurs De Veuze); Christian LeMaître; Archetype; Celtic Fiddle Festival; Bagad Kemper.*

PIERRE CRÉPILLON, LAURENT BIGOT, PATRICK MOLARD AR SAC'H LER *(Escalibur, 1989) Interesting variation on the piping tradition, full of beautiful melodies and dance tunes played on biniou, bombarde and Highland bagpipes.*

KOUN AN DRO: DANSES BRETONNES *(Keltia, 1995) As pretty an album of Breton dance music as you'll find, this features the uilleann pipes in a Breton context.*

YOUENN LE BIHAN & PATRICK MOLARD ER BOLOM KOH *(Gwerz Pladenn, 1995) Marches, dances, and song airs played by master pipers in traditional "couple" style. Also includes the uilleann pipes and the piston, a low bombarde.*

ANDRÉ LE MEUT & HERVÉ RIVIÈRE BOMBARDE ET ORGUE *(Keltia, 1995) Bombarde and pipe organ used to play songs and hymns from the repertoire of André's father Jean Le Meut. A beautiful, unusual CD.*

VARIOUS ARTISTS FEST DEIZ-FEST NOZ *(Arfolk, 1997) Compilation from the Printemps de Châteauneuf festival showcasing some of the best "couple" playing on biniou and bombarde, along with kan ha diskan singing.*

VARIOUS ARTISTS JEUNES SONNEURS DU CENTRE BRETAGNE *(Arfolk, 1996) A collection of the younger bagpipe and accordion players, including Yann Simon and Teddy Molard, excellent musicians with dozens of awards to show for it.*

VARIOUS ARTISTS SONNEURS DE VEUZE EN BRETAGNE *(ArMen, 1989) One of the only collections to concentrate on the veuze, this features excellent field recordings and comprehensive liner notes.*

BRITTANY: FIDDLE

The violin has been much less central to the folk revival in Brittany than in Ireland and Scotland. Like the veuze, the "violon" is an instrument shared by Brittany with the rest of France, and this made it less likely to be championed by the pro-Celtic organisations of the early folk revival. Nevertheless, the violin has an important tradition in Haute-Bretagne, and is widely played in folk revival bands.

The fiddle is referred to as "violon" in both French and Breton – no distinction is made between the classical instrument (the violin) and its folk counterpart (the fiddle). In French, classical violinists are "violonistes" while folk fiddlers are

Banner text: ODADEG AR SONERION / NTER-KANT VLOAZ E SERVIJ MUZIK BREIZ

■ *Bagad Kemper at Brest, 1997.*

"violoneux".Traditionally the violin has mostly been played as a solo instrument, for dancers. This has led to a lively, syncopated playing style that makes frequent use of open drones and double-stops, both for the sake of volume and for rhythmic emphasis. The violin is also sometimes played in a "couple" with hurdy-gurdy, clarinet, accordion or second violin. In the revival, violins are most commonly heard in fest-noz, folk and folk-rock bands.

Evidence for violin playing in Breton traditional music goes back to the 17th century, and references to it are sprinkled through historical documents for the next 200 years. By the 19th century the violin was one of the most widespread instruments in Brittany, and by the early 1900s reached the height of its popularity. After World War I, however, the violin was all but replaced by the accordion, and in the 1970s only about 40 violoneux were active in Brittany. This has led most revival players to seek other models for their playing, most importantly from jazz and Irish fiddle music.

Probably the best known violin player now active in Brittany is **Christian LeMaître**. He has been a member of the bands Kornog and Pennou Skoulm, as well as the violin ensemble Archetype, all of which toured beyond Brittany. He has also appeared in Europe and the US as a member of the Celtic Fiddle Festival tour, playing alongside Kevin Burke from Ireland and Johnny Cunningham from Scotland.

For his traditional Breton repertoire, LeMaître takes much of his inspiration from singers and bombarde-biniou pairs; he also composes his own tunes, and plays Irish reels and Bulgarian horos. He has one solo recording, and plays on albums by all the various groups already mentioned. Another of Brittany's important violin players is **Jacky Molard** who was in the bands Gwerz and Pennou Skoulm, as well as the Celtic-jazz-rock fusion group Den. He has also played as a trio with his brother Patrick Molard (the aforementioned piper) and Jacques Pellen.

Archetype was an unusual instrumental formation made up of six violins, with a cello and a double-bass for accompaniment. It contained mostly musicians who were members of other bands: Molard and LeMaître were both there, as were Pierrick Lemou (from the bands Strakal and Gwenva), Fañch Landreau (from Skolvan) and several others. The music they made was harmonically rich and generally mellifluous; it was mostly Breton music, with some original compositions, Irish reels and klezmer tunes thrown in as well. Although they no longer play together very much, they do have an excellent album available.

There are, of course, many fine violoneux among the current generation of musicians. Most of them play in bands rather than as soloists, and in fact the number of solo violin albums in Breton music is quite meagre. Look for names such as Hervé Bertho, Jean-Yves Bardoul and Yvon Rouget to ensure that an album or band features top-notch fiddling.

RECOMMENDED RECORDS

ARCHETYPE ARCHETYPE *(Escalibur, 1990) Very fluid and harmonically rich music by six all-star Breton fiddlers.*

CELTIC FIDDLE FESTIVAL ENCORE *(Green Linnet, 1998) This second CD by LeMaître, Johnny Cunningham and Kevin Burke also features Breton guitarist Soïg Siberil and is almost half Breton music, some played by Burke and Cunningham.*

CHRISTIAN LEMAÎTRE BALLADE À L'HOTESSE *(Escalibur, 1995) At once traditional and exploratory, LeMaître takes inspiration from singers and bombarde-biniou pairs. Stately but insistent rhythm and full tone make his liquid playing great.*

TRIPTYQUE TRIPTYQUE *(Gwerz Pladenn, 1993) Jacky Molard (fiddle, tenor guitar and mandolin), Patrick Molard (flute and three different bagpipes) and Jacques Pellen (guitar) play progressive Breton music, both traditional and original.*

VARIOUS ARTISTS SONNEURS DE VIOLON TRADITIONNELS EN BRETAGNE *(ArMen, 1993) Thirteen traditional fiddlers from French-speaking Haute-Bretagne play avant-deux, ronds, polkas and wedding marches, recorded between 1956 and 1990.*

BRITTANY: ACCORDION

The accordion is the most popular instrument in Breton music, although it was not common in Brittany until about 1875. Once it did arrive it gained popularity quickly, for several reasons.

Since it was mass-produced, the accordion was the cheapest of all traditional instruments, and by far the most durable. It required less care and maintenance to keep in order than biniou, bombarde, veuze or fiddle. Since it could be played solo – unlike the biniou or bombarde – it was less costly to hire an accordionist than a traditional pair of sonneurs. It is an easy instrument on which to learn the basics, much easier than biniou, veuze or bombarde on which it can take a player hours of practice just to produce a steady tone.

Finally, the accordion had a certain amount of sex appeal. The traditional dances of the Breton countryside were all line-dances and round-dances, and couples did not dance together. But the accordion was associated with other styles of dance from outside: waltzes, mazurkas, contradances and polkas, danced, as the Bretons say, belly to belly. This gave it great cachet in some circles – and got it banned as "the Devil's box" in others.

By the 1920s the diatonic accordion – what in England is called the melodeon – was changing Breton music. Repertoires adapted to the piping scales were being modified, biniou and bombarde "couples" were out of work, and it seemed the only way to make it as a musician was as an accordionist.

When the chromatic accordion arrived in the 1930s the influence of jazz brought in saxophones, banjos and drum kits, and these were teamed up with accordions to form a new kind of band. The most influential was the "jazz-Menez" formed by accordionist **Yves Menez** in 1936. He was one of the few jazz bandleaders to interpret traditional Breton dance music on the chromatic accordion – and the current groups Ti-Jaz, Tammles and Maubuissons bring the influence of this style into the modern era. Since the 1950s, several cultural organisations such as La Boueze have made a concerted effort to revive the older diatonic accordion. With their help, the instrument eventually settled into a comfortable place on the Breton scene in both solo and band contexts.

Before concentrating on the diatonic accordion, **Alain Pennec** learned to play bombarde and bagpipes. Since the 1970s he has been playing music in pipe-bands, in ensembles like the Trio Pennec and Tammles, and solo. His solo playing covers a lot of ground musically, but is still firmly planted in Breton traditions: his tunes come from the bagpipe tradition, from the repertoires of accordion players and fest-noz groups that he has encountered over the years, from collections and archives of folk music, and from the pens of composers including Pennec himself.

A similar story applies to **Bruno Le Tron**. Originally a biniou player, he learned the accordion to expand his harmonic capabilities. He founded the Breton-jazz crossover group Maubuissons, as well as La Compagnie du Beau Temps, a non-Breton group that performs folk music of central France. As a solo artist, he is influenced not only by Breton and French styles but by other European folk music and by jazz.

Patrick Lefebvre plays traditional dance music from Central Brittany, particularly the Monts d'Arée region, on both chromatic and diatonic instruments. His repertoire was learned from other accordionists and singers, such as the great kan ha diskan vocalist Bastien Guern, and Jean Coateval, a student of Yves Menez.

Yann-Fañch Perroches started to play the accordion in the 1970s. He since founded Skolvan, one of the best Breton bands on the scene, and Cocktail Diatonique, an accordion quartet. He has also played and recorded as a solo artist, performing music that adds a touch of jazz to traditional Breton melodies. All told, he is one of the most active musicians on the Breton scene.

Yann Dour, whom we met earlier as a singer, is also an excellent example of an accordionist from the Pays Gallo. Setting him apart is his repertoire of various ronds and en-avant-deux, traditional dances from the Gallo country, and his ability to accompany his own marvellous singing on the accordion.

More accordionists you may wish to listen out for include Etienne Grandjean, Jacques Beauchamp, Ronan Robert and Frédéric Lambierge playing diatonic accordion, or Loïc Leborgne and Éric Richard playing chromatic. All are excellent musicians and appear on many recordings.

BRITTANY: HARP

Although there was a medieval Celtic tradition of harp playing in Brittany – Richard the Lionheart brought Breton harpists over to play at his coronation – the practice had completely died out by the 18th century.

The idea of the Breton harp (or telenn) was revived in the early 20th century by regionalists asserting the Celtic heritage of their province. They imported Celtic harps from Ireland, Scotland and London.

In the 1930s Gildas Jaffrenou attempted to build a distinctively Breton harp and in 1946 turned for inspiration to the plans of the 14th-century Irish "Brian Boru" harp (also the model for the harp on Irish money and Guinness bottles). He passed these plans on to Jord Cochevelou, who experimented over a number of years and had a working prototype by 1953. The first person to play that prototype in public was his nine-year-old son Alan, who would one day be world-famous under his pseudonym, **Alan Stivell**. Stivell was one of the earliest innovators on the harp, and the instrument is played now by many individuals and groups.

Stivell's use of the Breton harp has many characteristics. He plays solo Breton music, as well as airs from Ireland and Scotland; he uses the harp to accompany his

■ *Alan Stivell pictured in 1976.*

own singing in Breton and Gaelic; and he includes the harp in bands influenced by everything from hard rock to new age. His early albums *Reflets* (Fontana, 1970) and *Renaissance De La Harpe Celtique* (Philips, 1971) are seminal recordings for the harp, and particularly deserve to be heard – but the same could be said for many of his records over the years. Perhaps the best known harp act next to Stivell is **An Triskell**, a group led by the twins Pol and Hervé Quéffeléant.

Their music shows a marked influence from Stivell's work. Like Stivell they favour the wire-strung harp, played with the nails for a crisp and brittle sound. Their musicianship is excellent, and their Celtic pop has stood the test of time, with their mid 1970s work better than the synth-heavy albums they produced in the 1990s.

Kristen Nogues is a similarly innovative harp player, having synthesised traditional music, pop and jazz into her singing and playing. A veteran of many groups including Nevenoe and Celtic Procession, Nogues has not recorded many solo projects. Listen for her voice and harp playing on compilations and in bands.

There are many artists using the harp in a more conservative solo context, playing airs and dance tunes. To mention a few, Dominig Bouchaud, Gwenola Roparz and Job Fulup all have excellent recordings available.

BRITTANY: CLARINET

The clarinet was invented in 18th century Germany, and soon became part of the standard classical orchestra. From there it was adopted into military and municipal marching bands, which put it into the hands of amateur musicians in Brittany. It became a part of traditional music in the 19th century, and continues to be a folk instrument today. On both sides of the language line people have the same nickname for the clarinet: it is tronc d'chou in French, and treujenn-gaol in Breton, but both mean "cabbage stalk".

The most common cabbage stalk in Breton music is different from the standard orchestral instrument. While the orchestra or jazz band uses a 24-key fully tempered instrument, the treujenn-gaol usually has only 13 keys, and sometimes as few as six. Over the years, as classical and jazz musicians moved up to more state-of-the-art instruments, they sold their old 13-key and six-key instruments at bargain prices to folk musicians. Later, the folk players decided they liked the unique scale of instruments with fewer keys, and this became part of the tradition.

Perhaps the most popular playing style is for two clarinets to play together, in the style of kan ha diskan singers or sonneurs de couple. The clarinet has also been played in small ensembles where it is heard alongside accordions and violins; a group like this could keep wedding guests happy by playing old Breton dances in the "couple" style, and then playing waltzes and mazurkas influenced by jazz and Parisian musette.

Finally, the clarinet was sometimes adopted into proper jazz bands with saxophones and drums, and these groups sometimes played Breton tunes as well as jazz. More recently, the clarinet has been part of several important folk-revival bands, most notably Gwerz and Quintet Clarinettes, both of which feature the best known clarinet player in Breton music, **Erik Marchand**. Other bands using the clarinet include Strobinell, L'Echo and Cabestan. While there are not too many Breton CDs featuring solo or duet clarinet playing, some anthologies have been released. Also, each of the bands mentioned has recordings that feature the clarinet, played by such fine musicians as Bernard Subert, Jil Lehart and Michel Aumont.

BRITTANY: FLUTES AND WHISTLES

The wooden transverse flute came to Breton music via Ireland, and one of the first people to bring the Irish flute into Brittany was Alan Stivell. He was soon followed by **Jean Michel Veillon**, a child prodigy on the bombarde who switched to playing the wooden flute nearly 30 years ago.

Since then Veillon has been one of the leading musicians of Brittany, in groups like Kornog, Pennoù Skoulm, Den and Barzaz, and he has brought the wooden flute to prominence in Breton music.

Veillon also recorded the very first album devoted to Breton music played on the wooden flute, a milestone on the Breton scene and perhaps the culmination of his effort to have the flute recognised as part of the Breton instrumental line-up. Soon after that, Veillon teamed up with guitarist Yvon Riou, and the duo have released several CDs of mesmerising, subtle Breton dance music.

Following the example of Veillon and the very successful bands he has played in, many other musicians have taken up the wooden flute and played it in a group context. Most notable are Hervé Guillo of the group Storvan, Yannig Alory of Carré Manchot, Yann Herri Ar Gwicher of Strobinell, and the young player Carolyn Langelier of Tud.

Tin whistles are to be found in several Breton groups. Stivell brought them into his groups in the 1970s, several dance bands such as Strobinell play them, and the folk-rock group Tri Yann makes a feature of them. The most recent trend in flute playing in Breton music is to use Asian and Amazonian flutes. In Barzaz, David "Hopi" Hopkins plays South American cane flutes, and Asian bamboo flutes are played by J Pol Huellou on several recent recordings.

BRITTANY: GUITAR

Although it is not a traditional instrument, the guitar is well established in Breton music. From the 1970s onward guitars appeared on the majority of band albums to emerge from Brittany, beginning with groups such as Tri Yann and Sonerien Du, and chanteurs engagés like Servat and Glenmor often featured guitars in their backup

■ *Albums (left to right) by: Various (An Triskell); Soïg Siberil; Jacques Pellen; Alain Pennec; Quintet Clarinettes; Various (Sonneurs De Clarinette).*

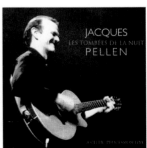

groups. But as a lead instrument, the guitar goes back to Alan Stivell's bands of the 1970s, and to the brilliant guitarist **Dan Ar Braz**.

Ar Braz discovered the guitar through rock'n'roll in the early 1960s, but he soon fell in with Stivell and spent a decade in the harpist's groups, playing Celtic music on both acoustic and electric guitars. He emerged in the late 1970s to found his own bands and record his own albums of guitar-based music, borrowing elements of Celtic music, rock and new age. From 1976 to 1977 Ar Braz joined the well-known English folk-rock band, Fairport Convention, then returned to Stivell's band for a brief stint, and a little later struck out on his own, spending some time in the studio to record the brilliant album *Douar Nevez* (Hexagone, 1977).

After passing some difficult years in the 1980s, during which he nevertheless recorded fine albums on both acoustic and electric guitar, Ar Braz emerged at the forefront of the Breton scene in 1994 with a big band and a big-production album titled *Héritage Des Celtes* (Sony/Columbia, 1994). The group he led on that recording – which included well-known Breton singers and musicians such as Gilles Servat, Yann-Fañch Kemener, Jacques Pellen and the entire pipe-band Bagad Kemper – went on to record three more albums, all released on the Sony label and culminating with a double-CD in 1998.

The best-known acoustic guitarists in Brittany are **Soïg Siberil** and Jacques Pellen. Siberil discovered the guitar through the influence of American folk and bluegrass, but soon turned his attention to Breton music. He plays in a style influenced by British and Irish guitarists, using the DADGAD tuning so common in Celtic music.

Siberil was a founder of the bands Kornog, Gwerz, Pennou Skoulm, Den, and Kemia, before beginning a solo recording career; his three excellent solo projects show him to be both technically proficient and deeply imaginative.

Jacques Pellen comes from a jazz background. His major contribution to Breton music has been Celtic Procession, a loose assemblage of 20 or so musicians who play music influenced by Breton traditional music and jazz. Celtic Procession has appeared in many different forms, from a trio to an orchestra, and has recorded several CDs as a group. Pellen has also recorded with Jacky and Patrick Molard as Triptyque. Other

guitarists to listen for include Arnaud Maisonneuve, who plays blues guitar behind Breton songs, as well as Nicolas Quemener and Gilles Le Bigot, who provide rhythm and harmony on backup guitar in various Breton bands.

Mandolins, citterns and bouzoukis all came to Breton music through the influence of American, Irish and Scottish folk. They can be heard in bands devoted to Celtic crossover music including Kornog and Tri Yann, in some fest-noz bands like Tud and Strakal, and in experimental bands such as Kemia. It is very rare to hear soloists on these instruments in Brittany.

RECOMMENDED RECORDS

AN TRISKELL LA HARPE CELTIQUE *(Le Chant du Monde, 1990) Retrospective compilation of harp music. Includes straight playing of traditional airs, plus an acoustic "Celtic ensemble" featuring Irish flute, Scottish bagpipe and Breton bombarde.*

COCKTAIL DIATONIQUE COCKTAIL DIATONIQUE *(Keltia, 1992) Four top diatonic accordion players including Yann-Fañch Perroches and Ronan Robert collaborate on lively traditional tunes and jazz. Also includes biniou and vocals.*

JACQUES PELLEN LES TOMBES DE LA NUIT, A CELTIC PROCESSION LIVE *(Naïve, 1999) Breton-jazz hybrid featuring brilliant guitar playing by Pellen and Dan Ar Braz, with other instruments and vocals.*

QUINTET CLARINETTES MUSIQUE TETUE/BAZH DU *(Silex, 1995) A double-CD collecting this group's two albums. Five clarinettists including Erik Marchand play traditional and original melodies inspired by the treujenn-gaol tradition.*

SOIG SIBERIL ENTRE ARDOISE ET GRANIT *(Gwerz Pladenn, 1996) This was the brilliant second solo CD by the guitarist of Gwerz, Kornog, and Pennoù Skoulm, featuring contemplative pieces and dance tunes on ringing, open-tuned guitar. With Jacques Pellen, Jacky Molard, Jamie McMenamy.*

ALAN STIVELL RENAISSANCE DE LA HARPE CELTIQUE *(Dreyfus, 1971) This album revealed the Breton harp to the world. Stivell's small orchestra plays Breton, Gaelic and Welsh music, with Dan Ar Braz on electric guitar.*

JEAN-MICHEL VEILLON E KOAD NIZAN *(Gwerz Pladenn, 1993) The first Breton flute album, this maintains a balance between the pulse and lilt of dance music and the smouldering intensity of slower tunes.*

VARIOUS ARTISTS ACCORDEONS DIATONIQUES EN BRETAGNE *(Keltia, 1990) This upbeat compilation featured the work of Alain Pennec, Yann Dour, Jacques Beauchamp, Etienne Grandjean, Bernard Lasbleiz and Christian Desnos, together amounting to some of Brittany's top melodeon players.*

VARIOUS ARTISTS SONNEURS DE VIELLE EN BRETAGNE *(ArMen, 1993) Originally a double-LP, this CD anthology of ethnographic recordings is the best source of information on the Breton hurdy-gurdy and includes detailed notes in French.*

Jacques Pellen at Cardiff, 1998.

BRITTANY: BANDS

Bands have always existed in Brittany. In the 19th century a common example was the "couple" of biniou and bombarde, accompanied by a simple snare-drum, while the jazz band was prevalent in the 1920s and 1930s. But it was not until the 1960s that the idea of a band playing traditional Breton music from a concert stage was born. **Alan Stivell** was one of the originators of this Breton folk-band movement. The experiments that led to his early albums – *À L'Olympia* (Fontana, 1972), *Chemins De Terre* (Fontana, 1973) and *E Langonned* (Fontana, 1974) – that were among the earliest leading to the creation of a Breton folk ensemble. Stivell drew on the Irish and Scottish folk revival, importing harps, tin whistles, flutes and Irish-style fiddle along with Scottish bagpipes and drums. He incorporated arranging techniques from Irish groups such as The Chieftains, Sweeney's Men and Planxty as well from folk-rock groups like Fairport Convention and Horslips. From American folk he took such instruments as dulcimers and guitars, and indeed his later album *Journée À La Maison* (Keltia, 1978) owes much to American music.

The greatest folk groups to emerge in Stivell's wake were Kornog and Gwerz, and they continued to use the other music alongside Breton tradition. **Kornog** included fiddler Christian LeMaître, flute player Jean-Michel Veillon, guitarist Soïg Siberil and singer/bouzouki player Jamie McMenamy. The international appeal of their music derives partly from its similarity to Irish and Scottish styles. From Irish music came the guitar with strings tuned DADGAD, the bouzouki and the wooden flute, while McMenamy, a former member of Scotland's Battlefield Band, sang Scottish songs. Kornog toured the US and their album *Première* (Green Linnet, 1984) was recorded live in Minneapolis. Their music demonstrated the shimmering, complete and joyful sound that a simple quartet can achieve.

Unlike Kornog, **Gwerz** never achieved much popularity beyond France. The use of biniou, bombarde and clarinet, as well as Erik Marchand's piercing vocals in Breton and French, made them more strictly Breton in feeling and therefore less broad in appeal. Still, their music is powerfully affecting and well worth hearing. Marchand is a singer of startling power, and some of his songs are frighteningly intense. Their instrumentals are more varied in mood than Kornog's work: gloomy, dark melodies are interspersed with upbeat dance music and reflective, gentle guitar pieces. Gwerz recorded four albums in the 1980s, then broke up. They re-united briefly in 1992, resulting in an excellent live CD.

In some ways, the spiritual heirs to Kornog and Gwerz were **Barzaz**, a band that existed for most of the 1990s. While their repertoire was almost entirely Breton traditional music, none of the instruments they used – wooden flutes, cane flutes, guitar, and fretless bass – had been present in Brittany until relatively recently. Kornog's flute player, Jean-Michel Veillon, was a member, as was Kornog's second guitarist, Gilles Le Bigot. David "Hopi" Hopkins played percussion and cane flutes, while Alain Genty's fretless bass added jazzy fluidity. The one traditional aspect of Barzaz's sound was the singing. Yann-Fañch Kemener was the vocalist, and the band achieved the effect of overlapping lines found in kan ha diskan by using Veillon's flute as diskaner. Meanwhile, brittle-sounding percussion, rolling bass and breathy bamboo flute combined well with Le Bigot's subtle guitar work.

Most live appearances by Gwerz, Barzaz and Kornog were held in concert halls and on festival stages. That was true also of Stivell's bands of the 1970s and 1980s, but another type of live show for all of these groups has been the fest-noz, or night

▪ *Members of Kornog.*

party. The fest-noz has been responsible for the creation of a new genre of music, related to the "folk-Breton" music of groups like Stivell, Kornog and Gwerz, but more specialised. It exists primarily for the purpose of playing at festoù-noz, and is mostly instrumental, played on some combination of violin, diatonic accordion, bombarde, flute, clarinet, bagpipes, guitar and bouzouki. The influence of the Irish tradition and of the Celtic revival on this style is clear, but the music remains Breton through the overlapping melody lines characteristic of kan ha diskan and of sonneurs de couple.

The most illustrious of the fest-noz bands is **Pennoù Skoulm**, formed when members of Kornog and Gwerz coalesced around their common member, guitarist Soïg Siberil. During their lifetime as a group, Pennoù Skoulm played for hundreds of dances but only released a single self-produced cassette. After they broke up, the band's material was remixed by Escalibur Records, with added snippets recorded at other times, and released on CD. Their complex and subtly interwoven melody lines create a musical tapestry. The closer you listen, the more intricate it seems.

Ensemble Gwenva is another group that has played innumerable festoù-noz. They have the most traditional sound of any of the groups in this sector of Breton music, due to their reliance on the tradition of sonneurs de couple in their arrangements. The group is made up of Jean Baron and Christian Anneix, one of Brittany's best-known "couples", along with Etienne Grandjean on diatonic accordion and Pierrick Lemou on violin. The four represent some of the greatest individual talents of the Breton folk revival, so it is no surprise that their album, *Le Paradis Des Celtes* (Ethnic, 1992), is a thoroughly satisfying example of Breton fest-noz

■ Bleizi Ruz on-stage at Pont L'Abbé, 1987.

music with deep connections to the tradition. The group **Skolvan** asserted their connection to Brittany's musical traditions by including on one of their albums a snippet of singing by a certain Mme Bertrand field-recorded in 1959. Alongside this they play new music from Irish-bred, English-born accordionist Johnny Whelan (whom they met in New Jersey) as well as various Breton composers. They also explore the legacy of jazz left by American servicemen and native French jazz geniuses, inviting brass players to join for several sets of tunes. They even enticed the kan ha diskan pair of Kemener and Guillou to sing. All this innovation – along with the unrivalled skill of musicians Youenn Le Bihan on bombarde, pistoñ and biniou, Fañch Landreau on violin, Yann-Fañch Perroches on diatonic accordion and outstanding guitarist Gilles le Bigot – makes Skolvan the pinnacle of fest-noz bands.

There are many other fine fest-noz bands out there. Strakal emphasise melodic fluidity, with accordion, bombarde and two fiddles. Carré Manchot have a more rhythmically driving sound, propelled by rhythm guitar and bass underlying flute, bombarde and accordion. Storvan achieve a pulsating, lively sound using violins and woodwinds backed by bouzouki, while Strobinell concentrate on wind instruments of varied timbres and pitches, giving their music a unique and breathy quality. Early fest-noz bands like Ar Sonerien Du and Diaouled Ar Menez were more experimental, if a bit sloppier, and tried everything from chromatic accordion and bombarde duets to choppy electric guitar behind banjo and fiddle.

While Alan Stivell was influential in the formation of the folk ensemble and the fest-noz band, more revolutionary still was his importation of rock instruments into Breton music. He was once again following pioneers from outside of Brittany: groups such as Fairport Convention and Steeleye Span in England and Horslips and Sweeney's Men in Ireland had already "plugged in". Stivell's similar move, exemplified on the early-1970s albums *À L'Olympia* and *Chemins De Terre*, started the folk-rock scene in France. One of Stivell's guitarists from these sessions, Gabriel Yacoub, founded **Malicorne**, who are France's most influential and important electric folk ensemble. The other guitarist, Dan Ar Braz, went on to become an influential rock performer in his own right.

Currently the best known Breton folk-rock group is **Tri Yann**. They formed as a folk trio in 1971 and went electric in 1976. Concentrating on folksongs from the Gallo-speaking regions of Brittany, Tri Yann were already unlike other groups in their rejection of the "Celtic language only" rule that prevailed in much of the early folk scene. By their third album, *Suite Gallaise* (Marzelle, 1974), they were more confident, and their fourth, *La Decouverte Ou L'Ignorance* (Marzelle, 1976), established Breton, American folk and Irish influences with electric guitar, bass and drums.

A string of successful albums followed, including *Urba* (Marzelle, 1978), *An Heol A Zo Glaz* (Marzelle, 1981), *Café Du Bon Coin* (Marzelle, 1983), *Le Vaisseau De Pierre* (Marzelle, 1988), *Belle Et Rebelle* (Marzelle, 1990) and *Portraits* (Marzelle, 1995). They have become more of a rock band over the years, but their concerts and albums always feature bagpipes, tin whistle, fiddle, bombarde and many other sounds from the Breton tradition. The band have a fascination with history, and so their albums will remain important statements on the meaning of being Breton – as well as making good, enjoyable listening.

Tri Yann means "three Johns" in Breton, and the band was, in fact, founded by three men named Jean. Their original name, Tri Yann an Naoned, "three Johns from Nantes" made clear their origin too. Another recent Breton/Gallo folk-rock band, also from Nantes, are **Les 4 Jean**. Whether this name is an act of homage to Tri Yann or one of defiance is hard to tell. But they do have serious credentials. Their singer is Roland Brou, and Alain Pennec plays several instruments. The music turns out to be a beautiful balance of traditional and rock sounds.

Another well known Breton folk-rock group is **Bleizi Ruz**. They have been around since 1973, and play gavottes and cercles circassiens as well as songs taken from the rich Breton tradition, with many of their original compositions also clearly in Breton styles. Most of their arrangements centre on Loic Leborgne's chromatic

■ *Members of Tri Yann on-stage.*

accordion and Eric Liorzou's vocals, aided in call-and-response sequences by Bernard Quillien's bombardes and whistles, and underpinned by Liorzou's guitar and mandola, along with electric bass. They have often featured a full drum kit as well, but now use an array of world-music percussion.

We'll finish with the youngest of the folk-rock crowd, **Armens**. Although they feature chromatic accordion and fiddle, they demonstrate little grounding in traditional music, and at heart are really a rock band. They have the potential to become the next Tri Yann, but they need to work on their overall musicality and the traditional component of their music before that will happen.

Recent developments in Breton music are moving it toward house music, world beat and hip-hop – much like the Afro Celt Sound System. But that's for another chapter. What is important is that the Breton music tradition, like its counterparts in the other Celtic countries, is living, growing and changing as it confronts the new century with pride.

■ *Albums (left to right) by: Alan Stivell; Kornog; Tud; Pennoù Skoulm; Bleizi Ruz; Skolvan.*

RECOMMENDED RECORDS

BARZAZ AN DEN KOZH DALL *(Keltia, 1992) The songs range from historical ballads to frisky drinking songs, from grisly murder ballads to lively dance songs, and the fine singing is complemented perfectly by mesmerising arrangements.*

BLEIZI RUZ CELTIC TRIP *(Shamrock, 1996) Highlights original lyrics and melodies in various Breton dance rhythms, and features world music percussion by David Hopkins who adds subtlety to the arrangements.*

GWERZ LIVE! *(Gwerz Pladenn, 1993) It is hard to imagine a better Breton album: this record is charged with intense energy and vitality as top folk-revival musicians play and sing before an adoring audience.*

KORNOG PREMIERE *(Green Linnet, 1984) Brittany's greatest instrumentalists teamed with Scottish singer/instrumentalist Jamie McMenamy. Pulsating Breton tunes, Scottish ballads and live ambience make this Kornog's best album.*

LES 4 JEAN LES TISSERANDS *(Boucherie, 1999) Gallo folk-rock band's second CD with a fine mix of traditional and rock sounds, fronted by Roland Brou (vocals) and Alain Pennec (accordion, flute, bombarde, biniou).*

PENNOÙ SKOULM FEST-NOZ *(Escalibur, 1994) Lively dance music that flows smoothly and easily, but is also complex, intricately arranged and densely layered.*

SKOLVAN SWING & TEARS *(Keltia, 1994) Infectious fest-noz music with a twist. All manner of brass instruments fill out the more jazz-inspired arrangements, and Jamie McMenamy guests on bouzouki.*

ALAN STIVELL ZOOM 70/95 *(Dreyfus, 1997) A double-CD compilation presenting 25 years of Stivell and showing off his various innovations, from solo harp to folk, Celtic, jazz, and rock arrangements.*

TRI YANN INVENTAIRE 1 / INVENTAIRE 2 *(Marzelle, 1996) Two volumes (sold separately) compiling 40 tracks from Tri Yann's many albums make the best introduction to this historically crucial band.*

VARIOUS ARTISTS DAÑS, MUSIQUE À DANSER DE BRETAGNE *(Iguane/Adipho, 1987) This is an appealing compilation of 1980s fest-noz bands, including Storvan, Carre Manchot, Strakal, Strobinell, Skolvan, BF15 and Pennou Skoulm. It amounts to a great place to begin your explorations.*

CELTIC IBERIA

BY ANDREW CRONSHAW

To a listener abroad who has caught a set by one of the roots bands bursting out from Galicia or Asturias, it might seem that in northern Spain there exists music which is broadly similar to that of Ireland or Scotland, but with an exotic southern tinge. That certainly was the impression gained by an American journalist who saw a show by Carlos Núñez and his band. "It was," he wrote, "as if some madcap bartender in Dublin had slipped a shot of Spanish wine into the stout."

There are indeed friendly, collaborative relations across the Bay of Biscay, and northern Iberia does have a Celtic history. But much of this initial impression of Irishness or Scottishness probably derives more from the surface texture of the music of many of the present wave of touring bands rather than from its deeper structure or cultural context. One of the most prevalent traditional dance forms in Galicia and Asturias is the muiñeira, in a jig-like 6/8 rhythm, and among the concert bands of today it is common to find "pan-Celtic" fretted instruments such as bouzoukis and guitars combined with the indigenous instrumentation, in which bagpipes and percussion dominate.

As the tourist advertising used to say, Spain is different – and that applies just as well to the origins, functions and forms of its musical traditions. A term increasingly used is "the Atlantic regions" which has the great virtue of sticking to geography, implying maritime connections, and avoiding racial assessments.

Northern Iberia does have considerable Celtic credentials, which seem to have persisted while major changes took place in more southerly parts of the peninsula. Given the lack of hard early evidence it is difficult to determine which (if any) characteristics of its present-day and recent traditional music can be considered "Celtic". But the possible Celtic origins of the musics, particularly bagpipe music, have been discussed in their homelands for at least a couple of centuries.

A BRIEF HISTORY

About 600 BC proto-Celtic peoples arrived in Iberia from the area of the Rhine and upper Danube and mingled with the existing population. When in the early years of the 1st century AD the Roman Empire expanded to include the whole of Iberia, regional culture was generally not suppressed. Latin, the power language, overwrote the Iberian Celtic languages – but failed to kill off the pre-Indo-European, non-Celtic language of the Celtic north Iberians' eastern neighbours, the Basques.

■ *Galician singer (opposite) pictured accompanying herself on pandeiro.*

When the Romans withdrew at the beginning of the 5th century AD Germanic Suevi took over the north-west but seem to have had virtually no linguistic or cultural effect. By the beginning of the 8th century the Moors ruled south and central Iberia, but never controlled the extreme north, from Galicia to the Pyrenees, which at that time constituted the Kingdom of Asturias, or Galicia and Asturias. So the north's culture remained to some extent distinct from that of the rest of Iberia throughout Roman, Visigothic and Moorish eras, and there was substantial inter-Celtic contact across the Bay of Biscay by adventurers and fishermen.

Around 810 AD an event occurred that was to have a huge effect on the culture, including the music, of Iberia's entire northern strip. It was claimed that the remains of one of Christ's apostles, Saint James, had been found in Galicia. The alleged relics conveniently provided a rallying icon for Christendom in its fight against the Islamic "infidels" (who, though seen as the enemy, contributed greatly to Spanish and Portuguese culture, technology and even diet). Saint James became Santiago Matamoros and the site of the miraculous discovery became the city of Santiago de Compostela, the greatest pilgrimage destination of the Middle Ages. Pilgrims arrived in many thousands from the whole of Europe, from as far afield as Scandinavia. They travelled the length of northern Spain through what is now Navarra, Euskadi,

■ *Ricardo Portela, gaiteiro of Viascón, Pontevedra, Galicia.*

Cantabria, Asturias and Galicia. These green, rocky Atlantic western outposts of Europe were opened up to a two-way stream of Europe's medieval culture.

And where there were people gathered together along the pilgrim way there was music. Local and foreign styles mingled. We can only speculate on the texture, form and spirit of that music, but a few manuscripts have survived. They include the seven Cantigas de Amor of the 13th-century Galician poet and musician **Martín Codax**, and these display some of the characteristics still found today in Galician music. By this time, and probably many centuries earlier, bagpipes were in use. When the reconquest was complete, at the end of the 15th century, Asturias-León had developed into the Kingdom of Castile, which stretched south from Galicia's Finisterre to the Mediterranean. But despite centuries of administrative union with the south, the lands behind the northern mountain chain -– from the River Miño to the Pyrenees – have to the present day maintained a very marked cultural distance from the rest of Spain, which is much more Arabic-influenced, and after the death of Franco gained varying degrees of self-government.

With partial autonomy came official status for three of Spain's regional languages, Euskara, Catalan and Galego, in addition to Castellano, or peninsular Spanish. There is pressure in Asturias for similar status for its language. Because Galego and Asturianu are spelt differently, from each other and from Castellano, the spelling of musical terms in this chapter is variable. Indeed Galicia and Asturias are themselves Castellano words; in their own languages they are Galiza and Asturies.

CELTIC IBERIA: PIPES

In the traditional music of both Galicia and Asturias the dominant melodic instruments are the gaita (bagpipe) and the voice. Gaitas were flourishing and professional players were earning a living playing them by the 15th and 16th centuries. There was a renaissance in the 19th century, a gradual decline during the 20th, and there is now another great renaissance. It began at the end of the 1970s and gathered pace dramatically in the late 1990s, with international major-label success for the first album by the Galician gaiteiro Carlos Núñez, *A Irmandade Das Estrelas – Brotherhood Of Stars* (RCA Victor, 1996). This was followed by the Asturian Hevia and his *Tierra De Nadie* (EMI, 1998) which has so far achieved over a million sales, more than any other Spanish album of any genre in the same period.

The bagpipe is sometimes seen as an identifying feature of music with a Celtic background. It may be that ancient Celts played them, but bagpipes were common to many countries of Europe, to the Islamic world, and to India. The instrument's sound – normally a continuous reed tone, usually over drones – strongly shapes the music it plays, and so it is that musicians from different countries and traditions are likely to find common ground whenever they happen to meet... whatever their historical, cultural or racial links.

Bagpipe traditions in Iberia are not restricted to Galicia and Asturias. Various forms of the instrument are known in Aragón, Huesca, Catalunya, Mallorca, León, Zamora and in the Trás-os-Montes region of north-east Portugal. The word "gaita" means a bagpipe in Galicia and Asturias and several other parts of Europe, but elsewhere in Spain and abroad can mean just a musical pipe of some sort, without a bag, often but not always with a double reed.

■ *Asturian gaiteru Margolles (1880-1963) and tamboriteru José Manuel Junco.*

Euskadi's traditional strident shawm, like a fat bagpipe chanter and somewhat like Castilla's dulzaina, is called a gaita, while in several regions such as Salamanca and Extremadura the name is applied to a three-hole whistle, a tabor-pipe. Galician, Asturian, and Trás-os-Montes gaitas are in general shape and construction similar to Scotland's Great Highland Bagpipe, but with fewer drones.

The player mouth-inflates the gaita's bag by means of a tube fitted with a non-return valve. By pressure from his left arm, the air is driven into the chanter (Galego: punteiro; Asturianu: punteru). This is fitted with a double reed, two blades of reed between which the air passes, like that of a shawm or oboe. The chanter has a conical bore, with seven finger-holes on the front – three for the left hand; four for the right – and one for the left thumb at the back. The bass drone (ronco or roncón) rests on the player's left shoulder. It is pitched two octaves below the tonic (key note) of the punteiro and has, like most bagpipe drones, a single reed made from a cane tube out of which the vibrating tongue is split.

A Galician gaita has from one to three drones. In addition to the ronco some have a much shorter drone, the ronquillo or ronquilla, which sticks out from the bag rather than going over the shoulder. It plays a note an octave above the ronco. Some also have an even smaller third drone, the chillón.

The tonic of the punteiro is played with the top six holes and the thumb hole covered. By progressively opening holes from the bottom the basic scale is a diatonic octave. (Also, depending on the tuning of the particular punteiro and the chosen style of the player, "open fingering" or "closed fingering" may be used.) By cross-fingering and in some cases half-holing, the extra notes to make a chromatic scale can be obtained. Then, with the aid of an extra kick of pressure on the bag, the reed can be pushed into the second octave, giving a compass of an octave and a half from tonic to top note. In addition, closing the seventh hole with the little finger of the right hand gives a semitone below the tonic.

Traditionally, Galician gaitas are said to be in one of three pitches: C (called a redonda), D (grileira) or B-flat (tumbal). But these are just approximate classifications, and there have been and continue to be variations and experiments. Low-pitched gaitas in A were often used by corales, the vocal-and-gaita ensembles of the 20th century.

Asturian gaitas are similar in most characteristics to Galician, but they usually have only one, or sometimes two, drones. The gaita-de-foles of Portugal's Trás-os-Montes has a single drone, and the scale of the punteiro is much more variable; it is played solo, with only drone and drum accompaniment, and so does not have to be in tune with any other melody instrument. The exact intonation of the notes of the gaita-de-foles' scale and the player's fingering is decided by maker and player: whatever gels well with the drone and sounds pleasing to the player. It is also usually close to the scale in which he would sing – which can be far from the equally-tempered scale. Trás-os-Montes music is a precious and fragile reminder of the days before the development and needs of western classical harmony.

In Galicia, for dancing and processions, the gaita has traditionally appeared singly or in a pair, alongside a tamboril (a usually wooden, natural-skinned side drum with gut snares, played with a pair of sticks) and a bombo (a bass drum struck with a single stick). When playing together, gaiteiros use the same sort of harmony as singers, either in unison or parallel thirds, producing a wonderfully strong, thrilling sound.

In Asturias the basic traditional unit is the pareya, a duo of gaita and tambor. In Trás-os-Montes the format is a trio of a single gaita, caixa (tamboril) and bombo, and there it is only in the Terra de Miranda region that the tradition survives, in the hands of fewer than ten players. There are, however, signs of the beginning of a resurgence in interest among a few young Mirandês. Despite the similarity of the instrumental line-up to that in Galicia to the north, members of the Mirandês group Galandum Galundaina, most responsible for maintaining the skills and energy of the tradition, reject the idea of Celtic connections in their music, preferring to cite influences from Portugal's long Arabic history.

There is now a renaissance in gaita playing. The new music is strongly attached to the old, with all the brilliant new young players having great respect for and knowledge of their predecessors' music. But the playing context has changed. The celebratory events at which gaitas were an essential component in many cases either dwindled or changed in nature during the second half of the 20th century. The Civil War of 1936-39 did of course have a great effect, as did the ensuing Franco regime which was, to put it mildly, unfriendly toward strong manifestations of regional culture. "Colourful folkloric spectacles" were tolerated, but the public use of languages other than Castellano was heavily suppressed and the songs were only safe as long as they stayed away from current social or political comment. The result was a tendency by the young to regard the world of gaitas as old-fashioned folksiness.

When the lid was taken off Spain's cultural diversity after Franco's death in 1975, languages which had continued to be spoken in private emerged abundantly in public and in print, and people looked again at their music. The young found that there were still old maestros from whom they could learn. In Asturias, gaita-playing had almost disappeared by the 1950s, while in Galicia the very strong gaita tradition had diminished but survived; in both regions the resulting renaissance put new young gaiteiros on the streets, playing in the old way.

A large part of the upsurge centres on stage performances and recordings. The new tunes being made tend to reflect the changes. As in Scotland and Ireland, what was essentially dance music is now often performed to a seated audience. The music is frequently given arrangements that can maintain the interest of static, observing listeners rather than spur on the dancers. As a result, the structures on which most of it is based are not always obvious from the new music. What follows is a summary of the main gaita tune forms. It is impossible to describe adequately the shape, spirit and feel of this music in words. The ideal is to be around gaitas at a fiesta or romería, but failing that a listen to recordings of one or two gaiteiros playing with traditional percussion will make things much clearer than trying to deduce its basic structures from the arranged music of progressive bands.

Individual gaiteiros are famous for their style and technique, but there is no tradition of completely solo, expressive, lyrical non-dance playing of bagpipes as there is with Scotland's piobaircachd and Ireland's slow airs – though with the new wave there are signs of something similar emerging. Nor has there been substantial

Hevia pictured in concert.

military use of the gaitas, although there are now big marching pipe and drum bands – largely based, controversially, on the Scottish model. The gaita has been almost entirely associated with dancing, the singing of dance-songs, and with secular and religious processions, virtually always with percussion.

Gaita music is therefore divisible into tune types associated with the rhythms of particular dance movements or the requirements of processions. The melodies of Galician and Asturian tunes are varied, shapely and memorable, not just to an instrumentalist but also to a singer; most are songs too, and gaitas and voices are frequent companions, either together or taking turns within a tune. The commonest tune type, in both Galicia and Asturias, is the muiñeira, the name of which derives from muiñeiro, the word for a miller. The springy 6/8 "deedle-di-deedle-di" rhythm is widespread in European folk-dance music, including Scottish and Irish jigs, but muiñeiras are more swingy than most jigs, less full of notes, and less tightly tied to a consistent stress pattern from bar to bar. There are other 6/8 tunes which are in effect muiñeiras but with different steps; in Galicia they include the ribeirana, carballesa, redonda, chouteira and contrapaso.

The word alborada signifies a song to or at sunrise, or one which starts a day's activities or celebrations. Normally written down in 2/4, occasionally in 3/4, an alborada is usually instrumental, a winding sort of tune often characterised by a series of descending turning phrases, a kind of formalised lark-song. A pandeirada has the rhythm of a dance, so even though it isn't a gaita tune it is appropriate to mention it here; it is essentially sung just with pandeiro or pandeireta. The foliada is a song that is generally associated with romerías (community picnic festivities at a local shrine) and is particularly joyful, usually in a swinging, swirling 3/4. Since the name relates more to the function than to the form, though, other types of tune are occasionally called foliadas.

Generally the word for a social dance is baile, but there are also formation dances such as danzas de espadas (sword dances), danzas de palillos (stick dances) and danzas de arcillos (dances with decorated arches). These dances occur in many parts of Iberia – as they do elsewhere in Europe, and indeed in the British Isles – and have specific tunes.

A pasacorredoiras or pasacalles (Asturianu: pasucáis) is a street marching or walking tune, and marchas procesionales are connected with religious or secular processing. Gaitas are used in some church events, including the misa de gaita, a gaita mass. A very popular dance and song form throughout Spain is the jota, which originated in Aragón. Considerably modified in Galicia and Asturias, jotas in 3/8 are almost as common as muiñeiras.

Other widespread Spanish dances have been absorbed and transformed in the repertoires of gaiteiros and dancers, most popularly the fandango, which is usually in 3/8, and the pasodoble in 2/4. Some have come from further afield. The polca arrived in Galicia in the 19th century, causing some consternation because it entailed close contact between members of the opposite sex. The mazurca entered the tradition from elsewhere in Europe. The rumba came from South America, where several countries have large populations of emigrants from north-west Spain.

The tune styles mentioned so far are found in Galicia. Asturias has its own distinctive melodies and regional variants, but many of the same dance forms appear – including the muñeira (sometimes called a gallegada), alborada, jota, fandangu, pasudoble, pasucáis, marcha procesional – as well as a range of others such as the giraldilla (in 3/4), pericote (2/4), xiringüelu (2/4), saltón (2/4), diana, respingu and more. Before beginning a tune, a gaiteiro will often play a short free-rhythm introduction, known as a cadencia, preludio or in Asturianu a floréu. It acts as a run around the scale to check tuning, fingering and grace-noting and the functioning of the reeds. It is essentially improvised, with each musician favouring particular runs and turns, but the patterns tend to be picked up in the same way as tunes and are therefore to some extent formalised.

Recordings of gaitas have been made since very early in the 20th century, so it is still possible to hear some of the legendary masters. The Do Fol label is planning to remaster many of the century's most important Galician recordings for a CD series *Clássicos Da Música Galega*. A leading name in the first half of the century was **Perfecto Feijoo**, known as a gaiteiro as well as a hurdy-gurdy player, a collector of shepherds' horns and one who cherished Galicia's rich traditions. Like several other gaiteiros during the 20th century, Feijoo sometimes played with corales, the folk-choral vocal groups. In the 1960s and 1970s the leading figure was **Ricardo Portela**, a major influence on today's young gaiteiros and on bands such as Milladoiro which formed at the beginning of the current upsurge.

In Asturias the most famous gaiteru in the latter part of the 19th century was **Ramón García Tuero**, known as El Gaiteru Libardón, of Villaviciosa. He was also a noted singer, and is considered the last of those who combined the roles of gaiteru, juglar (musical entertainer) and poet. Tuero travelled widely in Spain and abroad, performing in France, Mexico and Cuba, and recording to disc in Italy.

Maintaining the Asturian tradition into the second half of the 20th century were a handful of pipers, including **José Remis Ovalle** of Margolles who at a competition in 1956 run by Xixón town council was named Gaitero Mayor de Asturias, and became Gaitero Mayor de España in 1970. Ovalle also travelled abroad, performing and recording in many South American countries and in the US. His father, José Remis Vega, El Gaiteru Margolles, was the creator of a school of gaita playing considered the most important in Asturias in the 19th century. **José Antonio García Suárez**, El Gaiteru Veriña, was significant in carrying the tradition through to today's young players.

The most celebrated Asturian gaiteru now is **Hevia** (José Ángel Hevia Velasco). His 1998 EMI album *Tierra De Nadie / No Man's Land* swept the Spanish media – in 2000, for example, he was seen piping windswept on a hilltop during the title sequence of one of Spain's top sporting fixtures, the Gira de España cycle race. Such success often generates envy and derision among colleagues, but most gaita players and aficionados recognise the opportunities Hevia has created for others – and that there's much more to him than just high-powered major-label marketing.

When Hevia began playing there were not many to learn from. He tells in the album's notes how in 1977 he began to pick up fingering from an old gaiteiro "who fingered a stick as his pupil sat in front fingering the puntero". A year later he met

■ *Carlos Núñez and band.*

Armando Fernández, who became his teacher. Gaiteiros did not have a very positive image; the day before his first public performance his mother cried. "She didn't want to see her son going from romería to romería, always at the cider stall and 'noise-making among thieves'," writes Hevia. "The elders called the few of us fools who began to play la quinta del biberón [roughly 'the class of the baby's bottle']. Teaching ourselves, we made our own education with blind men's sticks, with hesitations, advances and setbacks, asking the impossible of luthiers. In 20 years I changed gaitas 20 times. In time I stopped designing every single gaita I play. Later came schools, bandas de gaitas and hundreds of students. Some of us gaiteros went professional, something which hadn't happened since the Civil War."

By 1991 Hevia had co-written the exemplary book *La Gaita Asturiana - Método Para Su Aprendizaje*, published by the Asturian government, the Principado de Asturias. During the 1990s he was among the bunch of young players who grouped and regrouped in a series of bands which found a new expression for traditional music, drawing inspiration and ideas for augmented instrumentation from Galicia, Scotland, Ireland, Brittany and elsewhere.

Hevia developed his skills, not just on gaitas but on the low whistles that had appeared in Spain in the hands of Davy Spillane and others. He also explored the technology, and on *Tierra De Nadie* did most of the percussion programming as well as using the electronic MIDI gaita he co-developed. The album does fit into a "world-groove" genre, although to some that might suggest no more than an unsubtle collage of samples or a bland piece of opportunism. The record is in fact a varied, richly-textured, constantly interesting work by an excellent player of vision and determination who has worked long and hard on his music. It incorporates much that is Asturianu in form and technique, including vocals from the very fine traditional singer Mari Luz Cristóbal Caunedo and the Colectivu Muyeres.

Gaitas feature in the majority of the new wave of Asturian folk bands, and it is not just Hevia who has emerged as a leading player. **Xuacu Amieva** is a respected and in-demand gaiteiro who was a member of the 1980s band Ubiña and has taught several of the pipers now in other bands. But, disappointingly, on his album *Tiempo De Mitos* (Resistencia, 1999) flute rather than gaita predominates.

Tejedor are a family trio from Avilés consisting of gaiteiro and flute player José Manuel Tejedor, his brother Javier who plays diatonic accordion, percussion and gaita, and sister Eva singing and playing percussion. The Tejedor brothers have won all the Asturian prizes, and each has won the Macallan bagpipe award at Festival Interceltique in Lorient, Brittany. Their album *Texedores De Suaños* (Resistencia, 1999) has traditional and Tejedor-original material. Scottish accordionist Phil Cunningham produced, played and in some cases arranged; session players include uilleann piper Michael McGoldrick, fiddler Duncan Chisholm and drummer James Mackintosh.

Traditional music had declined in Galicia, one of the world's bagpipe strongholds, although gaitas were still to be heard in villages and in cities. But when interest grew again in the late 1970s among the young, there were still many more living players from whom they could learn than in Asturias. A fine field recording by Roberto Leydi, *Foliadas Das Rias Baixas – Folk Songs & Music Of Spanish Galice* (Albatros), provides something of that atmosphere, with the hubbub of a Galician fishing village in fiesta in 1970. Three years earlier I'd found myself in the thick of a similar event in another west coast fishing village. Gaitas, tamborils and bombos escorted big-headed cabezudo figures in the streets; moving into the bars, they alternated with the powerful, thirds-harmony singing of foliadas, alalás, pandeiradas and muiñeiras, the singers rattling pandeiretas and scrubbing cunchas. For a British teenager it was an unforgettable experience of the energy of a living tradition.

Leydi's recording was made at the fiesta on the island of Arousa. It includes the wild, strong playing of the gaita-and-percussion group Os Airiños das Rias Baixas,

■ *Xosé Manuel Budiño.*

from Villagarcia, featuring Berjillo Diaz Diaz (gaita), Enrique Diaz Diaz (tamboril) and José Fonte Reys (bombo), plus bar singing, fireworks and church bells. There's a dance-band from Pontevedra mixing gaita with trumpet, clarinet, saxophone, maracas and drum-kit at a village dance, and Os Airiños d'o Parque de Castrelos, recorded in Vigo's public gardens, with Juan Manuel Gonzalez Alonso and Manuel Davila Alonso (gaitas), Ricardo Silveira (tamboril and vocal), Wenceslao Cabezas "Polo" (pandeireta, pandeiro and vocal) and Severo Davila Fernández (bombo).

The town of Ortigueira with its festivals, classes and courses has been a significant influence in the traditional music renaissance. Its first Festival Internacional Do

Mundo Celta took place in 1977, and a double-LP recorded at the 1980 event was released by the small Guimbarda folk-music label. It features Os Airiños do Parque de Castrelos, along with zanfonas (hurdy-gurdies), pitos & requintas (whistles and flutes) and a massed gaita band from its own Escola de Gaitas. Foreign performers came from Wales, Brittany and Ireland.

Young Galicians who were becoming more interested in their indigenous music began travelling around fiestas and festivals, playing with and learning from trios and quartets such as Os Campaneiros, Os Irmáns Graceiras, Os Areeiras and Os Rosales. In 1979 some of them formed the band **Milladoiro**, and in the years that followed they and several more new folk-rooted bands took gaitas and other traditional instruments and music from the fiesta to the concert stage, creating a rejuvenated image and the foundations for the current boom.

Most of today's leading exponents were impressionable teenagers at that time. Some of this new generation came from traditional musical families. Others found that it had become possible to learn about the instruments and techniques by joining gaita bands, or by attending certain educational institutions – and one in particular was to prove highly influential in the lives of many young players.

At the Universidade Popular de Vigo a workshop was set up for experimenting with and teaching the construction and playing of the instruments used historically in Galician music. It was under the directorship of instrument-maker Antón Corrál, and had leading makers and musicians as teachers.

In 1989 **Carlos Núñez** took me into the spacious, high-ceilinged hall that housed the workshop. On the benches, in various stages of construction or dismemberment, were a panoply of the tools of Galician music through the centuries, including gaitas, zanfonas, pitos, requintas, harps and percussion instruments. Antón Corrál explained the work they were doing, and demonstrated Galicia's equivalent of Australia's lagerphone, the struck-string, floor-thumped, jingle-rattling charrasco. A tour-de-force triple-LP box set titled *Instrumentos Musicais Populares Galegos* (Sonifolk, 1987) featured the workshop's armoury, played by Corrál, Núñez, Carlos Corrál, Ramón Casal, Anxo Pintos, Santiago Cribeiro, the banda de gaitas Xirabal, famous gaiteiro Ricardo Portela, pandeiro and pandeireta player Wenceslao Cabezas "Polo", and a number of others.

Carlos Núñez was born in Vigo in 1971. He began playing the gaita at the age of eight, when he was also studying classical recorder, for which he won top marks at the Royal Conservatory in Madrid. By the age of 13 he was appearing in Shaun Davey's *Pilgrim Suite* at Lorient. At 16 he was a leading player of gaitas, pito, tarrañolas and crumhorn on the Vigo workshop's box-set project, and in his 18th year he played with The Chieftains on the soundtrack to the film *Treasure Island* and became a teacher of gaitas at Vigo Conservatory. The Chieftains connection greatly elevated his profile at home as well as abroad, and he went on to tour worldwide with them and play on several of their albums, including *Santiago* (RCA Victor, 1996). At the beginning of the 1990s, Núñez and his Universidade Popular colleagues Anxo Pintos and Santiago Cribeiro founded the six-piece band Matto Congrio. They toured with The Chieftains and in 1992 released an acclaimed album, with Paddy Moloney as guest uilleann piper.

Núñez then assembled a band, including two ex-members of Matto Congrio, which became the nucleus of the large cast of musicians who appeared on his very ambitious first solo album, the hugely successful *A Irmandade Das Estrelas / Brotherhood Of Stars* (RCA Victor, 1996). It sold over 100,000 copies in Spain in its first few months. Much was made in the major-label publicity of the foreign stars who appeared on this album – Ry Cooder, The Chieftains, La Vieja Trova Santiaguera and others – but at its core are many Galician musicians. In addition to Núñez's basic band, they include zanfona player Amancio Prada, traditional percussionists Wenceslao Cabezas "Polo" and Núñez's young brother Xurxo, ex-Milladoiro violinist Laura Quintillán, and the eight women singer/pandeireteras who form the group Xiradela, as well as leading players and singers from other parts of Iberia. On the set of tunes from the repertoire of Perfecto Feijoo, Núñez plays Feijoo's own B-flat gaitas, borrowed from the Pontevedra Museum.

Most who listen to the album are likely to be unfamiliar with Galician traditional music and so would not recognise some of the links Núñez makes between the musics of Galicia, other parts Iberia, Ireland, and Cuba, one of the destinations of Galician emigration across the Atlantic. Indeed he probably attempts more cultural cross-referencing than is feasible, but the result is splendidly melodic and rich. In addition to erudition, charm, impeccable technique and a fine sense of fun and showmanship, Núñez's great strength is his over-riding passion for a strong melody – and the ability to communicate it.

His next album was *Os Amores Libres* (RCA Victor, 1999). Here he continued to remember and point out connections with other "Celtic countries", with flamenco, with Balkan and Irish gypsies, with Irish fighters against Franco, and connections between North Africa and the west of Ireland, between Bretons and Berbers. The record features over 100 guests, a fact trumpeted by the press release but likely to make the listener check the sleevenotes to see who, where and why – and strain to hear the contribution some of them make.

He brings in people from interesting parts of the Galician tradition, and explains who they are, revealing the riches of the Galician tradition and his clear enthusiasm and feeling for them. There is traditional singer Divina, from the area of Manzaneda, Galicia's highest mountains, and Xiradela, a group of pandeireteras/singers "who go to villages at weekends to learn from elderly farmers and sailors the songs of their youth". The dance group Xacarandaina with their leader Enrique Peón are "the great group of folklore investigation and performance of our time who observe the dying

■ *Susana Seivane.*

rural tradition in an intelligent, direct and constant manner". Wenceslao Cabezas "Polo" is here again, on pandeireta, pandeiro, scythe, and aturuxo (which means "encouraging shouts and screams"). He is "the great master of tambourine in Galicia, who keeps the dance traditions which were so popular in the 1940s and 50s alive".

Also on hand is the bell ringer of San Salvador de Manzaneda, "one of the last rural bell ringers who still masters the language of the varied tolling which was used to inform the neighbours; amongst those sounds, in Galicia we find the traditional muiñeira, which always announces a celebration".

There is the muiñeiro (miller) of Folón, who "restored a beautiful old mill, abandoned and unused since his youth, with his own hands; with his rhythmic sound he captures the legendary origins of the muiñeira". Percussionist Dionisio Aboal is the "great lover of Galician folklore; for almost half a century he has travelled around the villages of Galicia collecting endless unusual percussion instruments", while Antonio Río, practitioner of the art of brindo, improvises humorous singing, "a sort of ancient rap", and there is also to be heard an in-studio performance of the Danza de Palillos of Ancéu.

The drum group Treboada de Tomiño are featured, too. "In Galego, 'treboada' means 'thunder', which is also the name of the enormous drums we can find on the border with Portugal; these elderly musicians told us that in the past almost a hundred of these drums used to play in unison." All these players, plus Núñez's band and the other guests, are crammed into 12 audio tracks lasting 74 minutes. An entire television series could be made from the Galician contributions alone, plus several more on the cultural connections. Live, of course, this sort of thing is not physically or financially possible; the Carlos Núñez Band is a small, tight unit delivering an exciting and entertaining show.

Xosé Manuel Budiño is, like Núñez and several other leading players, a graduate of the workshop at the Universidade Popular de Vigo, and he was the gaita soloist with the Banda de Gaitas Xarabal that appeared on the 1987 triple-LP set. In 1991 Budiño won the Galician section of the Lorient festival's Macallan solo gaita prize, while the cuarteto de gaitas Campaño of which he was a member won the Pontearas competition. In addition, in 1992 his band of the time, Fol de Niu, won the Best Folk Band prize at the Santiago festival.

"One of our aims was to go out, to travel abroad, to get to know other cultures and express our own" says Budiño. "At the beginning one very much liked to find out about Irish music, Scottish music, Breton music, but later you arrive at the time when you return to Galicia and to searching for the traditional music – because it's your music, your own culture that you want to express. Fifteen years ago there were very few groups coming out of Galicia. There was Milladoiro, but very few others. There weren't enough musicians to export our music. Festivals in Galicia had to have a Breton group, or a Scottish or Irish one; without that the festival wouldn't be a success. But these days the top of the bill has to be Galego. If not," he laughs, "people don't go."

While undoubtedly encouraged by lingering kisses with Irish, Scottish and Breton music, Galician-rooted music now seems to be emerging with a new vision. A clear example is Budiño's debut album *Paralaia* (Resistencia, 1997), a record richly varied, full of ideas, with energy and immensely tight playing, and constantly refreshed by light and shade. Budiño plays gaitas, uilleann pipes and whistles with a core band of bouzouki and mandola, accordion, bass and percussion, plus Breton guests Jacky Molard (fiddle) and Soïg Siberil (guitar), as well as Euskal trikitilari Kepa Junkera.

There's no sense here of a bunch of hot international session musicians simply doing a workaday job with tunes they met as they walked into the studio. They all pull their weight and get right inside the material. The sound is hefty sometimes, with Xan Hernández's bass and Leandro Deltell's robust percussion, but it is never leaden. The instrumental tunes, all Budiño compositions, are intricate, developing traditional forms but never losing sight of a shapely melody. The style draws on other cultures, but is very clearly Galician. There are songs, too, largely written or found by the magnificent, wild-sounding Galician traditional singer Mercedes Peón, who made her long-awaited recording debut here.

Budiño's second album, *Arredor* (Virgin, 2000), features his band with collaborators including Peón, Scots guitarist Tony McManus and Capercaillie's Donald Shaw. It includes 'Compostela', which was the piece that was written by Budiño for the millennium international TV link-up in which he and the pandeiretera/singers of Leilía performed perched high on the roof of the mighty Cathedral of Santiago de Compostela.

Susana Seivane emerged as a top-line gaiteira in 1999 with her very fresh eponymous album on the Do Fol label, full of interesting, shapely tunes played with great snap and sparkle. The living, evolving tradition is evident in the material which includes muiñeiras, jotas, pasodobles, a processional march and a sung alalá. These were learnt largely from living players and tune-makers or, in the case of the rumba 'Sabeliña', composed by Seivane. The variety in the tunes is enhanced by the arrangements which feature primarily guitar, bouzouki, diatonic accordion, violin, hurdy-gurdy, flutes, bass and mostly traditional percussion. Sonia Lebedynski's very attractive singing features on two pieces, and in one of them – 'Maneo' – Seivane too makes a vocal appearance, taking the second part.

It was clear from the photo on the front of the CD and the fashion-shoot poses throughout the booklet that Seivane is seen as a bagpipe babe. Actually, she was just that: her grandfather Xosé and father Alvaro are famous gaita-makers, and a couple of family snaps do indeed show the three-year-old Susana already looking confident with a tiny gaita.

All the legendary pipers of the past were male, as indeed were the tamboril and bombo players who completed a trio or cuarteto de gaitas. But today there is a growing presence of female players. "A few years ago there weren't so many women who played the gaita," says Seivane, "and in the past there were very few. But in Galicia now there are equal numbers of boys and girls, gaiteiros and gaiteiras. There might even be more girls."

Seivane was born in 1976, in Barcelona. When she was 12 her family moved back to Galicia where she met two big influences, the famous elder gaiteiros Ricardo Portela and Nazario González. She joined the band Raxumeiros, led by gaiteiro Bieito Romero who now leads Luar na Lubre, and she played on television with Milladoiro. Rodrigo Romaní from that band produced her album, and three other Milladoiro musicians were on the session team, which also included Berrogüetto's Anxo Pintos, Os Cempés percussionist Beto Niebla, flautist Xosé Liz from the band Beladona, and accordionist Brais Maceiras. After the album a touring band was assembled, with long-time Seivane collaborators Maceiras and Sonia Lebedynski, plus bouzouki, guitar and percussion. "We aren't a strictly traditional group, because we have guitar, bouzouki and so on, and they're not traditional," she says. "We play in a traditional style, though. But there are other ways, like the trios or cuartetos de gaitas, with bombo and tamboril – they're the most traditional. We say we play 'music from before but speaking of now,' because times change. We have something more modern, more up to date." She doesn't identify particularly with the Celtic tag. "I think it's a label, to sell more. What we do is Galician music."

Another young gaiteira becoming prominent is **Cristina Pato**. Born at the beginning of the 1980s, she was a member of the band Mutenrohi, recording two albums with them before making her solo CD *Tolemia* (Fonofolk, 1999) and subsequently touring with her own band. She has great respect for musicians such as Budiño, Núñez and Hevia, and is influenced by the Scottish bands Capercaillie and Shooglenifty. "But I want to move a little away from Galicia and Scotland," says Pato, "a little toward Africa and also Brazil, to change the evolution of the traditional sound of the gaita." *Tolemia* only contains two tracks with traditional themes. The rest, seven of which were written by Mutenrohi violinist Raquel Rodriguez, have nothing to do with Galician folk music, she says. "Their only connection is the sound of the gaita."

RECOMMENDED RECORDS

XOSÉ MANUEL BUDIÑO PARALAIA *(Resistencia, 1997) This wonderfully accomplished, varied and exciting debut album of new tunes proves that the tradition doesn't stop here. Here is dazzling playing from a tight ensemble, as well as wild, real-thing vocals from the superb Mercedes Peón.*

HEVIA TIERRA DE NADIE / NO MAN'S LAND *(EMI Odeon/Higher Octave, 1998) Powerful, rich, danceable million-seller by Asturian gaiteiro José Angel Hevia Velasco.*

HEVIA AL OTRU LLAU / AL OTRO LADO / THE OTHER SIDE *(EMI Odeon, 2000) Huge commercial success can be hard to follow, but this jubilant celebration of Asturian melody and rhythms succeeds admirably.*

CARLOS NÚÑEZ BROTHERHOOD OF STARS *(RCA Victor, 1996) This first solo album from the first of the new wave of great young gaiteiros is eclectic, connection-making and*

internationally star-studded, and marked the beginning of "el boom" in Galicia. And a very melodic and varied listen it is.

CRISTINA PATO TOLEMIA *(Fonofolk, 1999) Young player experimenting with the gaita in non-traditional music forms.*

SUSANA SEIVANE SUSANA SEIVANE *(Do Fol/Green Linnet 1999) Very fresh, melodic and up-front, further stirring international interest and establishing Seivane as a brand leader in the new wave of skill and energy in gaita-playing.*

CELTIC IBERIA: VOICE

The tradition-rooted musical upsurge that began at the end of the 20th century was largely led by instrumental music, but singing constitutes an important part of tradition throughout Iberia. Following a period when singers tended to be immersed in a band rather than prominently featured, individual voices are now emerging. The old, strong vocal styles and textures are being re-evaluated and are reappearing in the new wave through singers such as Mercedes Peón or the group Leilía in Galicia, or the Colectivu Muyeres in Asturias.

Singing is a hands-free activity, and so in Iberia as elsewhere people have sung while working, alone and together. And since it doesn't require instruments, singing is natural at times of communal leisure and celebration. Sometimes the singing was free-rhythm and expressive, sometimes it turned into and accompanied dancing. Music that moves the soul tends to move the body, too.

Rhythmic singing was accompanied by the rhythmic sound of the work, or with percussion instruments, most commonly pandeiros or pandeiretas in Galicia and Asturias. Many gaita tunes are songs too, and people sing along or in alternation with the gaitas. Singing against percussion or gaitas involves a good deal of strong vocal projection, and throughout Spain the classic traditional singing voice, of both sexes, is powerful and resonant.

The subject range of traditional songs is wide. Many are secular, covering day-to-day life, love, marriage, death, lullabies, children's songs and seasonal customs, as well as songs about work or accompanying work, including fishing, milling, drawing

■ *Albums (below, far left to right) by: Tejedor; Hevia; Various (Foliadas Das Rias Baixas); Xosé Manuel Budiño; Escola de Gaitas de Ortigueira; Carlos Núñez; Susana Seivane; and Os Rosales.*

water, reaping, sowing and mining (the latter particularly in Asturias). Songs can be historical or legendary, of kings and heroes and magic, of the romancero ballad traditions which spread around Europe in the middle ages, aided by the pilgrimage traffic on the Camino de Santiago. Or they may have religious connections, used in church or associated with religious festivals. There is also a continuing poem-song tradition. New lyrics or words of respected poets such as Galicia's most famous, Rosalía de Castro, are attached to existing or modified tunes.

The melodies, scales and modes of the songs are also varied. Some sound definitely "Spanish" to foreign ears (an impression which often derives from the use of the phrygian mode). Some may use similar scales to other European melodies, but a tonal emphasis or a vocal or instrumental texture nevertheless define them as distinctively Galician or Asturian. They are very much Iberian, but with less of an Arabic feel than those from further south. Virtually none is significantly reminiscent of Scottish or Irish music, though of course there has been contact by sea with other countries of the Atlantic seaboard since fishermen first set sail.

The popularity of contemporary roots music from Scotland, Ireland and Brittany certainly has an audible effect, however, on the shapes, rhythms and arrangements of much new Galician and Asturian roots music. Just as in the past influences arrived with pilgrims and sailors, the songs being made now reflect influences from whatever local or distant music a musician hears.

An adequate analysis of Galician and Asturian song would take a whole book, but in addition to the dance-songs already described in the pipes section we will just mention a couple of notable and distinctive Galician traditional forms. The alalá derives its name from the sound of its refrain. It is a slow song, moving and passionate, performed unaccompanied. Alalás are sung solo or, as when sung by the corales, in harmony of parallel thirds. A pandeirada is an energetic, up-tempo song coasting across a very fast "takata-takata-takata" rhythm on pandeiretas or pandeiros.

For centuries throughout Europe individuals have been collecting and writing down folk songs they found in their own country or abroad. Sometimes they were recorded simply as personal aide-mémoires, but often because it was felt that the songs might be lost. In some parts of Iberia groups of people who wanted to perpetuate their songs, and perhaps also enhance their status, formed into folk choirs. In Galicia these coros or corales had male and female singers and often a trio or cuarteto de gaitas. It was one of these corales, **Aires d'a Terra** from Pontevedra, that in 1904 performed on the first commercial recordings of Galician music. Many others would make recordings throughout the 20th century.

The idea of "folk choirs" might suggest some sort of effete, pompous folk music, and in some cases that was true. But the corales were major forces in the collection, performance and continuation of the riches of Galician music. For most of the century they existed alongside and interacted with the folk tradition. These singers

■ *Mercedes Peón.*

and musicians were not taking music from the people to the concert hall; they were the people themselves. In many corales they sang with vibrant, grainy, traditional technique, not classico-choral prissiness.

The corales faltered during the Franco era when the ability of folk song to comment on real life was severely curtailed. And if all one can sing about is the inoffensive and historical, one becomes perceived as irrelevant. The corales and the image of the gaita tended to be described as folclorico, a word which had come to mean a colourful folksiness for public show and tourism, in contrast to the real underlying culture of the people. Nevertheless the best of the corales, such as

Cantigas da Terra (founded in 1916) and **Coral de Ruada de Orense** (1919), continued to make a magnificent sound, with strong rich voices and moving, melismatic solos, male and female. The corales also gave the great gaiteiros such as Perfecto Feijoo the opportunity to perform. As Xosé Manuel Budiño says, "Playing with the corales was [the gaiteiros'] way of getting their music out, because they couldn't have their own groups. It was a beautiful sound, the mix of the voices and the deep-pitched gaitas in A."

There were corales in Asturias, too, as well as miners' choirs similar to those in Wales but featuring melismatic Asturian vocal solos. As in Galicia, some tended to sweetened choral arrangements and new compositions that were nostalgic rather than the robust traditional sounds, but others had the gritty power to move the soul. Often found among the choral tracks on LPs with postcard-style folkloric sleeves are recordings of fine solo singers and great gaiteiros such as José Remis Ovalle. These records were probably designed chiefly as reminders of home for exiles, including those who formed émigré corales in South America and elsewhere.

Choirs still exist, but in the next stage of the folk music relay the baton was taken by the folk bands which began to form in Galicia in the late 1970s and in Asturias during the 1980s. Most of them focused on gaita tunes, instrumentals and arrangements, and the role for singing diminished.

Gradually, though, individual singers have emerged, the majority women. Since many perform in concert using amplification there was a move to a quieter, less hard-edged vocal sound. But in the closing five or six years of the 20th century came a new focus on old-style voice projection and the strong sound of groups of singing pandeireteras. This has coincided with the rise of the new gaita stars and bands, many of whom feature fine traditional-style singers and pandeiretera groups on their recordings and in concert.

Albums (below, left to far right) by: Uxía; Muyeres; Emilio Cao; Pancho Alvarez; Obradoiro de Gaitas & Zanfonas, Universidade Popular de Vigo; Coral "De Ruada" de Orense; Various corales (Galicia Canta).

The regal **Uxía** (Uxía Senlle) became prominent in the late 1980s as singer with the band Na Lúa. In the mid 1990s, at the time of her album *Estou Vivindo No Ceo* (Nubenegra, 1995/ Intuition, 1997) and a subsequent joint album with Sudanese singer Rasha, Uxía gained international repute and became involved in more solo projects and collaborations within and outside Galician music. Well grounded in

traditional music, she has the powerful, hard-edged voice when she needs it, but also an intimate, silky warmth.

The serene vocals of Sonia Lebedynski (Galega despite her Polish name) are a key feature of Susana Seivane's band. Guadi Galego has brought a new dimension to Berrogüetto; Chouteira has the stirringly full-blooded Uxía Pedreira, and Luar na Lubre the impressive Rosa Cedrón. In Asturias one of the first folk bands of the 1980s was Ubiña, with the high silver-edged voice of Marta Arbas. She stayed with the band when it metamorphosed into Xaréu, and by the turn of the millennium had joined Brenga Astur.

Guesting on Hevia's *Tierra De Nadie* (EMI/Higher Octave, 1998) is the magnificent traditional voice of **Mari Luz Cristóbal Caunedo**. She also delivers a classic unaccompanied performance – and plays gaitas – on the double-CD *Muyeres II* (Fono Astur, 1997). This, like the first *Muyeres* album, is devoted to Asturian female singers and vocal groups who collect and perform traditional songs, many of them accompanying themselves on pandeiros or pandeiretas. After the first album in 1994 an organisation was formed, Música Tradicional Muyeres, as well as a touring performing group, Colectivu Muyeres, which also appears on *Tierra De Nadie*.

In both Asturias and Galicia such groups of young women singers and pandeireteras are being increasingly heard in performance and on recordings. Leilía is the most prominent, with two albums of their own and appearances with Budiño and others, while Cantigas e Agarimos have performed and recorded with Berrogüetto, and Xiradela appear on both of Carlos Núñez's albums.

The first solo album by **Mercedes Peón**, *Isué* (Resistencia, 2000), will surely be regarded as a turning point in Galician music. Peón is a magnificently bold young singer in the old, hard-edged, passionate style that is the natural partner to the wildness of pipes and percussion; indeed she is also a pandeiretera and distinctive self-taught gaiteira.

Though she had sung upon occasion with Matto Congrio, Peón did not record with them. Declining encouragements to make a solo album she continued to spend her time learning from the old people in the villages, making thousands of hours of recordings of them. Some of these are released on Trompo, the label she set up with

Nando Cruz. Her own recording debut came on Xosé Manuel Budiño's *Paralaia* album (Resistencia, 1997). She and Budiño have particular musical empathy, sometimes collaborating in songwriting and guesting live with one another's bands.

After *Isué*, Peón gathered a band together to perform live shows. On-stage she is a mesmerising figure with a dancer's body language, surrounded by an eight-strong team of great skill and adaptability that includes multi-instrumentalist Victor Iglesias, her percussionist and dancer brother Henrique, and singers Sonia Reborido and Rocío Barreiro.

All the singers mentioned here are women, but of course the male voice is heard in bands, and there are plenty of able male singers. On the current scene, though, men tend to be instrumentalists first, and – as yet – relatively few are best known for their singing.

RECOMMENDED RECORDS

MERCEDES PEÓN ISUÉ *(Resistencia, 2000) Totally modern while revelling in the richness and spirit of traditional song, this is a turning point, a mightily bold expression of deep roots and of the charismatically individual.*
LEILÍA I É VERDADE, I É MENTIRA *(Virgin, 1999) Most prominent of the new wave of Galician pandeiretera groups.*
UXÍA DANZA DAS AREAS *(Virgin, 2000) Latest release from a major Galician and international singer. Here she is joined by Catalan singer Maria del Mar Bonet, Portuguese Dulce Pontes and João Afonso, Capercaillie's Karen Matheson, and instrumentalists including Susana Seivane, Xosé Manuel Budiño, Michael McGoldrick, Donald Shaw.*
VARIOUS ARTISTS MUYERES *(Fono Astur, 1994);* MUYERES II *(Fono Astur, 1997) Songs, dance-songs, ballads from various Asturian pandeiretera groups, including on II (a CD-ROM enhanced with video performance footage) a magnificent solo from Mari Luz Cristóbal Caunedo.*

CELTIC IBERIA: PERCUSSION

The capabilities and limitations of the instruments used by musicians have a powerful effect not just on the sound and texture of a tradition but also on its melodies and rhythms. Players will choose their tools from among whatever is available, bending them to the music they want or need to play and also bending the music to suit the instruments. Today's professional musicians can choose from a huge range of the world's instruments, but if they are attempting to work with a particular musical tradition they usually take its previously used instruments as a starting point.

This is a brief summary of most of the other traditional instruments that are or have recently been used in the geographical region of Galicia and Asturias, though not necessarily throughout the area. To avoid too many confusing parentheses the Galego or English form of the names are used, with some of the more marked divergences between the Galego and Asturianu also indicated.

The tamboril (sometimes called redoblante or redobrante) is the usual drum used with gaitas. It is a small snare-drum, natural-skinned with snares usually made of gut, rope-tensioned or screw-tensioned, with wooden or occasionally metal hoops. It is played with two sticks, and hangs from the player's belt. In Galicia, and sometimes in Asturias, the rhythm section accompanying gaitas is completed by a bombo, a natural-skinned bass drum played with one stick. However, the new Scottish-style massed pipe-bands have been moving to high-tension plastic-headed drums and clicky rat-tat-tat press-roll playing.

The pandeiro (Asturianu: panderu) or pandeiro cuadrado (panderu cuadráu) is a square double-headed drum, usually with a few pieces of wood or beans that rattle around inside. (In Portugal something very similar is called an adufe.) Held square- or diamond-wise in front of the player, it is played with the fingers of both hands. This drum is typically used by a female singer or group of singers for self-accompaniment, as is the pandeireta, a relatively large natural-skinned tambourine.

Cunchas means "shells". Scallop shells are not only the symbol of pilgrimage to Santiago; a pair of the knobbly "vieira" kind rubbed together back to back constitute a percussion instrument, used for accompanying dance-songs. Tarrañolas (Asturianu: tejoletas) are strips of wood, like wooden "bones", held between the fingers and clattered together. In Asturias there exists a big, deep-sounding form of castañuelas which are held facing upward in the palms of the hands, and are traditionally used in a dance by men.

The charrasco is a pole with a frame on top bearing tambourine rattles. The player hits and rubs a string stretched along the pole with a stick, while thumping the pole on the ground. Seen less frequently are the canaveira, a length of cane split so its halves crack against one another, the carraca, a football-type rattle. Work implements have naturally been used as percussion instruments, for example the payella or payecha of western Asturias, a frying pan with a long roughened handle that is scraped with a key.

CELTIC IBERIA: WIND INSTRUMENTS

A pito is a wooden conical-bored whistle similar in general appearance to a recorder, with seven finger-holes on the front and one on the back. Some have an extended double-reed-shaped mouthpiece. The fingering is similar to that of a gaita punteiro, making it a possible first step to gaita playing. The last old makers made them in E-flat but Antón Corrál revived and modified the instrument, making pitos in D that play accurately chromatically.

A requinta is a fife, a short six-hole conical-bored transverse flute, sometimes with a single key over a seventh hole. Usually it is in G, occasionally high C. Other flute-type instruments include the ocarina and the chifre, small panpipes carved out of a solid block of wood. In the past, shepherds played various animal horns as trumpets. The clarinet is a relatively recent introduction but has been played with gaitas.

The diatonic accordion arrived in the region late in the 19th century and joined the gaitas in playing for dance music, particularly the newer forms such as waltzes and rumbas, even though the tuning between the two instruments was often approximate. The birimbao is not the Brazilian berimbao but the jew's harp.

CELTIC IBERIA: STRINGED INSTRUMENTS

Despite the prevalence of fretted instruments in other parts of Iberia they were not used in Galician and Asturian traditional music until the advent of the modern folk bands – and even then tended to be foreign-style guitars, bouzoukis and mandolins, not usually Iberian instruments. Gypsies in the north do not play flamenco; as Carlos Núñez points out, one is more likely to see them playing brass to accompany a strange circus-type routine involving a goat on a high stool. But Galician guitarist Xesús Pimentel uses Galician material to make flamenco-style music.

Likewise when the violin is used now, as it is in a number of folk bands, most of the influence on technique comes from European classical or Irish or Scottish music. However, earlier in the 20th century blind fiddlers would move from fair to fair playing traditional tunes and pieces by Sarasate and others, and would make up topical and satirical songs. Fiddler and multi-instrumentalist **Pancho Alvarez** based his album *Florencio, O Cego Dos Vilares* (Do Fol, 1998) on the life and repertoire of one of the last of these.

The zanfona (hurdy-gurdy) had been played since the Middle Ages but nearly died out in the 20th century. In 1904 Perfecto Feijoo played it on what are thought to be the first hurdy-gurdy recordings ever made. In the middle of the century **Faustino Santalices** began its revival, publishing a booklet and performing for a record, and in the 1970s young musicians continued his work and re-established the instrument. Antón Corrál and students at the workshop of the Universidade Popular de Vigo championed the zanfona, even reconstructing the two-player organistrum from carvings on the Portico de la Gloria at Santiago cathedral. Other leading players instrumental in its revival include Xosé Lois Rivas, of Fuxan os Ventos and now of A Quenlla, Anxo Pintos of Berrogüetto, Antón Seoane of Milladoiro, Amancio Prada, and Faustino Santalices junior.

Also used in the Middle Ages was the small Celtic-style harp. In the 1970s **Emilio Cao** rekindled interest by using the instrument to accompany himself in songs that are a continuation of the Galego- and Portuguese-language poetic traditions

■ *Members of Celtas Cortos.*

stretching back at least to the trovadores. Encouraged by harp revivals in Brittany, Scotland and Ireland the instrument began to be made and played again in Galicia. Other significant harp players include Rodrigo Romaní, who in 2000 left Milladoiro to pursue a solo path, and Quico Comesaña of Berrogüetto.

RECOMMENDED RECORDS

PANCHO ALVAREZ FLORENCIO, O CEGO DOS VILARES *(Do Fol, 1998) Based on the songs and tunes of the last of the blind fiddler-singers, with multi-instrumentalist Alvarez singing and playing all the instruments. A couple of the melodies here, including a garland-arch dance, are akin to English country-dance tunes.*

EMILIO CAO CARTAS MARIÑAS *(Sonifolk Lyricon, 1992; later reissued on Do Fol)*
Singer/harpist/zanfonist/multi-instrumentalist Cao plus Pimental, Núñez, Leilía and others in
Cao's settings of poems by 20th-century Galician sailor-poet Manuel Antonio.

**GRUPO DIDÁCTICO-MUSICAL DO OBRADOIRO-ESCOLA DE GAITAS E
ZANFONAS, UNIVERSIDADE POPULAR DO CONCELLO DE VIGO**
INSTRUMENTOS MUSICAIS POPULARES GALEGOS *(Sonifolk, 1987) A clear and richly
melodic introduction to the range and sounds of Galician traditional instruments, solo as well
as in traditional and expanded ensemble line-ups. Features many young players who have
since become leaders of the new wave.*

XESÚS PIMENTEL MÚSICA DE GALICIA *(Do Fol, 1999) Flamenco-style guitar but using
Galician traditional themes.*

RODRIGO ROMANÍ ALBEIDA *(Do Fol, 2000) Leading harpist and Director of the
Conservatorio de Música Tradicional at the Universidade Popular de Vigo, Romani left
Milladoiro after 22 years in 2000. His solo career begins with this release, named after his
home village. It features Susana Seivane, Anxo Pintos, Laura Quintillán, the gaita band
Treixadura, choir Fiadeiro, Orquesta Camerata Viguesa, and Prague Symphony Orchestra.*

CELTIC IBERIA: BANDS

The present-day style of folk band didn't arise in Galicia until the late 1970s, and in
Asturias not until the 1980s. Spain has never been one homogeneous culture, and
with the death in 1975 of Franco and the change to a democratic monarchy there
was a greatly increased freedom for people to explore and manifest their cultural
variety, making new growth on old roots.

Partly stimulated by the "folk scare" in the US which had begun in the 1950s and
gathered political steam in the 1960s, Britain and then several other countries of
Europe during the 1960s and 1970s had seen folk music revivals. So it was that many
of the young Spanish musicians seeking to arrange, perform and record the material
they were finding were able selectively to borrow ideas from these existing models.
It is a matter of debate as to whether these were good or appropriate influences, but
it is largely as a result of contact with incoming new ideas and of changes in society
that any musical tradition evolves.

In Galicia there was still a living tradition, so while new folk bands did appear
there, putting together instruments and making arrangements of traditional and new
material, there was a continuing interchange between new and old. Two of the first
and most influential of the new bands were Fuxan os Ventos and Milladoiro.

Fuxan os Ventos were song-centred rather than gaita-led, and their motivation
was strongly socio-political, aiming to promote respect for the Galego language and
the culture of the economic underclass. In a note to Pancho Alvarez's album
dedicated to the blind fiddlers, the band's founder, singer and zanfona player Mini

(Xosé Lois Rivas; now a member of A Quenlla) described his childhood in the 1950s and 1960s as "the heavy years of Franquismo and national-Catholicism".

He continued: "Those who spoke Castilian with some fluency were pretty and nice kids, those who spoke 'Castrapo' (a combination of Castilian and Galician) were boorish and, above all, poorer. Radio and orchestra music was the best; bagpipers and songs by the peasant and the elderly were considered old-fashioned and illiterate. Choirs with 'gallegadas' were avoiding the purge because they used polyphony, and thus the upper class quietened the country's conscience."

In a recent interview, Mini said: "The essence of Fuxan os Ventos was to combine traditional music, or sometimes composed music with traditional elements, with words of combat." Musically, Fuxan os Ventos constituted a bridge between the rich, powerful vocal sound heard in the strongest corales and the arranging skills of the new folk bands who used zanfona, flutes, violins, Spanish guitar and traditional percussion. The group made a string of albums between 1976 and the mid 1980s, and there is a 1999 CD compilation on Fonofolk.

Milladoiro, the name for the piles of stones left by Santiago pilgrims to mark the path, was the title of a 1977 album by Antón Seoane and Rodrigo Romaní. It consisted of traditional and Seoane-composed music arranged largely for zanfona, ocarina, harp and traditional percussion, with some gaita, guitar, acoustic keyboards, crumhorn, recorder and fretted instruments. A varied collection, it moved between robust traditional and more delicate early-music styles.

Meanwhile three musicians, Xosé V Ferreiros, Fernando Casal and Ramón García Rei, had been delving into the music of the old gaiteiros. They formed a trio called Faíscas do Xiabre and recorded a tribute to the music and sound of the famous early-20th-century cuarteto de gaitas Gaiteiros de Soutelo. *In Memoriam* (Guimbarda, 1979) mainly features two gaitas, tamboril and bombo in a line-up like the Soutelo quartet, but on some tracks they add further instruments.

Seoane and Romaní guested on that record, and in May 1979 – following the recruitment of violinist Laura Quintillán and antique music researcher, flautist and recorder-player Xosé A. Méndez – Milladoiro gave their first show. Their debut album, *A Galicia De Maeloc* (Dial, 1980), contained eight traditional tunes and some new compositions by band members, including a tribute to poet Rosalía de Castro. There were also two Irish tunes on the record, O'Carolan's 'Si Bheag Si Mhor' and 'John Ryan's Jig', featuring uilleann pipes. The sleevenotes spoke of British Celts in the 5th century driven by Anglo-Saxon invasions to look for and settle in new lands in Brittany and Galicia.

By *Milladoiro 3* (Sony, 1982) the group had incorporated occasional contributions from synthesisers and from Scottish Highland bagpipes. Album four in 1986 was recorded in Dublin, at Windmill Lane studio, with Paddy Moloney guesting, and two years later the band were guests alongside Breton, Scottish and Northumbrian musicians on the 'Millennium Celtic Suite' track featured on the *Chieftains Celebration* album (RCA Victor, 1989). More collaborations and appearances with The Chieftains have since followed.

There have been Milladoiro albums of music made for the theatre, for an art exhibition, and album eleven, *Iacobus Magnus* (Discmedi, 1994), was an orchestral suite about the pilgrimages to Compostela, recorded at Abbey Road studio in London with the English Chamber Orchestra. Album fifteen, *Auga De Maio* (Discmedi Blau,

■ *Luar na Lubre.*

1999), was a return to a simpler style, and to largely traditional Galician music, with just two guests, singers Olga Cerpa from the Canary Islands band Mestisay and Ana Belén from Spain.

Meanwhile, first Galicia and more recently Asturias have spawned large numbers of bands. Many have recorded, some have become popular live acts, some have shrivelled and died, or regrouped to rise transformed.

Many connections have been made with "Celtic" music in other countries. A few musicians have flirted with the new age music that was for a time popular in Spain – and in record shops one is still likely to find both "Celtic" and "world" music racked under "nueva era". There has been chamber-folk, synth-washes and folk-rock. The dust-stirring Galician-tinged Valladolid folk-rock band **Celtas Cortos** (named after a brand of cigarette) topped the Spanish singles chart early in the 1990s, while in the last five or so years of the 20th century came the remarkable rise of the star gaiteiros and "el boom"

Nowadays Galician and Asturian musicians are looking for ideas and cross-references not just to the north and east, but to the south. This is not just to North Africa, the Atlantic islands or West Africa, but to nearby Portugal, with which Galician culture in particular has strong connections that for political reasons have been little celebrated during the 20th century. Formed in 1980, Galician band **Na Lúa** have moved through stylistic and personnel changes but have consistently made a bridge of rapprochement across the river Miño. Produced by famous Portuguese musician and traditional experimenter Júlio Pereira – and featuring the magnificent Uxía in full voice – *Ondas Do Mar De Vigo* (Do Fol, 1988) was an ambitious work that reached out in all directions both technologically and geographically, and particularly into Portugal.

If it were released for the first time now, the album would still make waves with its energy and skill, its flowing diversity of references, and its lucid, snappy production. Though not frequent live performers, Na Lúa continue to explore. Their most recent album, *Feitizo* (Do Fol, 1999), is full of memorable traditional melodic shapes and rich-textured instrumentation, rattling skipping pandeiretas, thudding bombo, thrumming fretted strings and Antón Rodríguez's and Cándido Lorenzo's skirling gaitas and reeds. Vocals are handled by the band plus guests Aloia Martínez and the female vocal group As Donicelas.

Studying and working together for several years at the instrument workshop of the Universidade Popular de Vigo were three young musicians: piper, zanfona player and multi-instrumentalist Anxo Pintos; accordionist Santiago Cribeiro; and Carlos Núñez. At the beginning of the 1990s they formed the folk-rock band **Matto Congrio** which made one very well received album, *Matto Congrio* (Sonifolk, 1993) before splitting in half.

Two members, Pancho Alvarez and Diego Bouzón, went to join the band that Núñez was forming, while the other three, Pintos, Cribeiro and drummer Isaac Palacín, got together with violinist Paco Juncal, harp and bouzouki player Quico Comesaña and guitarist Guillermo Fernández to form **Berroguetto**. The band were seen as something of a supergroup, and their first album *Navicularia* (Do Fol, 1996) lived up to expectations, elegantly produced with dense, often swinging arrangements and full-throated traditional-style guest vocals from the seven pandeireteras of Cantigas e Agarimos.

Quim Farinha replaced Paco Juncal on violin, while the lively vocalist Guadi Galego has joined, and the band is one of Galicia's most popular live roots performers. The second album, *Viaxe Por Urticaria* (Do Fol, 1999), was recorded like the first in Euskadi, and features Euskal (Basque) musicians guesting on txalaparta and saxophone. A new album is scheduled for 2001.

Both Berroguetto and Na Lúa use gaitas in some of their music, and a lot of traditional shapes, rhythms and references, but they have moved far outside the structure of an augmented, expanded, traditional ensemble. There is an important place, though, for modern musicians to continue to play the sort of music to which people can sing and dance. A healthy, living tradition needs to be extending on the outside and full on the inside. Os Cempés and Chouteira are a couple of notable bands in that general territory, using largely traditional-style tunes and instrumentation but ever-developing. Both use a basis of gaitas, tamboril and bombo with accordion, zanfona and pandeireta, plus male vocals in Os Cempés, and female in Chouteira (from Uxía Pedreira).

In the notes to their 1998 anniversary compilation *20 Anos De Camiño*, **Muxicas** said of one of their seven earlier albums: "This is a strongly vindicative period which will place Muxicas at the head of the movement for the dignification of Galician music against foreign aggressions, a stance which will give them more than one headache (of which they happen to be particularly proud)." This kind of declaration no doubt causes the "sparks" to which the band's name translates.

However, Muxicas have made lively, robust and considerably inventive music, using male and female vocals, gaitas, zanfona, accordion, traditional percussion, and occasionally marching brass and fife band. Even the cussed can make fine music, and it is often the cussed who have kept many a tradition alive during the thin times before the next revival.

Luar na Lubre were formed in 1986, and on their fifth album, *Cabo Do Mundo* (WEA, 1999), they make the kind of music that Muxicas's main man Xosé Manuel Fernández Costas might hate. Guitar, driving bouzouki, bodhrán, djembe, some Clannad-style breathy synth, a set of Irish tunes featuring a guest who played uilleann pipes on the soundtrack to the film *Titanic*, some Stivell-type ripple'n'soar, even a song set to a version of the Martin Carthy/Simon & Garfunkel arrangement of the 'Scarborough Fair' tune. If it were less impressively done it would be easy to dismiss. But here is a band who know how to grab an audience in these days of big, lush, pan-Celtic landscapes. The record is powerfully produced, and possesses the great assets of leader Bieito Romero's gaita playing and Rosa Cedrón's singing. It carries all, or most, before it. Like its predecessor *Plenilunio* (Warner Spain, 1997), *Cabo Do Mundo* went gold, and the song 'Chove En Santiago' won a national award for best song of the year in Galego, alongside a track from Carlos Núñez's album and one from Cristina Pato's former band Mutenrohi.

Camerata Meiga, which evolved in 1999 from the band Xeque Mate, combine traditional instruments, piano, soprano sax, violin, cello, double bass and drums in complex, rich-textured arrangements with prominent bowed strings. Splendid Portuguese singer and fado-style songwriter Amélia Muge provides the vocals on Camerata Meiga's first album *Habelas Hailas* (Resistencia, 1999) and joins the band for performances.

Over in Asturias the revival started from a slimmer surviving tradition, and later than in Galicia. There are not yet quite so many bands, and apart from Hevia they have not yet enjoyed huge sales. Llan de Cubel and Felpeyu in particular have been touring a great deal and creating interest abroad. Others are on the way, including Brenga Astur, which now features Marta Arbas, who was the singer in 1980s Asturian groups Ubiña and Xaréu. **Llan de Cubel**, named after a mountain in Cuieru county, formed in 1984. They seek out and play all-Asturian material and

Members of Muxicas.

have two gaiteiros, but adopted a style not dissimilar to some of the Irish bands, using Donal Lunny-style driving bouzouki chording with fiddle, flutes, whistle, guitar, accordion, bodhrán and traditional percussion. They played excellently and tightly, though, and could integrate so well with Scottish and Irish music and musicians that they made many friends. Their fifth album, *Un Tiempu Meyor* (Fono Astur, 1999), contains more vocal items than before, features orchestral arrangements from the Orquesta Sinfónica del Principado, and has Hevia guesting on a couple of tracks. By this time, after several changes, the line-up of the six-piece included Scottish fiddler Simon Bradley.

The current Llan de Cubel guitarist Xel Pereda came to the band from **Felpeyu**, which released its first album *Nel Cantu La Memoria* in 1994 on the Fono Astur label, home to much Asturian roots music since the beginning of the revival. Xuan Nel Expósito plays gaita, but chooses to concentrate largely on diatonic accordion, and is joined by two fiddles, bouzouki, guitar, bass and percussion, with members of the all-male band taking vocals.

Across the eastern border of Asturias is the smaller Cantabria, where musicians are also seeking out their traditions, and making some Celtic connections – or at least feeling part of the Atlantic culture. **Luétiga** are a band that split and reformed with a new line-up between 1998 and 1999, while some previous Luétiga members formed another Cantabrian roots band, **Atlántica**. Like many of their Galician contemporaries and Asturian colleagues, both outfits use pan-Celtic instruments. One wonders, then, if it is the sound of chording guitar, bagpipes and fiddle, or if it is the shapes of the music they play, that caused people at the Chicago Irish Festival to remark to Luétiga, "Your music sounds Irish… but not just that." Which is more or less where this chapter came in.

RECOMMENDED RECORDS

ATLÁNTICA LA LUZ DEL IVIERNU *(El Tripulante, 2000) Second album by the band which is led by former Luétiga members Marcos Bárcena and Kate Gass, playing traditional material from Cantabria.*

BERROGÜETTO VIAXE POR URTICARIA (Do Fol, 1999) *Now with vocalist Guadi Galego, this second album shows them to be a focal turn-of-the-millennium band, expanding on traditional music but keeping its shape, power and drive.*

BRENGA ASTUR CANCIOS DEL GOCHU XABAZ *(Fonofolk, 2000) Second album by rising Asturian band, now featuring ex-Ubiña and Xaréu singer Marta Arbas.*

CAMERATA MEIGA HABELAS HAILAS *(Resistencia, 1999) Rich and varied arrangements for wide instrumentation, including strong contributions from Portuguese guest singer Amélia Muge.*

CHOUTEIRA GHUAUE! *(Do Fol, 1997) Gaita, tamboril and bombo, plus accordion, zanfona, pandeireta and the vocals of Uxía Pedreira, with traditional and new music.*

FELPEYU TIERRA *(Fono Astur, 1997) Xuan Nel Expósito does play gaitas, but in this widely-travelled band concentrates mainly on diatonic accordion, and is joined in largely traditional Asturian music by two fiddles, bouzouki, guitar, bass and percussion.*

FUXAN OS VENTOS SEMPRE E MÁIS DESPOIS *(Fonofolk, 1999) This compilation is drawn from the seven albums that were made during the 1970s and 1980s by this influential and culturally committed band.*

LLAN DE CUBEL UN TIEMPU MEYOR *(Fono Astur, 1999) Long-established largely acoustic band of gaita, guitar, fiddle, accordion, percussion, tambor Astur, bouzouki, bass*

■ *Albums (below, left to far right) by: Milladoiro; Fuxan Os Ventos; Berrogüetto; Muxicas; Na Lúa; Os Cempés; Llan de Cubel; Luar na Lubre.*

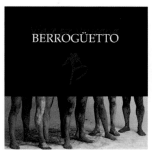

pedals, keyboards and vocals that has brought Asturian music to many foreign audiences. This fifth album includes orchestral arrangements and a guest appearance from Hevia.

LUAR NA LUBRE CABO DO MUNDO *(WEA, 1999) Powerfully-produced and big-selling album featuring Bieito Romero's gaita and Rosa Cedrón's cello and vocal.*

LUÉTIGA CÁNTABROS *(Luétiga, 1999) First album from the Cantabrian band's new line-up, with guests Kepa Junkera and Hevia.*

MATTO CONGRIO MATTO CONGRIO *(Sonifolk, 1993) Shortlived but acclaimed Galician folk-rock band, comprising Carlos Núñez, Pancho Alvarez, Diego Bouzón, Anxo Lois Pintos, Santiago Cribeiro and Isaac Palacín. It divided amoeba-like to produce the Carlos Núñez band and Berrogüetto.*

MILLADOIRO 3 *(Sony, 1982) CD-reissued taste of the early work of the veteran and influential instrumental chamber-folk ensemble. Parts sound a little plodding now, there's a lumpy touch of dated string-synth – and 'Greensleeves' – but otherwise classic gaita tunes in elegantly melodic arrangements.*

MILLADOIRO AUGA DE MAIO *(Discmedi /Green Linnet 1999) After a run of special projects, this was designed to re-focus the band – plus guest singers Ana Belén and Olga Cerpa – with predominantly trad tunes.*

MUXICAS 20 ANOS DE CAMIÑO *(Punteiro, 1999) Strong and varied retrospective taken from the previous seven albums by a band who develop and expand while sticking close to raw, characterful and energetic Galician traditions of instrumentation and technique.*

NA LÚA ONDAS DO MAR DE VIGO *(Do Fol, 1988) The band's masterwork, named after a verse by Martín Codax and sounding ever richer with the years. Produced by Júlio Pereira, it features Uxía in fine vocal form, plus guests including Portuguese star Fausto.*

OS CEMPÉS ¡¡OPA iii!! *(Do Fol, 1996) Memorable tunes, mostly trad, played live with no-nonsense exuberance by young musicians strong in the tradition of the gaita groups: Antón Varela's skirling gaita and Oscar Fernández Sanjurjo's chugging melodeon, plus rattling, thumping bombo, tamboril and pandeireta.*

TEJEDOR TEXEDORES DE SUAÑOS *(Resistencia, 1999) Asturian traditional and Tejedor-original material from gaiteiro and flute player José Manuel Tejedor, plus his brother Javier on diatonic accordionist, percussionist and gaiteiro, and singer and percussionist sister Eva, in conjunction with producer Phil Cunningham and other British guests.*

NEW DIRECTIONS

BY SUE WILSON

If Celtic music has proved one thing during its long and eventful history, it is that it is a cultural survivor. Its ability to recapture the imagination of successive generations has again been comprehensively demonstrated in the international upsurge of popular interest that has revitalised the Celtic scene around the turn of the 21st century. By common consent, among both pundits and musicians themselves, Celtic and Celtic-based music are on an unprecedented roll, whether measured in record sales, audience share, or the quantity and quality of new acts and recordings.

The most salient and dynamic feature of this new Celtic flowering, across virtually all the music's different home territories, is the proliferating incidence of cross-genre or cross-cultural experimentation. Traditional Celtic modes and material are mixed and matched with everything from improvised jazz to electronic dance music, Scandinavian and East European styles, and on to Latin, African and Caribbean influences. In part this is an organic response to a world dramatically shrunk by technology, and culturally by the "world music" movement. In part it is a generational process, arising from the ascendancy of Celtic musicians in their 20s and 30s, even their teens, who naturally bring with them all the wider interests and influences of their time, be it trip-hop or drum'n'bass, salsa or Afro-pop.

Scotland, for once stealing a march on its usually dominant Hibernian neighbour, has been a particular hotbed of such cross-fertilisations. The close-knit nature of the Scottish music scene, combined with the burgeoning and refreshingly internationalist cultural confidence that helped drive the country's progress toward winning its own devolved Parliament, continues to engender a sometimes bewildering profusion of interdisciplinary collaborations and hybrid styles.

The Highland group **Capercaillie** were one of the earliest and remain the best-known pioneers in this new fusion territory, having famously put a 400-year-old Gaelic song in the UK pop charts with their 1991 hit single 'Coisich A Ruin'. A polished, multi-textured melange of folk and pop stylings with acoustic and electric textures, their sound centres on the luminous vocals of native Gaelic speaker Karen Matheson, and also takes in funked-up versions of traditional jigs and reels, further enlivened with Mediterranean and African flavours on their latest release *Beautiful Wasteland* (Survival, 1997).

■ *Rag Foundation (opposite) pictured in concert during 2000.*

A more radical approach, however, is embodied by several other current Scottish outfits, most notably the Edinburgh-based sextet **Shooglenifty**. Their high-octane dancefloor attack employs a densely layered rhythmic framework closely allied to contemporary clubland grooves, overlaid by fiddle and mandolin melodies vying with a welter of ambient effects and industrial distortion. Their first two albums *Venus In Tweeds* and *A Whisky Kiss* (Greentrax, 1994/1996) were followed in 2000 by *Solar Shears* (Vertical, 2000).

Also generating a rave-like atmosphere at their gigs are **The Peatbog Faeries**, a six-piece from the Isle Of Skye who mix up bagpipe and fiddle tunes with a rock/jazz rhythm section and a cosmopolitan array of dancefloor flavours, from ambient and techno to African and reggae. Their sole recording to date is *Mellowosity* (Greentrax, 1996), although a new album *Faery Stories* was due at the time of writing.

The formerly dreadlocked, now shaven-headed (but still absurdly photogenic) **Martyn Bennett** is a top-class piper and whistle-player and a classically trained violinist who has ventured yet further toward integrating traditional and electronic dance music. From the techno-house soundscapes of his self-titled debut album on Eclectic, through the hip-hop and ethno-trance of *Bothy Culture* (Rykodisc, 1998), he has latterly been working in a harder, heavier groove, drawing on big-beat and breakbeat styles, with even a smattering (or should that be spattering?) of punk for his latest release *Hardland* (Cuillin, 2000). Away from the dancefloor, clarsach (Celtic harp) player **Savourna Stevenson** has expanded her instrument's range into jazz,

African and contemporary classical territory, often in compositions based on themes from history or legend. *Calman The Dove* (Cooking Vinyl, 1998), written to commemorate the life of Saint Columba, has her teaming up with Irish uilleann piper Davy Spillane. Even the more traditional style adopted by Shetland fiddler **Catriona MacDonald** reflects its contemporary context in subtle, underlying ways. Jazz tonalities and Scandinavian influences have long been a feature of her expansive, meltingly sweet-toned music, lusciously showcased on her debut solo album *Bold* (Peerie Angel, 2000).

One of Scotland's most successful current solo acts is **Tony McManus**. He has carved out a category virtually all to himself with his dazzlingly virtuosic renderings of traditional and less traditional tunes on acoustic guitar. His second album, *Pourquois Quebec?* (Greentrax, 1998) finds him collaborating with Breton musicians Alain Genty and Denis Frechette, while he recently recorded a breathtaking duo album with master fiddler Alasdair Fraser, *Return To Kintail* (Culburnie, 1999). Fraser's own recent work with his California-based band **Skyedance** strides boldly into Celtic-fusion territory. Into the melting pot goes everything from hard funk riffs to classical-style lyricism and Eastern-flavoured rhythms to contemporary Scottish anthems on their two highly accomplished albums, *Way Out To Hope Street* and *Labyrinth* (Culburnie, 1997/1999).

Scotland has also witnessed a series of experimental fusions of jazz and folk music. This goes back a decade to Savourna Stevenson's *Tweed Journey* and the emergence of groups such as Giant Stepping Stones, the Cauld Blast Orchestra, the Simon Thoumire Trio, and Bachué, as well as projects by musicians like reeds player Dick Lee, drummer Tom Bancroft and saxophonist Tommy Smith. The latest exponents of this particular fusion are John Rae's **Celtic Feet**, a band which combines a jazz quartet with Simon Thoumire's concertina and Eilidh Shaw's fiddle to startling effect on their debut album, *Celtic Feet* (Caber, 1999).

Looking across to Ireland, long the dominant player on the worldwide Celtic scene, by far the biggest phenomenon in its recent musical history is – of course – **Riverdance**. This was the outstanding example of Celtic traditions embracing both the modern world and other world-music styles. Within Ireland itself, the show's massive global success has helped tip the balance of debate decisively in favour of those who espouse a similarly broad-minded, 21st-century traditional music over those who would rather confine it in metaphorical glass cases.

That said, the influence of world music styles and other contemporary trends on Ireland's current folk scene has tended to be more diffuse and subliminal than overt or self-conscious – probably because traditional music, at least since the 1970s, has never really been out of the popular mainstream to the extent it has elsewhere, and so has seemed less in need of reinvention. Accordion virtuoso **Sharon Shannon** is one partial exception to this pattern, with several tracks on her second album, *Out*

■ *Members of Afro Celt Sound System on-stage.*

The Gap (Solid/Grapevine, 1994), having resulted from a fruitful collaboration with reggae producer Denis Bovell. Her third, *Each Little Thing* (Grapevine, 1997), spices its mainly Irish mix with such exotica as a Chilean tune, a Fleetwood Mac cover and a foray into electronic beats and drum-loops.

Shannon is also a regular guest with Donal Lunny's **Coolfin**, a six-piece line-up formed in 1998, which sees the legendary producer and bouzouki player carrying the impulse of Moving Hearts into funkier, more groove-based instrumental territory. Featuring fiddler Nollaig Casey and uilleann piper John McSherry, backed with bass, keyboards, drums and percussion, plus occasional soft-focus arrangements of Maighread Ní Dhomhnaill's singing, the band has released one self-titled album (Metro Blue/Capitol, 1998) which also featured a guest vocal by Eddi Reader.

The most assertively fusion-inclined outfit to have emerged from Ireland recently, however, is the Dublin-based seven-piece **Kila**, a raggle-taggle collective of multi-instrumentalists cooking up traditional, ethnic, rock, rap, dance and trance influences into a powerfully exhilarating blend of self-penned tunes and original Gaelic songs. Their second, breakthrough album *Tog E Go Bog E* (Kila, 1997) was followed by *Lemonade And Buns* (Kila, 2000), showing off a tightened sound that sacrificed none of the band's wildness.

Another exciting prospect are **Lunasa**, an all-instrumental outfit led by a glorious welter of fiddles, flutes, whistles and uilleann pipes, assertively backed with acoustic guitar and upright bass. As with many of the best new-wave Celtic bands, it is their rhythmic approach that is crucial, their driving grooves, interlocking cross-beats and nimble syncopations simultaneously buoying up the melodies and opening them to fresh interpretation. Their second album *Otherworld* (Green Linnet, 1999) combines formidable technical authority with thrilling lyricism and verve.

In many cases, however, the most innovative Irish-based fusion sounds have come from artists working outside Ireland. The leading figures are the **Afro Celt Sound System**, a London-centred assemblage of Irish and West African musicians whose debut release *Volume One: Sound Magic* (RealWorld, 1996) was one of the bestselling roots releases of the 1990s. A strong clubland sensibility making extensive use of programmed beats and synthesised atmospherics is a key ingredient in the Afro Celts' mix, together with Irish and African acoustic textures and the haunting sean nós singing of Iarla Ó Lionaird. Their second album, *Volume Two: Release* (RealWorld, 1999), is more smoothly integrated, featuring guest vocals from Sinead O'Connor, while **Iarla Ó Lionaird** has also gone on to record a solo album, *The Seven Steps To Mercy* (RealWorld, 1997), taking his ancient vocal style into subtly futuristic realms.

Michael McGoldrick, one of the guests on *Release* (as well as a regular touring member of Scotland's Capercaillie), is a Manchester-Irish flute player and uilleann piper fast being recognised as one of today's most exciting Celtic talents. Having established his credentials with a superb, traditional-style debut, *Morning Rory* (Aughrim, 1996), he went on to indulge a wide range of tastes and influences on his second, *Fused* (Vertical, 2000), a magically seamless interweaving of Irish, jazz-funk and hip-hop strands.

Across the Atlantic is ex-*Riverdance* fiddler **Eileen Ivers**, a first-generation product of New York's vibrant Irish community. She takes an impressive tour of contemporary urban and world music styles – Latin, Caribbean, African, jazz, flamenco, hip-hop – on her latest album *Crossing The Bridge* (Sony Classical, 1999) which positively fizzes with Ivers's characteristic energy and invention, even if not all the experiments come off. Chicagoan fellow fiddler **Liz Carroll** recently announced her return from an extended maternity sabbatical with her stunning third album *Lost In The Loop* (Green Linnet, 2000) featuring mainly traditional instrumentation but a thoroughly modern approach to arrangements and rhythm.

No contemporary survey of Irish music would be complete without mention of US-based fiddler **Martin Hayes**. His groundbreaking work with American guitarist **Dennis Cahill** might at first seem to head in the opposite direction to the kind of fusion under discussion. But Hayes's method is to dig deeper and deeper, with exquisite technique and feeling, into the innermost recesses and nuances of traditional tunes, and to string them together in extended medleys that last up to half an hour. Combined with Cahill's minutely sensitive yet free-ranging accompaniment, this revisiting of the musical bedrock underlines an acute understanding of traditional music's place in the modern world and – on an equally subtle level – reflects Hayes's

Simon Thoumire at Queen's Hall, Edinburgh in 1996.

previous experience working with US rock and jazz outfits. The duo's *The Lonesome Touch* (Green Linnet, 1997) is one of the essential releases of the 1990s.

Staying in North America, the Scottish cultural outpost of Cape Breton Island in Canada has seen a number of its emergent artists making their mark on the international Celtic scene in recent years, chief among them the vivacious young fiddler **Natalie MacMaster**. While remaining firmly allied to the tradition she inherited from her uncle, the legendary Buddy MacMaster, her latest album *In My*

Hands (Greentrax, 1999) also works in rock accompaniments, electronic back-beats and pop-style arrangements. **The Rankin Family**, too, enjoyed considerable success throughout the 1990s with their beguiling blend of folk, pop and country sounds, releasing a string of hit albums before disbanding in 1999.

Cape Breton's self-styled "fiddle slut" **Ashley MacIsaac** is becoming better known these days for his controversy-wreaking interviews than his music, but his first non-traditional recording *Hi, How Are You Today?* (A&M, 1995), an adrenaline-fuelled barrage of Celtic tunes with grunge-rock, funk-metal and hip-hop backing, remains a landmark in the island's musical evolution. It was as a guest on this album that Gaelic vocalist **Mary Jane Lamond** first won wider recognition, but she's since been forging ahead in her own career, crafting silky, pop-tinged arrangements of traditional songs. All these and eight other current Canadian-Celtic acts – including the marvellous Quebecois big band, La Bottine Souriante – are featured on *Fire In The Kitchen* (Wicklow, 1998), brought together by Ireland's legendary traditional ambassadors, The Chieftains.

Back on the Atlantic's eastern seaboard the musical profile of the Continental Celtic regions – Brittany and Galicia/Asturias – has increased significantly in recent years, particularly through the success of **Dan Ar Braz**'s Breton-based extravaganza *L'Heritage Des Celtes* (Columbia/Dan Ar Braz, 1994), featuring upward of 70 musicians representing all of Europe's Celtic traditions, and the increasing international exposure of Galician piper Carlos Núñez. A primary focus of musical activity in both regions is the local outdoor festivals which take place in myriad profusion throughout the warmer months, featuring a mix of dance bands, vocal ensembles and pipe bands, meeting a seemingly insatiable demand among both young and old for traditional dancing. The events also provide regular work for proliferating numbers of bands, including a younger generation who stick largely to traditional material while experimenting with different instrumentation and sometimes a harder, rockier edge.

Albums (below, left to far right) by: Various (Fire In The Kitchen); Capercaillie; Michael McGoldrick; Shooglenifty; Lúnasa; Rag Foundation; Kíla; and The Peatbog Faeries.

Among Brittany's more progressive artists, much current activity centres on a loose group of musicians, teaming up in seemingly endless permutations. These include the brothers Molard – Patrick on bagpipes, Jacky on fiddle – as well as bass player Alain Genty, guitarist Soïg Siberil and singer/clarinettist Erik Marchand, all of

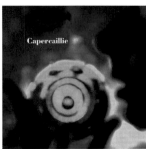

whom were members of the seminal Breton outfit Gwerz, which officially disbanded in 1989 but has continued to perform on an occasional basis. Other key figures are classically-trained pianist Didier Squiban, singer Yann-Fanch Kemener and guitarist Jacques Pellen. Between them, these artists have spun a spider's web of solo and collaborative projects and recordings over the last decade.

Triptyque (Gwerz Pladenn, 1993), featuring Pellen and the Molards, is a characteristic example, with its jazzy, improvisation-inspired approach to traditional Breton sources, while Genty's latest release *Le Grand Encrier* (Gwerz Pladenn, 1998) infuses Breton and Gaelic material with African and Oriental flavours, aided by the Molards (again) and Kemener's vocals. Squiban's collection of solo piano suites, *Molene* (L'Oz, 1997) steers a beautifully-poised course between traditional, jazz and classical idioms, while Pellen, too, has sought to bring a jazz aesthetic to Breton music with his continuing Celtic Procession project, recorded under the same title on Sony.

Most non-Spaniards hadn't even realised that there existed an Iberian Celtic connection until the charismatic young **Carlos Núñez** burst onto the scene in 1996, playing gaita (Galician bagpipes) and whistle. His success came with his platinum-selling debut *A Irmandade Das Estrellas / Brotherhood Of Stars* (BMG Classics, 1996), and his collaboration with The Chieftains on their *Santiago* (BMG Classics, 1996).

A wave of younger musicians has arrived in his wake, several of them experimenting with a variety of fusions, while Núñez himself has gone on to explore the links between Galician and flamenco music on *Os Amores Libres* (Wicklow, 1999). Chief among the young pretenders to his throne is **Xosé Manuel Budiño**. He plays uilleann pipes and low whistle as well as gaita, and weaves in a diversity of striking textures from dub-style bass grooves to Moorish influences on his debut album *Paralaia* (Resistencia, 1997). Close on his heels is another accomplished young piper, **Susana Seivane**, her calling-card release being *Fonsagrada* (Do Fol).

Traditional music in Wales, meanwhile, seems at last to be shaking off a popular image dominated by harps, eisteddfods and male voice choirs, spurred by the mainstream success of Welsh rock and pop groups like Catatonia, Stereophonics and the Super Furry Animals. The best known of the new folk acts is **Fernhill**, fronted by the atmospheric, richly-hued vocals of born-again Welshwoman Julie Murphy

183

(she's originally from Essex). Also juggling accordion, pibe cwd (Welsh bagpipes), guitar and clarinet, the trio create a highly distinctive marriage of traditional and contemporary songs sung in Welsh, Breton and English, the latest of their three albums being *Whilia* (Beautiful Jo, 2000).

Another Fernhill member, piper Ceri Rhys Matthews, has been instrumental in setting up the Fflach Tradd label, dedicated to promoting the increasingly diverse vitality of the country's folk scene. *Minka* (Fflach Tradd, 1999) was the debut release from **Rag Foundation**, currently the most talked-about new roots act in Wales. Powerfully reworked arrangements of classic traditional songs are their primary material, imbued with a hard-edged, emphatically modern sensibility. Also making waves are **Carreg Lafar**, a Cardiff-based band combining a varied instrumental line-up with vibrant twin lead vocals. Their album *Hyn* (Sain, 1998) is witness to their growing confidence and polish.

Last and, it has to be said, still least, are the oft-forgotten Celtic pockets of Cornwall and the Isle Of Man, but even here there are stirrings of musical revival. The key development in Cornwall has been the creeping, organic spread of regular informal pub sessions, now taking place at least weekly in virtually every main village, and recently given an extra focus by the Revival 2000 campaign. This aims to improve communication and networking among musicians, and to organise so-called Grand Sessions that bring together musicians from different localities. The mix of styles to be heard at these gatherings is healthily broad, from traditional folk to acoustic pop acts. **The Porters**, whose lively self-penned songs fall largely into the latter category, are tipped as the brightest current prospect from this scene.

The main impetus for the Isle of Man's nascent revival has been the budding international reputation of **Emma Christian**, who plays harp, recorder and sings in Manx Gaelic, her speciality being ethereal, candlelit performances in historic venues. She is also half of the partnership behind Manx Celtic Productions, which beside releasing in 1994 Christian's sole recording to date, *Beneath The Twilight*, organises the annual Isle Of Music Festival, established in 1996. This has featured such major international artists as La Bottine Souriante, Carlos Núñez and Ladysmith Black Mambazo. The company also released a compilation CD of current Manx acts, *The Best That's In*, again reflecting the growth of a local session scene.

RECOMMENDED RECORDS

AFRO CELT SOUND SYSTEM VOLUME 1: SOUND MAGIC *(RealWorld, 1996) The UK's leading folk-fusionists, with African, Irish, trad and techno energised by new ideas.*
DAN AR BRAZ L'HERITAGE DES CELTES *(Columbia/Dan Ar Braz, 1994) A landmark in the Breton revival, featuring over 75 musicians from Europe's Celtic territories.*
LUNASA OTHERWORLD *(Green Linnet, 1999) Exhilarating second album from the band dubbed "the hottest Irish acoustic group on the planet", with a melodic richness and flair underpinned by driving, precision-honed rhythm work.*
NATALIE MACMASTER IN MY HANDS *(Greentrax, 1999) Striking a thoughtful balance between tradition and innovation, the Cape Breton fiddler's sixth album features a diverse range of guests including Sharon Shannon and bluegrass star Alison Krauss.*
MICHAEL MCGOLDRICK FUSED *(Vertical, 2000) One of the finest examples to date of fully-fledged Celtic fusion, with McGoldrick's lissom flute, whistle and uilleann pipes sounding entirely at home against a jazz/clubland backdrop.*
CARLOS NÚÑEZ A IRMANDADE DAS ESTRELLAS / BROTHERHOOD OF STARS *(BMG Classics, 1996) Introduced today's Galician sounds to the wider Celtic world: Núñez's fiery gaita and whistle alongside stellar guests including The Chieftains and Ry Cooder.*
SHARON SHANNON SPELLBOUND: THE BEST OF SHARON SHANNON *(Grapevine, 1997) A sparkling retrospective of the Irish accordionist's brilliant career so far, including previously unreleased tracks featuring members of Donal Lunny's Coolfin band.*
SHOOGLENIFTY VENUS IN TWEEDS *(Greentrax, 1994) Killer grooves, gorgeous melodies and a wilfully distorted maelstrom of acoustic and electronic textures on this debut release from the Scottish pioneers of roots-based rave music.*

ARTIST INDEX

Page numbers in *italics* indicate illustrations